THE
BOOK TREE

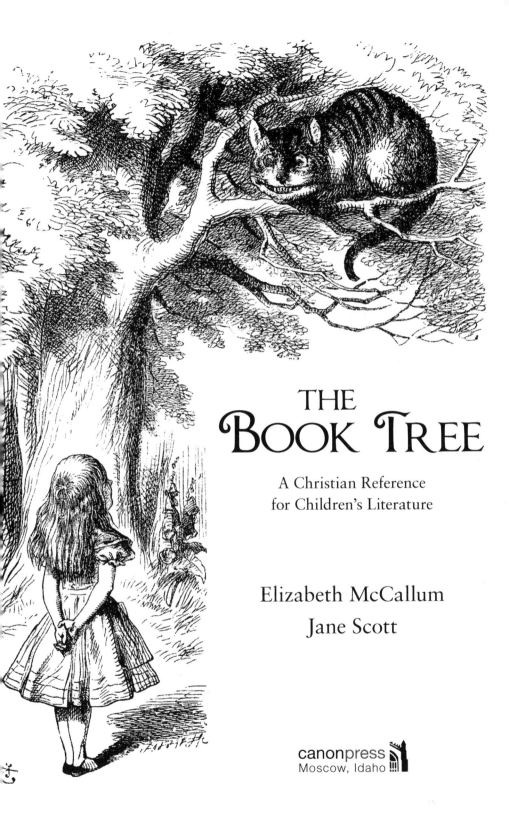

THE
BOOK TREE

A Christian Reference
for Children's Literature

Elizabeth McCallum
Jane Scott

canonpress
Moscow, Idaho

ILLUSTRATIONS
previous: *Alice's Adventures in Wonderland,* illustrated by John Tenniel (London: MacMillan & Co., 1898), see page 62.
opposite: *The House at Pooh Corner,* illustrated by Ernest Shepard (New York: Dutton Children's Books, 1928), see page 58. Used by permission.

Published by Canon Press
P.O. Box 8729, Moscow, ID 83843
1.800.488.2034 | www.canonpress.com

The Book Tree: A Christian Reference for Children's Literature
Copyright © 2001, 2008 by Elizabeth McCallum and Jane Scott.
Second edition.

Cover design by Rachel Hoffmann.
Interior layout by Laura Blakey.
Printed in the United States of America.
Illustration permissions: Page 5—From *The House at Pooh Corner* by A.A. Milne, illustrations by E.H. Shepard, © 1928 by E.P. Dutton, renewed © 1956 by A.A. Milne. Used by permission of www.penguin.com. All rights reserved.
Page 163—From *Daniel Boone* by James Daugherty, © 1939, renewed © 1967 by James Daugherty. Used by permission of www.penguin.com. All rights reserved.

Library of Congress Cataloging-in-Publication Data
McCallum, Elizabeth
    The Book tree : a Christian reference for children's literature / Elizabeth Mc-Callum, Jane Scott. -- 2nd ed.
    p. cm.
Includes bibliographical references and index.
ISBN-13: 978-1-59128-050-7
ISBN-10: 1-59128-050-8 (pbk. : alk. paper) 1. Children's literature--Bibliography. 2. Christian literature for children--Bibliography. 3. Children--Books and reading--United States. I. Scott, Jane, 1969- II. Title.

Z1037.M287 2007
[PN1009.A1]
011.62--dc22   2007041724

13 14 15 16 17 18   9 8 7 6 5 4 3 2

"Before beginning a Hunt, it is wise to ask someone what you are looking for before you begin looking for it.
A.A. Milne
Pooh's Little Instruction Book

DEDICATED TO
young people (and their parents) who are always looking for a good book.

ILLUSTRATIONS
Heidi, illustrated by Jessie Willcox Smith
(Philadelphia: David McKay Company, 1922), see page 82.

CONTENTS

ILLUSTRATIONS
The Merry Adventures of Robin Hood, illustrated by Howard Pyle
(New York: Charles Scribner's Sons, 1911), see page 148.

FOREWORD

ACCORDING TO RICHARD HOGGART, WE now live in a "post-literate society." It is an opinion shared by many. As a result, it has become commonplace for prognosticators of the future to herald the impending demise of literature, of books, indeed, of the printed word.

Such dire warnings are not without warrant. There can be little doubt: electronic mass media have become the dominating means of conveying and purveying modern culture today. Television has become America's drug of choice—a kind of electronic Valium. And virtually everyone across this vast land is using it. More than ninety-eight percent of all households have at least one television set. In fact, more American households have televisions than have indoor plumbing. Not surprisingly, American children watch an inordinate amount of programming. Preschoolers watch an average of more than twenty-seven hours each week—more than four hours per day. On school nights, American teens are limited in their television consumption to only about three hours per night. In contrast though, they spend about fifty-four minutes on homework, less than sixteen minutes reading, about fourteen minutes alone with their mothers, and less than five minutes with their fathers.

The family that puts great stock in reading is, therefore, quite happily a breed apart. It is not that such folk are elitists, snobs, or ivory tower parvenus. On the contrary, they are often

9

the most down-to-earth enthusiasts in any given community at any given time. It is just that over the course of their lives they have developed a taste for quiet reflection and substantive expression. They have acquired the habits of inquisitiveness and thoughtfulness. They appreciate rip-roaring yarns as much as harmonious nuances of narration; they relish well-drawn characters as much as graceful and temperate prose; they celebrate redolent imagination as much as clear articulation. They love words, ideas, and stories. They love to laugh and cry. They yearn for grace and consolation. They care passionately about beauty, goodness, and truth. They have learned the joyous journey of literary affections. They are, indeed, a breed apart.

Literary affections naturally give way to literary habits. Families who love to read will find the time to read—the distractions of life are simply crowded out. Even amidst the tyranny of the urgent which seems the natural accompaniment to modern life, they seem to be able to catch moments of quiet, snatches of solitude, brief interludes of attentiveness to the ideas and ideals of literature. Invariably, this relentless prioritizing of time leads to a necessary prioritizing of content. At some point every serious reading family comes to the realization that they will never be able to read everything they wish to, and so they turn their attention to read everything they ought to—they refocus their attention on the enduring masterworks: the classics.

As a result, such families invariably become inveterate and unapologetic list makers. There are lists of books that must be read. There are lists of books that must be reread. There are lists of books that must be read by others. There are lists of books that must be bought. There are bestseller lists. There are best-of-the-best lists. There are the indispensable book lists—those titles readers might profess to be their preferred companions were they stranded on a desert isle. It seems that list-making simply goes with the territory—it is the natural accompaniment to the shelf life.

Thus, this book will most certainly appeal to that breed apart—all those who nurture literary affections. It will sate even the most inveterate of list makers. How appropriate that a mother and her daughter—Elizabeth McCallum and Jane Scott—should have given us such a delectable treat. They have provided a guide to the best of children's literature serviceable for both veteran reading families and those just beginning their great journey of the imagination. I think you'll find that their accurate descriptions, careful recommendations, and cogent insights will prove to be as delightful as they will be invaluable.

I love books about books. I particularly love great books about great books. That is why I am so happy to commend this volume to you and your family—it does a great job of introducing the great books to those of us who find ourselves in that happy literary breed apart.

GEORGE GRANT
Professor of Moral Philosophy at Bannockburn College
and author of *Shelf Life* and *The Micah Mandate*

ILLUSTRATIONS
The Magic Fishbone, illustrated by F.D. Bedford
(New York: Frederick Warne & Co. Ltd., 1922), see page 93.

PREFACE
TO THE FIRST EDITION

THIS PREFACE IS YOUR ROADMAP for using *The Book Tree*. The following paragraphs will show you why this book was written and who can benefit from its information. It will give you some details about the selections we chose, including the layout of the book and our selection criteria. In short, this preface should help you make the best use of the information the book contains.

Good Children's Literature Is Essential

We wrote our book because a book of this sort is greatly needed. *The Book Tree* is a recommended reading list for all ages, from preschool through high school, and it includes several unique features. It contains a selective array of excellent books for each age group. We believe with Walter de la Mare that "only the rarest kind of best of anything can be good enough for the young," so we have spent many years researching and reading old books and new, classics as well as recent releases. In this book, we provide a recommended list of classic books, as well as books by Christian authors, some little-known books by great writers and poets, and a sizable collection of inspiring biographies. Of course, we do not think that these are the only books worth reading. In fact, we are discovering new favorites all the time. We are simply sharing with you some of the books that we have especially enjoyed.

Another special feature is that each book we recommend is accompanied by a summary that seeks to capture the flavor of each selection in order to spark children's interest in the book. One of the main reasons we wrote *The Book Tree* was to encourage young people to cultivate a life-long love of reading. Cultivating a love of good books enriches our hearts, our minds, and our souls.

The question is sometimes raised, Why should we read *fiction*—shouldn't Christians be more concerned about reading what is *real*? We believe one answer to this question is that good literature can vividly confirm and nurture a knowledge of what is good and true. Good fiction allows us to vicariously experience conflicts between good and evil and thereby grow in wisdom. Jesus used parables not only to confuse the wicked but also to make a profound impact on His disciples.

Futhermore, a good story or an excellent biography inspires, instructs, and opens up new worlds of interest and activity. Children's characters and beliefs are deeply strengthened by the books they read. That is why it is imperative that their books be of high caliber. Good books not only supply excellence in content and literary structure but also provide challenging reading. Quality children's books are written by authors who, in the words of C.S. Lewis, "meet children as equals in that area of our nature where we are their equals. . . . The child as reader is neither to be patronized nor idolized: we talk to him as man to man."[1]

This Book Is for You

The Book Tree will be a helpful resource for every member of the family. Thousands of children's books are currently available, and we have done some of the legwork for you: we have narrowed the books down to a recommended selection and given you an interesting taste of each book. *The Book Tree* not only allows young people to browse through a great selection

---

[1] C.S. Lewis, *On Stories and Other Essays on Literature* (New York: Harcourt Brace Jovanovich, 1982), 42.

of books but also helps homeschooling parents and teachers look for good books to supplement curriculum.

As you select books for your children, we strongly suggest that you avoid cartoon versions of classic children's stories that water down the story visually and verbally. We also recommend that readers read unabridged books, and we have therefore excluded all abridged editions with the exception of a fine abridgment of *David Copperfield* for young readers that was written by Dickens himself and a truncated version of *Les Misérables*, which would otherwise have extremely limited appeal.

We also warn parents that children's sections of bookstores and the local public libraries are no longer safe places for young children to browse unsupervised. The latest children's literature reflects a tendency to focus upon sordid themes.

Preschool Children

Parents of little ones will use this book to find good stories to share with their children. Reading at this tender age is such a wonderful thing—for parents and children alike. Unfortunately, many people assume that the quality of children's books is not important, and they are content to allow their little ones to read whatever comes to hand. As a result, sensitive, thoughtful children are fast becoming a rarity. We encourage parents to choose books of the highest caliber for their children and to read to them daily! You will find rich enjoyment and create happy memories as you read great books together. As children cultivate the habit of reading at an early age, they are more likely to be readers all their lives. The time you spend introducing your young ones to reading is a wonderful investment that will yield lifelong fruit.

Preschool children need to be read stories that are beautifully written and beautifully illustrated. Both the sounds and the illustrations in children's books nurture their aesthetic sense. Young children love fairy stories and stories about talking animals and children engaged in simple tasks. They love enchanting rhythms and repetition. They want stories that reassure them about the love of God, love of parents, stability of home, and orderliness of the world God has made. They need stories that praise good behavior. And, of course, they love to laugh.

Elementary Children

Parents, keep reading to your children throughout their growing up years. If you develop the consistent habit of reading good stories to them on a daily basis, they will *always* love hearing good stories. Elementary children are beginning readers and should be given character-building stories as well as stories that celebrate the simple joys of childhood. Their books should be those that reward the good and punish the wicked, that never condone or gloss over sinful behaviors, and that depict authority figures—such as parents, teachers, and pastors—in a positive light. Children of this age love animal adventure stories, mythology, Arthurian legends, fables, and books about the heroes of our faith and our American heritage. Also realize that when children are read to, they can comprehend at a higher reading level than when they read to themselves.

Middle School Children

The Book Tree will be helpful for middle school students looking for good books for reports or extra reading for pure enjoyment! Middle schoolers should be voracious readers. They should read an unabridged *Pilgrim's Progress* and every other good book they can get their hands on. The key at this age is to introduce children to a great deal of variety in their reading. Make sure that the books they read are worth reading. So much "junk food" juvenile fiction is available, and because these books are so easy to read, they are addictive. Children's creative imagination should be cultivated with lots of well-written fantasies. Middle schoolers love narratives about growing up, as well as thrillers, mysteries, and science fiction. They should also be given a steady diet of biography and historical fiction. Parents, keep reading to your older children. They need those special family times as much as you do, and they will love having you read the books that are sure to become some of their own favorites.

High School Students

The older we get, the more our tastes are defined, and the more help we need to find the books we like. If high schoolers can find their fiction niche, they will love to read. They should be encouraged to read old books—great classic novels, plays, and poems—*as soon as, and not before, they are old enough or ready to relish them.* And they often relish them far earlier than we tend to think. They should not make the mistake of shying away from old books, assuming that they won't understand them. In his essay "On the Reading of Old Books," C.S. Lewis comments that classics are often easier to understand than modern books, and that "the only palliative (for the mistakes of our age) is to keep the clean sea breeze of the centuries blowing through our minds, and this can be done only by reading old books."[2]

Young people who develop this love of good books are building the kind of character that will lead the future. The vast majority of people reach adulthood as non-readers. However, those who cultivate the life-long practice of reading good books will be characterized by a sharp intellect, an analytical mind, and a well-tuned sense of humor.

Homeschooling Parents and School Teachers

Teachers (both traditional and homeschool) will find *The Book Tree* a valuable resource. Standard literature textbooks do not adequately represent the classics, and teachers must constantly supplement their curriculum with great literature. *The Book Tree* will help teachers select books that are worth teaching and that students will enjoy. In addition, students routinely question teachers about books to read, or they want to know about the content of certain books. *The Book Tree* will allow them to browse, pick out a book that sounds good, and keep them coming back for more. Many young people become discouraged when they stumble upon books that do not interest them. After all, we all have different tastes and

---

[2] C.S. Lewis, *God in the Dock: Essays on Theology and Ethics* (Grand Rapids: Eerdmans, 1970), 202.

interests. Hopefully, *The Book Tree* will aid the book selection process and guide children to the kind of books they will read and reread.

Grandparents, Aunts, Uncles, and Friends
The Book Tree is also a useful resource for anyone giving books to grandchildren, nieces, nephews, or young friends. One of the best presents you can give anyone, for any occasion, is a great book, and this guide will help you pick out just the right one. Not only will our book save you time looking at the endless titles on the bookstore shelves or browsing online bookstores, but it will also help you make a thoughtful choice—"I picked this out for you because it's about . . . and I thought it sounded like something you would enjoy."

An Overview of What's Inside
We have placed our selections in broad categories in order to indicate general levels of reading. These categories are as follows:

- Preschool Literature
- Elementary Fiction (generally for readers in grades 1–5)
- Middle School Fiction (generally for readers in grades 6–8)
- Elementary and Middle School Biography
- High School Fiction (generally for readers in grades 9–12, and up!)
- High School Biography

Obviously, these categories will not apply to all readers alike. We encourage you to browse through all the categories to make sure you are not missing any treasures. C.S. Lewis wisely stated that "a children's story which is enjoyed only by children is a bad children's story. The good ones last."[3] Do not avoid "harder" selections simply because of the age or grade label; young people should be constantly challenged by more difficult books. Some students have even shifted their reading level up one full category (middle schoolers reading

[3] Lewis, *On Stories and Other Essays on Literature*, 33.

from High School Fiction; elementary students reading from Middle School Fiction).

We have also included four indexes at the end of the book. These will allow you to look for books by title, by author, by illustrator, or by subject.

Our Criteria

Our criteria include the following:

1. **Well-written literature.** We looked for well-written literature because excellence in language pleases our Creator. Of course, the books we have included reflect a range of literary skill.

2. **Reader-friendly literature.** We avoided complex books that need formal instruction and guidance in order to thoroughly understand and enjoy the text. We wanted to make our list as user-friendly as possible.

3. **Ethical standards.** We recommend books that uphold Christian morality. We therefore did our best to select wholesome books and to eliminate those with blatantly objectionable content, language, or perspective. This is not necessarily to say that such books should be avoided altogether; however, they generally require critical, Christian analysis provided by mature readers, such as parents or teachers. Although we have omitted obviously objectionable books, we have included important texts by non-Christian authors, such as London, Conrad, Hardy, Crane, and Twain, whose books belittle Christian thinking in subtle ways. Readers must approach these books as they should read all literature—with the discernment of biblical faith.

4. **Visual appeal.** In the case of preschool and elementary books that include illustrations, we recommend books that are visually appealing, because pictures have perhaps as profound an impact on young minds as the stories they illustrate. When such books have multiple editions, we selected the edition that we feel best illustrates the story.

5. **Accessibility.** Except for books that were too good to pass by, we kept our selection of books as current as possible. We have also worked hard to provide up-to-date publication

information on each book. You have several options for obtaining a book that is hard to find. Don't stop your search at the local bookstore. Out-of-print book search services are available, especially online. In addition, public libraries are filled with books that are currently out of print. If you continue to come up empty-handed, we encourage you to contact us, and we will be glad to help.

We hope that you will find our recommendations useful as you look for favorites of your own. May you find our selections delicious and return often to *The Book Tree* to pick yourself a good book!

Soli Deo gloria,
ELIZABETH MCCALLUM & JANE SCOTT

PREFACE
TO THE SECOND EDITION

IN PREPARATION FOR THIS SECOND edition of *The Book Tree,* we have made some exciting discoveries and included many new titles. We hope this new expanded edition will help families as they browse for more books to enjoy. We suggest that readers look through titles in several categories because taste and reading competence vary widely with every child.

Although we are delighted with the new good books we were able to find, we must warn our readers that the caliber of contemporary children's books has declined alarmingly. Many book stores and libraries offer increasingly objectionable material; for example, one major chain has added a teen section that contains books dealing almost exclusively with pre-marital sex, homosexuality, the occult, and dysfunctional families. Such books reverse the distinction between good and evil, beauty and ugliness, integrity and depraved behavior, and they subtly, sometimes blatantly, encourage teenagers to embrace corrupt values. In addition to immoral themes, many new children's books are tastelessly illustrated, and a number are downright ugly. The Bible sets the standard for all we do, including our reading habits. In order to select books for our children that inspire, encourage, and uplift, we must consider God's standards of beauty and order: "Whatsoever things are true . . . honest . . . just . . . pure . . . lovely . . . and of good report, think on these things" (Phil. 4:8).

Illustration: *Alice's Adventures in Wonderland,* illustrated by John Tenniel (London: MacMillan & Co., 1898), see page 62.

Another concern is the increasing prevalence of rewritten or abridged books. It seems as though every classic book has been retold in order to accommodate the rising national illiteracy. These retold versions are usually poorly written and trite; they fail to capture the beauty and depth of the original. Children should read unabridged editions of the classics. If they are not old enough to enjoy a particular book, let them wait a few years. It is counterproductive to introduce a child to a retold classic before he or she is sufficiently mature to enjoy the original.

A tragic consequence of the poor quality of children's literature is that young people who love reading are a rare breed, which is heartbreaking because reading stimulates the imagination and develops a taste for reflection and evaluation. More than ever, concerned parents need good reference books to help them and their children make informed choices about reading.

Finally, parents should be aware that the literary canon— books that are most excellent and most representative of their particular culture—is under attack. Books once considered classics are rapidly being replaced by books that are worthless and often harmful. As a result, the search for good children's literature has become increasingly difficult. We would like to challenge parents, teachers, and everyone who cares about good books to reverse this alarming trend by insisting on classic literature in your libraries and book stores and by passing on to your children a love for great literature.

Please email us at *TheBookTree@canonpress.com* if you want suggestions about a particular author or book, or if you have any other questions about our favorite subject—reading!

Soli Deo gloria,
ELIZABETH MCCALLUM & JANE SCOTT

ILLUSTRATIONS
The Tale of Peter Rabbit, illustrated by Beatrix Potter
(London: Frederick Warne & Co., 1902), see page 54.

1

PRESCHOOL
LITERATURE

ADVENTURES OF LITTLE BEAR
written by Else Holmelund Minarik, illustrated by Maurice Sendak
When Little Bear plays outside in the snow, he is cold, so he asks his
mother for a coat, a hat, and finally snow pants, but when he discovers that he already has a fur coat of his own, he suddenly isn't cold at
all! You will also enjoy *Little Bear's Friend* and the other stories in the
Little Bear series of easy readers. [HarperCollins]

THE ADVENTURES OF THE BRAVE COWBOY
written and illustrated by Joan Walsh Anglund
This little cowboy has all sorts of exciting adventures. He rounds up
cattle rustlers and bank robbers. He kills mountain lions and bears,
he drives covered wagons across the prairie, and he lassoes bulls at the
rodeo. The book includes several stories about the brave cowboy as well
as pictures of his imaginary adventures. [MJF Books]

ALLIGATORS ALL AROUND
written and illustrated by Maurice Sendak
This book will teach you your alphabet while you laugh at green
alligators doing funny things. [HarperCollins]

ALL THE PLACES TO LOVE
written by Patricia MacLachlan, illustrated by Mike Wimmer
When Eli is born, his grandmother wraps him in a soft wool blanket
and holds him before an open window, so what he hears first in the

> *M*y grandmother loved
> the river best of all
> the places to love.
> That sound, like a whisper,
> she said;
> Gathering in pools
> Where trout flashed like
> jewels in the sunlight.

world is the wind. Eli soon learns about the whispering river, the hills and the valley, cattails and turtles, blueberries and the open sky. When little sister Sylvie is born, Eli will show her all the places to love. "My grandmother loved the river best of all the places to love. The sound like a whisper, she said, gathering in pools where trout flashed like jewels in the sunlight." [HarperCollins]

ALL THINGS BRIGHT AND BEAUTIFUL
written by Cecil Frances Alexander, illustrated by Mary Morgan
"All things bright and beautiful, All creatures great and small, All things wise and wonderful, the Lord God made them all." This beautiful song of praise is sweetly illustrated with scenes of children enjoying God's creation. [Grosset & Dunlap]

AMELIARANNE AND THE GREEN UMBRELLA
written by Constance Heward, illustrated by Susan Beatrice Pearse
Ameliaranne Stiggins, who always comes up with good ideas, is upset because all her little brothers and sisters are ill and can't go to the Squire's tea party. At the party, she hides her own tea—jam tarts, iced cakes, and scones—in her umbrella to take home to the little ones. But what will happen when stern Miss Josephine finds out her secret? There are many wonderful Ameliaranne stories. They are currently out of print but well worth the search! [George G. Harrap]

ANDERSEN'S FAIRY TALES
written by Hans Christian Andersen, translated by Mrs. E.V. Lucas and Mrs. H.B. Paull, illustrated by Arthur Szyk
This is a collection of wonderful fairy tales about such unforgettable characters as an emperor who refuses to admit the naked truth about his pride, a self-sacrificing mermaid, and a one-legged tin soldier who never forgets to do his duty. [Grosset & Dunlap]

ANGUS AND THE DUCKS
written and illustrated by Marjorie Flack
The first in the series of "Angus" books. Angus is a Scottish terrier who is very curious about things. Above all, he wonders what is making the quacking noise that comes from the other side of the garden hedge. One day, Angus escapes from his house, dives under the bushes, and discovers what is making the strange sound. That's when Angus learns that it is best not to be too curious. You will enjoy other stories about this little dog, such as *Angus and the Cat* and *Angus Lost*. [Farrar, Straus & Giroux]

> He was curious about WHAT lived under the sofa and in dark corners and WHO was the little dog in the mirror.

ANT AND BEE AND THE ABC
written by Angela Banner, illustrated by Bryan Ward
One day, Ant throws away his hat because it is too big for him, and Bee throws his away because it is too small. But when they begin to miss their hats, they decide to go off looking for them. They go to the place where Lost Things Are Saved in Boxes. There they find boxes for every letter of the alphabet, containing all sorts of interesting things, but do they find their hats? There are many other great Ant and Bee stories. [Trafalgar Square]

APPLE PIE
written and illustrated by Kate Greenaway
This book describes everything you can do to an apple pie, from A to Z—especially E, to *eat* it! You will love Kate Greenaway's illustrations. [Frederick Warne]

AROUND THE YEAR
written and illustrated by Tasha Tudor
Beautiful illustrations convey the special joys of each month of the year. [Simon & Schuster]

AUTUMN STORY
written and illustrated by Jill Barklem
Here you will get to know the beautiful world of Brambly Hedge, where families of field mice busy themselves by harvesting seeds and berries, preserving jams, and storing up food for the winter ahead. On one of these harvesting expeditions, little Primrose wanders away from her father and goes on a little adventure of her own. But when night falls, will she ever find her way back to her snug little home? [Atheneum]

BABY FARM ANIMALS
written and illustrated by Garth Williams
The youngest in your family will love these sweet pictures of baby animals. [Golden Books]

BIG RED BARN
written by Margaret Wise Brown, illustrated by Felicia Bond
This story describes the different animals that live happily together in the big red barn. They play all day until the sun goes down. Then they sleep safely in the barn, and only the mice are left to scamper in the hay. [HarperFestival]

BIG SISTER AND LITTLE SISTER
written by Charlotte Zolotow, illustrated by Martha Alexander
This is the story of two sisters. Big sister looks after little sister and tells her how to do everything, until one day little sister decides to go off by herself. Then little sister learns that she is very glad to have a big sister to look after her. [HarperCollins]

BILLY AND BLAZE
written and illustrated by C.W. Anderson

Right from the very start Billy and his new pony seemed to like and understand each other.

Billy loves horses more than anything else in the world, and one birthday his father gives him the most wonderful present: a pony. Billy and his new pony, Blaze, become the best of friends and enter the local Horse Show Competition. Will they win the

Silver Cup? You will also enjoy other books about Billy and Blaze such as *Blaze and the Gray Spotted Pony, Blaze and the Lost Quarry,* and *Blaze and Thunderbolt.* [Simon & Schuster]

A BIRTHDAY FOR FRANCES
written by Russell Hoban, illustrated by Lillian Hoban
As Mother and Father prepare for Gloria's birthday party, her big sister Frances wishes it were her birthday. She sulks instead of helping her mother with the preparations for Gloria's birthday, and when she buys her sister a present—a chocolate bar—Frances finds it's very hard to give up her delicious gift. [HarperCollins]

BLUEBERRIES FOR SAL
written and illustrated by Robert McCloskey
Little Sal carries her tin bucket to pick blueberries with her mother. Each blueberry she drops in goes "kuplink!" because her pail never gets full! On the other side of Blueberry Hill, Little Bear has also come with his mother to eat blueberries. Somehow, Little Bear and Little Sal get mixed up, and both mothers get a big surprise! [Penguin Putnam]

BOOK OF NURSERY AND MOTHER GOOSE RHYMES
written and illustrated by Marguerite de Angeli
A collection of the nursery rhymes you love best—funny tales, sad songs, and pretty poems. You will enjoy reading about little Bo Peep and Georgie Porgie and Daffy-Down-Dilly, and you will also love the soft illustrations Marguerite de Angeli has drawn. These poems will take you all the way up the hill to fetch a pail of water and all the way home again, jiggity-jig. [Doubleday]

BREAD AND JAM FOR FRANCES
written by Russell Hoban,
illustrated by Lillian Hoban
At breakfast time, the badger family is eating soft-boiled eggs, but Frances eats bread and jam because she is very fond of jam, and she is not very fond of eggs. In fact, at every meal-time, Frances wants just bread and

Jam is tasty, jam is sweet. Jam is sticky, jam's a treat—
Raspberry, strawberry, gooseberry, I'm very FOND . . . OF JAM!

jam. Her mother finds a way to cure Frances of this bad habit. Also look for *A Baby Sister for Frances, Bedtime for Frances,* and *Best Friends for Frances.* [HarperCollins]

THE BREMEN-TOWN MUSICIANS
written by Jacob and Wilhelm Grimm, illustrated by Paul Galdone
A cruelly mistreated donkey runs away to Bremen to look for a job as town musician. Along the way, he meets a tired old dog, a dismal cat, and a rooster escaping the soup pot. The foursome go on together to Bremen. On their way, they come across a robber's house. Though they are strong and scary men, the robbers turn out to be no match for the Bremen-Town "musicians." [McGraw-Hill]

BROWN BEAR, BROWN BEAR, WHAT DO YOU SEE?
written by Bill Martin, illustrated by Eric Carle
This book will help you learn the colors while you enjoy pictures of brightly colored animals. [Henry Holt]

CAPS FOR SALE
written and illustrated by Esphyr Slobodkina
This is the story of a peddler who sells caps, and he carries all his caps on his head. When no one wants to buy the caps, he sits down under a tree and takes a nap. When he wakes up, all his caps have disappeared. Who do you think is wearing all his caps? [HarperCollins]

THE CARROT SEED
written by Ruth Krauss, illustrated by Crockett Johnson
A little boy plants a carrot seed. Then he waters and waits, weeds and waits, for the carrot to come up. Finally it does! [HarperCollins]

CHANTICLEER AND THE FOX
written and illustrated by Barbara Cooney
Barbara Cooney has retold this tale found in *The Canterbury Tales,* a collection of short stories that Geoffrey Chaucer wrote in the 1300s. This is the story of a proud rooster named Chanticleer who is especially proud of his crowing. A fox tries to take advantage of Chanticleer's vanity, but the clever rooster finally manages to outwit the sly fox. [HarperCollins]

CHICKEN SOUP WITH RICE: A BOOK OF MONTHS

written and illustrated by
Maurice Sendak

This book will teach you the months. It tells a story about a little boy who likes chicken soup with rice just about any month of the year! [HarperCollins]

> In January it's so nice while slipping on the sliding ice to sip hot chicken soup with rice.

A CHILD'S GARDEN OF VERSES

written by Robert Louis Stevenson, illustrated by Tasha Tudor

This is a collection of wonderful poems all children enjoy. It includes old favorites such as "My Shadow," "The Land of Counterpane," and "The Swing." [Henry Z. Walck]

THE CHRISTMAS MIRACLE OF JONATHAN TOOMEY

written by Susan Wojciechowski, illustrated by P.J. Lynch

Jonathan Toomey is such a mumbling, grumbling man that all the village children call him Mr. Gloomy. Mr. Toomey is a woodcarver, and one day the widow McDowell and her son Thomas come to his door asking him to carve a special nativity scene for Christmas. Mr. Toomey takes the job, and, before long, Thomas is sitting next to Mr. Toomey watching him carve the figures, while the widow McDowell quietly knits by the fire. [Candlewick Press]

> The only sounds that could be heard were the scraping of the carving knife, the humming of the widow McDowell, and the click-click of her knitting needles.

CITY CAT, COUNTRY CAT

written by Patricia Cleveland-Peck, illustrated by Gilly Marklew

Freckle is a little farm cat who loves to sleep in the sun, catch mice in the barn, and drink milk fresh from the cows. Charlie is a city cat whose chief delights are eating canned cat food and sleeping by the cozy fire. But each cat mysteriously spends hours away from home, nobody knows where. Discovering where they go is the biggest surprise of all. [Morrow Junior Books]

THE COLOR KITTENS
written by Margaret Wise Brown,
illustrated by Alice and Martin Provensen
The kittens Hush and Brush mix pails of paint to explore a wonderful, colorful world. They learn how they can mix different colors to make new ones and are delighted at all the colors, including "Purple as violets, purple as prunes, purple as shadows on late afternoons." [Golden Books]

CORDUROY
written and illustrated by Don Freeman
Corduroy longs for someone to buy him and take him home. He's a toy bear who lives at a big store. One day, a little girl sees him and asks her mother to buy him, but her mother notices that one of the buttons on Corduroy's green overalls is missing. Corduroy is determined to spruce himself up, so he searches everywhere in the store for his lost button. You will also enjoy *A Pocket for Corduroy*. [Viking]

> The store was always filled with shoppers buying all sorts of things, but no one ever seemed to want a small bear in green overalls.

COWBOY SMALL
written and illustrated by Lois Lenski
Cowboy Small takes good care of his horse, Cactus. Cowboy Small rides out on the range, rounds up the cattle, rides a bucking bronco, and does all the other things real cowboys do. There are several other fun books in this series. [Henry Z. Walck]

THE CRIPPLED LAMB
written by Max Lucado, illustrated by Liz Bonham
Joshua is unhappy because he is crippled and he can't play with the other lambs. Only Abigail the cow is kind to the little lamb. One day, the sheep are led to a new meadow, but Joshua is too slow. He has to return to the stable. While the lamb is sleeping, something wonderful happens in that stable, and Joshua learns that God has a special plan for all His creatures. [Word]

CURIOUS GEORGE
written and illustrated by H.A. Rey
George is a very curious monkey, and his curiosity gets him into all sorts of trouble, especially with the Man in the Yellow Hat. But George manages to get out of his scrapes. Look for all the other Curious George books. [Houghton Mifflin]

DINOS TO GO
written and illustrated by Sandra Boynton
These seven dinosaurs have unique personalities (rather like people). For instance, there's Zoomer who's full of energy and Tremble who's always afraid, Snort who's mean, and Smooch who's sympathetic and loving— "she's even fond of Snort from pretty far away." [Simon & Schuster]

THE DOLLS' CHRISTMAS
written and illustrated by Tasha Tudor
Sethany Ann and Nicey Melinda are two dolls who belong to Laura and Efner. They live in a large dollhouse with lots of rooms and a conservatory full of plants. At Christmas time, the dolls have their own Christmas tree and stockings filled with small presents. Every year, they give a three-course dinner party followed by a play for all their friends, and everyone has a lovely time. [Simon & Schuster]

EMILY
written by Michael Bedard,
illustrated by Barbara Cooney
A little girl is fascinated about the neighbor who lives in the yellow house opposite, a mysterious lady called Emily Dickinson who writes poetry. When Emily invites her mother to come and play the piano

> I crept quietly from the room. I tiptoed to the bottom of the stairs. My heart beat quickly as a little bird's. I started slowly up.

at the yellow house, the little girl meets Emily for the first time, and they exchange gifts. The little girl gives Emily some bulbs to plant in the spring, and Emily gives her a beautiful poem. [Bantam Doubleday Dell]

EMMA'S LAMB
written and illustrated by Kim Lewis
One day, Emma's father brings home a lost lamb. For a little while, Emma takes care of him, and they play hide-and-seek. You will love the pictures of Emma and her lamb having a wonderful time together. [Candlewick Press]

> He had pictures of pigs. He had books about pigs. Sometimes he even had pigs in his dreams. But he had never seen a real live pig.

EMMETT'S PIG
written by Mary Stolz,
illustrated by Garth Williams
Although Emmett is used to seeing all kinds of animals at the zoo and in the apartment building where he lives, he wants very much to have a different kind of pet—a pig. As his parents explain to him, it would not be practical to have a pig in their city apartment, but he continues to dream about owning a real live pig. Then one day, it is his birthday, and Emmett gets a Very Special Surprise! [HarperCollins]

EXODUS
written and illustrated by Brian Wildsmith
This is a gorgeously illustrated retelling of the Exodus and God's dramatic redemption of His people out of bondage. *Joseph* by Brian Wildsmith is just as lavishly illustrated and faithful to the biblical record. [Eerdmans]

FIREFLIES!
written and illustrated by Julie Brinckloe
Fascinated with fireflies as they light the summer sky, a little boy catches them in a jar, watches them in wonder, and sadly lets them go. [Simon & Schuster]

THE FLOATING HOUSE
written by Scott Russell Sanders, illustrated by Helen Cogancherry
In the early 1800s, Mary and Jonathan McClure and their parents sail their flatboat with a few other families down the Ohio River from

Pennsylvania to Indiana, along with their horse, cow, mule, and pig. The children's job is to watch for sandbars and other dangers. Every evening, the McClures and other families tie up their boats to get water from the river, hunt wild animals, and trade food and provisions. They travel south through Virginia and Kentucky, and when they reach Jeffersonville, the McClures purchase land and build their house, but Mary and Jonathan can always hear the soft sound of the river splashing and lapping. [Atheneum]

> **B**ears swam across the current, snorting, black eyes gleaming. And once the whole river was blocked by a churning carpet of squirrels.

FLOSS
written and illustrated by Kim Lewis
Floss the Border collie learns how to be an excellent sheepdog on the heather-covered hills, but the thing she loves best is playing ball with the children. [Candlewick Press]

FLY AWAY, FLY AWAY OVER THE SEA
written by Christina Rossetti,
selected and illustrated by Bernadette Watts
These poems are filled with sunny fields, peaches, rainbows, and rivers—all the beauty of God's world. [North-South Books]

THE FOOLISH TORTOISE
written by Richard Buckley, illustrated by Eric Carle
A foolish tortoise wants to get along faster than his shell allows him to travel, so he abandons his protective covering. He soon finds out, however, that the world is a dangerous place for a tortoise without a shell. The story of this discontented animal is told in charming rhyme: "Along his way our hero went / And almost had an accident. / A snake with open jaws slid near. / The tortoise backed away in fear." [Scholastic]

THE FOURTH WISE MAN
retold by Susan Summers, illustrated by Jackie Morris
This is a beautifully illustrated retelling of a story written many years ago by Henry Van Dyke. You know about the three wise men who

followed the star to see the baby Jesus, but you may not know about the fourth wise man who sells all he owns and sets off with three precious jewels to give to Jesus. On his journey, he is delayed many times in order to help others in need. He does not arrive in Bethlehem in time to visit the Babe in the manger, and he gives away his jewels. But for the rest of his life, this fourth wise man continues his search for the King of Kings. [Dial Books/ Penguin Putnam]

FREIGHT TRAIN
written and illustrated by Donald Crews
This book is a delightful way to learn colors. A freight train with bright cars runs along the track, through tunnels, and across trestles by day and by night. [Greenwillow Books]

A FRIEND IS SOMEONE WHO LIKES YOU
written and illustrated by Joan Walsh Anglund
All kinds of people and things can be your friend—a boy or a girl, a dog or a cat, a mouse, a tree, a brook, or even the wind. Friends are all around you. [Harcourt Brace]

FROG AND TOAD ARE FRIENDS
written and illustrated by Arnold Lobel

> One day in summer Frog was not feeling well. Toad said, "Frog, you are looking quite green."
> "But I always look green," said Frog. "I am a frog."

Frog and Toad are best friends, so they do everything together. They go for walks. They swim in the river. When Frog is sick, Toad puts him to bed, makes him a cup of tea, and tries to think of a story to tell him. This is one of a series of great early readers. [HarperCollins]

THE FUNNIEST STORYBOOK EVER
written and illustrated by Richard Scarry
When you read this book, you will enter the wonderful, crazy world of Richard Scarry, where banana thieves screech through the streets dodging hotdog stands, leaping over bridges, plowing into restaurants, and scattering banana peels everywhere. These amazing adventures fea-

ture such entertaining characters as Sergeant Murphy, Huckle the Cat, Uncle Willy, and Lowly Worm, the hero of the hour. [Random House]

GEORGE THE DRUMMER BOY
written by Nathaniel Benchley, illustrated by Don Bolognese
George is stationed in Boston with British soldiers while America is still a British colony. George goes along with his drum when the soldiers are sent on a secret task to Concord, and soon he's in the middle of a big fight. [HarperTrophy]

THE GIVING TREE
written and illustrated by Shel Silverstein
A tree and a boy are the best of friends. As a child, the boy climbs the tree, eats her apples, and plays in her leaves. And as the boy grows older, the tree grows old with him, providing what he needs at every stage in his life. [HarperCollins]

THE GLORIOUS FLIGHT:
ACROSS THE CHANNEL WITH LOUIS BLÉRIOT
written and illustrated by Alice and Martin Provensen
This is the story of a Frenchman called Louis Blériot and his determination to build a flying machine. Like all inventors, Blériot has many failures. He suffers broken bones and bruises, but he builds one aircraft after another. And one day, he becomes the first man to fly across the English Channel. [Puffin]

> Here is BLÉRIOT I. . . . It has a little motor to make the wings flap. Alas! It flaps like a chicken. Never mind.

GOD'S CREATION—MY WORLD
written by Regine Schindler, illustrated by Hilde Heyduck-Huth
Day, night, the ocean, the land, plants, animals, and finally man— God made them all. This book celebrates the six days of Creation, giving thanks to the Lord for all the wonderful things in our world. [Abdingdon Press]

GOOD-BYE, CHARLES LINDBERGH

written by Louise Borden, illustrated by Thomas B. Allen
The incident described in this book is based on a true story. In 1929, a Mississippi farm boy is riding his horse when he sees a biplane circle over his father's fields and land in a clearing. You can imagine the boy's thrill when he realizes that the pilot is none other than the famous Charles Lindbergh! [Simon & Schuster]

GOODNIGHT MOON

written by Margaret Wise Brown, illustrated by Clement Hurd
This may very well become your favorite bedtime story. A little rabbit is tucked into bed but must say goodnight to everything in the room. The room grows darker and darker until finally the little rabbit is fast asleep. [HarperCollins]

GOODY O'GRUMPITY

written by Carol Ryrie Brink, illustrated by Ashley Wolff
When Goody O'Grumpity sets out to make a cake, all the Pilgrim children of the village flock to her house, hoping to get a scraping of the bowl. They watch the flour and eggs and spices transform into a magnificent brown cake! The recipe is included at the end of the story. [North-South Books]

THE GUARD MOUSE

written and illustrated by Don Freeman
Clyde is a mouse who guards Buckingham Palace. One night, Clyde's friends, the Petrini family from New York City, come to visit him. Clyde gives them a tour of London town—Trafalgar Square, Covent Garden Market, London Bridge, and Big Ben, which nearly deafens them when it chimes. Then Clyde must scamper back to the Palace for the Changing of the Guard. [Viking Press]

GUESS HOW MUCH I LOVE YOU

written by Sam McBratney, illustrated by Anita Jeram
Little Nutbrown Hare and Big Nutbrown Hare find many ways to say how much they love each other. "I love you as high as I can hop!"

At the end of the day, Little Nutbrown Hare nestles safely in bed. [Candlewick Press]

HAILSTONES AND HALIBUT BONES
written by Mary O'Neill, illustrated by John Wallner
"Purple is a violet opening in the spring. Red is a hotness you get inside when you're embarrassed and want to hide. Green is a coolness you feel in the shade of the tall old woods where the moss is made." All the colors, says this poem, have a wonderful story to tell. [Doubleday]

THE HAPPY LION
written by Louise Fatio, illustrated by Roger Duvoisin
The happy lion lives at the zoo in a French town. All the friendly passers-by say "Bonjour" to him. One day, the happy lion walks around town, but his friends are no longer friendly. In fact, they are very scared. Finally, the zookeeper's son finds him, and the two of them walk back to the zoo together. [McGraw-Hill]

HAPPY LITTLE FAMILY
written by Rebecca Caudill, illustrated by Decie Merwin
Bonnie is a happy four-year-old who has lots of fun and adventures with her mother, father, sisters, and brother, and she is in a great hurry not to be little any longer. You will also enjoy the other three books in the series. [Bethlehem Books]

HAROLD AND THE PURPLE CRAYON
written and illustrated by Crockett Johnson
Whenever Harold wants something, he takes his purple crayon and draws it, whether it's a path to walk on, a very small forest (so he won't get lost), a balloon to stop himself from falling out of the sky, or a policeman to ask the way. Look for other Harold books such as *Harold's Circus*, *Harold's Fairy Tale*, and *Harold at the North Pole*. [HarperCollins]

He laid out a nice simple picnic lunch. There was nothing but pie. But there were all nine kinds of pie that Harold liked best.

HENNY PENNY
written and illustrated by Paul Galdone
Henny Penny is a hen (of course), and when an acorn falls from a tree onto her head, she decides to tell the king that the sky is falling. A lot of barnyard animals go with her, but on the way a sly fox lures them into his cave, and none of these foolish animals are ever seen again. Paul Galdone has also adapted and illustrated other fables including "The Three Little Pigs" and "The Three Bears." [Houghton Mifflin]

HIDE AND SEEK FOG
written by Alvin Tresselt, illustrated by Roger Duvoisin
Suddenly, without warning, a dense fog rolls in over a seaside village on Cape Cod, turning the world a mysterious gray. The children enjoy the chance to play endless games of hide-and-seek. [William Morrow]

HOLD MY HAND
written by Charlotte Zolotow, illustrated by Thomas de Grazia
Winter creeps in with sighing wind and black clouds, but two little girls play together in the snow, holding each other's hands. [HarperCollins]

> Mashed potatoes are to give everybody enough.
> Dogs are to kiss people.
> Hands are to hold.

A HOLE IS TO DIG: A FIRST BOOK OF DEFINITIONS
written by Ruth Krauss,
illustrated by Maurice Sendak
This is a little book of first definitions. What is a face? "A face is so you can make faces." And "A face is to have on the front of your head. Hands are to hold. A seashell is to hear the sea. Dishes are to do. A hole is to dig." [HarperCollins]

I LIKE TO BE LITTLE
written by Charlotte Zolotow, illustrated by Erik Blegvad
A little girl's mommy asks her what she wants to be when she grows up. The little girl replies that she just wants to be little so that she can sit under the table and pretend it's her house or go barefoot or watch the raindrops fall down the windowpane or jump in piles of leaves. It's such fun to be little! [HarperCollins]

JAMES THE RED ENGINE
written by the Rev. W. Awdry, illustrated by C. Reginald Dalby
This is a fun train story from the author of the famed Thomas the Tank Engine. James is an engine who pulls coaches and freight cars. Unfortunately, James behaves very badly. He is careless and eventually causes damage to a train. Sir Topham Hatt the railway owner is cross and refuses to let James do any more work until James is sorry for his bad behavior. Then one day James is the only engine who can pull the big express train. [Egmont Books]

JUST ME
written and illustrated by Marie Hall Ets
A little boy mimics all the animals on the farm. He waddles after Cocky the rooster, hoppity-hops like Rabbit, and even tucks in and hides like Turtle. But when he sees Dad untying his boat on the pond, he runs, just like himself. [Penguin Putnam]

JUST YOU AND ME
written by Sam McBratney, illustrated by Ivan Bates
When a storm comes, Little Goosey and Gander Goose look for a place to shelter, but other animals have found each hiding place, and Little Goosey wants Gander Goose to be with him during the storm. So they move on to find the right place for just the two of them. [Candlewick Press]

KATIE MEETS THE IMPRESSIONISTS
written and illustrated by James Mayhew
During a visit to an art museum with her grandmother, Katie climbs into several paintings by famous artists and has a wonderful time with the son of Claude Monet and other people who are featured in some great masterpieces. This is one of a series of books about art for young children. [Orchard Books]

> "Look at the flowers in the paintings," said Grandma.
> "I can only see spots," said Katie.

KATY AND THE BIG SNOW
written and illustrated by Virginia Lee Burton
Katy is a big red tractor that belongs to the city of Geoppolis. She can push dirt, repair roads, and plow snow. One winter day, a heavy snowfall brings the city to a standstill. Everything stops except Katy. Katy plows all the roads and airport runways so that life can go on again in the big city. Everyone in Geoppolis is very thankful for Katy. [Houghton Mifflin]

> How do you carry little Catherine Crocodile? Oh, do please tell me."
> "Why, I carry her on my back, of course!" said Mrs. Crocodile.

KATY NO-POCKET
written by Emmy Payne, illustrated by H.A. Rey
Katy is a mother kangaroo, but she is very unhappy because she doesn't have a pocket for little Freddy to ride in. Katy asks other animals how they carry their children, but that doesn't help her at all. The owl tells her to buy a pocket in the city, and there Katy finds the solution to her problem. [Houghton Mifflin]

LAURA CHARLOTTE
written by Kathryn O. Galbraith, illustrated by Floyd Cooper
A little girl called Laura can't fall asleep, so she asks her mother to tell her the story of Charlotte. Charlotte was her mother's toy elephant that Grandma had made out of scraps from her sewing basket. At the end of the story, which Laura has heard many, many times, Laura is fast asleep. [Philomel Books]

THE LITTLE AIRPLANE
written and illustrated by Lois Lenski
Pilot Small has an airplane, and he goes flying. He does all the things a pilot does as he flies high above the clouds. But during one ride, he has engine trouble and has to make a forced landing to fix his motor. [Henry Z. Walck]

THE LITTLE AUTO
written and illustrated by Lois Lenski
Mr. Small has a red auto, and he takes very good care of it. Then he goes for a drive and always obeys the traffic signals. [Henry Z. Walck]

LITTLE BAA
written and illustrated by Kim Lewis
Little Baa has a happy time frisking in the field with his mother. When he is tired, he takes a nap, and his mother wanders away to graze on the sweet grass. Then she sets off with the shepherd's collie Floss to find her Little Baa. [Candlewick Press]

THE LITTLE ENGINE THAT COULD
written by Watty Piper, illustrated by George and Doris Hauman
A tenacious little blue engine rescues a broken-down train and pulls it over the mountain, to the delight of everyone on board—the toys, dolls, and the funniest little clown you ever saw. [Penguin Putnam]

THE LITTLE FIR TREE
written by Margaret Wise Brown, illustrated by Barbara Cooney
A sick little boy looks at the trees outside his window and longs for a tree of his own. Out in the forest is a lonely fir tree, so at Christmas time the boy's father digs up the tree and places it by the child's bedside. Other children visit and sing about Christ's birth. [HarperCollins]

LITTLE FUR FAMILY
written by Margaret Wise Brown, illustrated by Garth Williams
A little fur family wears little fur coats and lives in a tree. The father works, the mother takes care of her child, and the little fur child plays in the wild, wild wood. [HarperCollins]

> And there was his father who put him to bed and they tucked him in bed all soft and all warm, and they held his paw and they sang him a song.

LITTLE GREY RABBIT GOES TO THE SEA
written by Alison Uttley, illustrated by Margaret Tempest
After Squirrel, Hare, and Grey Rabbit all catch colds and sneezes, even blackcurrant tea and hot soup don't cure them. Wise Owl recommends

an outing to the seaside. A splendid idea. They all pile into a caravan which takes them to the waves and the seagulls, where their sneezes are whisked away. [Ascherberg, Hopwood & Crew]

Note: Alison Uttley wrote many Little Grey Rabbit books, and they are all wonderful but hard to find; most of them are out of print. However, with a little work and patience, you should be able to locate some of them.

THE LITTLE HOUSE
written and illustrated by Virginia Lee Burton

The Little House lives in the country but is curious about the big city lights that twinkle far away. One day, a road is dug in front of the Little House, and before long she is surrounded by other houses, shops, and businesses, and finally by tall skyscrapers, an elevated train, and a subway. Now the Little House longs for the green fields and the daisies of the countryside. [Houghton Mifflin]

> She didn't like living in the city. At night she used to dream of the country and the field of daisies and the apple trees dancing in the moonlight.

THE LITTLE SAILBOAT
written and illustrated by Lois Lenski

Captain Small has a sailboat. He goes fishing and sailing, and he knows how to do all the things a sailor does even when it gets very dark and windy. [Henry Z. Walck]

LITTLE TIM AND THE BRAVE SEA CAPTAIN
written and illustrated by Edward Ardizzone

Tim wants very much to be a sailor, but everyone says he is much too young. One day, he gets his chance. He runs away to sea as a stowaway. So begins Tim's big adventure during which he nearly ends up in Davy Jones's locker! You will enjoy all of Ardizzone's "Tim" books, including *Tim in Danger*, *Tim to the Rescue*, and *Tim and Ginger*. [Lothrop, Lee & Shepard]

THE LORD IS MY SHEPHERD: THE TWENTY-THIRD PSALM

illustrated by Tasha Tudor

Tasha Tudor illustrates the King James Version of this beloved psalm with delicate watercolor paintings. [Penguin Putnam]

MADELINE

written and illustrated by Ludwig Bemelmans

Madeline and eleven other little girls go to boarding school in Paris. One awful night, Madeline has to be rushed to the hospital to have her appendix taken out. When the eleven other little girls visit her and see all her toys, they cry and want to have their appendixes out too. This is the first in a long series of Madeline books. [Penguin]

MAKE WAY FOR DUCKLINGS

written and illustrated by Robert McCloskey

This is the story of Mrs. Mallard's ducklings and their historic parade through the center of Boston. [Penguin]

MANY MOONS

written by James Thurber, illustrated by Louis Slobodkin

Princess Lenore is ill and cannot recover until her wish is granted: she wants the moon. None of the wisest men of the land can solve the King's dilemma. Then the Court Jester, who is the wisest man in the kingdom, proposes an ingenious solution. [Harcourt Brace]

MAY I BRING A FRIEND?

written by Beatrice Schenk de Regniers, illustrated by Beni Montresor

When the King and the Queen invite a little boy to tea at the royal palace, they are perfectly agreeable to is bringing a friend. So every day, the boy comes to tea and one by one brings with him a giraffe, a hippo, an elephant, and a seal—not

> The King and Queen
> Invited me
> To come to their house
> On Sunday for tea.
> I told the Queen
> And the Queen told the King
> I had a friend
> I wanted to bring.

to mention monkeys and lions. Of course, the animals must return the invitation, so the King and Queen join them for tea—at the zoo. [Simon & Schuster]

A MEDIEVAL FEAST
written and illustrated by Aliki
When the King and the Queen come to Camdenton Manor, many preparations must be made, because kings and queens do not travel alone! Everyone at Camdenton, from the lord and lady of the manor to the serfs who work the land, pitches in to prepare for the exciting royal visit. Detailed illustrations give you a picture of medieval life—hunting, hawking, dancing, and feasting! [HarperCollins]

MIKE MULLIGAN AND HIS STEAM SHOVEL
written and illustrated by Virginia Lee Burton
The terrific tale of the great tasks Mike and his prized steam shovel Mary Anne can accomplish. Mike and Mary Anne are determined to dig the foundation of the new town hall of Popperville—in one day! Mike is sure that his trusty machine is up to the job and that Mary Anne can out-dig the new Diesel shovels. But when Mike and Mary Anne finish the foundation on time, they still have a problem: how are they going to get out? [Houghton Mifflin]

MILLIONS OF CATS
written and illustrated by Wanda Gag

Cats here, cats there,
Cats and kittens everywhere,
Hundreds of cats,
Thousands of cats,
Millions and billions and trillions of cats.

Once upon a time, there was a lonely old man and a lonely old woman. The man sets off to find the old woman a cat, but instead he finds hundreds and thousands and millions of cats. He brings them all home to the old woman. The old woman is dismayed, but she finds a way out of their dilemma. [Putnam]

MISS RUMPHIUS

written and illustrated by Barbara Cooney

Miss Rumphius has always wanted to visit faraway places and live by the sea. At last she fulfills these desires, but she also follows her grandfather's advice and makes the world more beautiful. She plants flowers everywhere she goes until the whole land is covered with pink, blue, and purple blossoms. [Viking]

> ou must do something to make the world more beautiful," said her grandfather.
> "All right," said Alice. But she did not know what that could be.

MISS SUZY

written by Miriam Young, illustrated by Arnold Lobel

Miss Suzy is an industrious squirrel who lives at the top of a big tree. One day, some selfish squirrels chase her away from her little house. She is without a home until she joins forces with some toy soldiers and sets up housekeeping in an abandoned dollhouse. [Simon & Schuster]

THE MITTEN

written and illustrated by Jan Brett

While playing outside on a snowy day, Nicki loses one of the white mittens his grandmother has just knitted for him. While he is searching everywhere, a little mole finds it and crawls inside. Other animals join the mole in this snug, warm nest, and with each new animal the mitten gets bigger and bigger. [Penguin Putnam]

MITTENS

written and illustrated by Clare Turlay Newberry

Richard is terribly upset when his kitten is lost, and even a newspaper advertisement fails to locate his new pet. [HarperCollins]

MOG THE FORGETFUL CAT

written and illustrated by Judith Kerr

Mog is a forgetful cat. She forgets to use her own special door to get back into the house, so she tramples on the window box flowers and meows to be let back in. She is always in the way. Some of the people in the house don't seem to like her, but one night Mog does something very remarkable for her family. [HarperCollins]

MOUSEKIN'S ABC
written and illustrated by Edna Miller
Mousekin learns his alphabet by means of the Acorns under the oak tree, the little brown Bat with his small pug nose, Cottontail who lives in the clover, and all the other creatures and flowers of Mousekin's beautiful world. [Prentice-Hall]

> **W**ell, she likes yellow," said the little girl. "Yellow," said Mr. Rabbit. "You can't give her yellow."

MR. RABBIT AND THE LOVELY PRESENT
written by Charlotte Zolotow, illustrated by Maurice Sendak
A little girl doesn't know what to give her mother for a birthday present, so she asks Mr. Rabbit for help. Mr. Rabbit makes a lot of impractical suggestions but then suggests giving her mother red apples, yellow bananas, green pears, and blue grapes. The little girl puts all the fruit in her basket, and it makes a lovely present. [HarperCollins]

A NEW COAT FOR ANNA
written by Harriet Ziefert, illustrated by Anita Lobel
Anna's mother is poor, so she decides to sell her few treasures to buy the things they will need to make a new winter coat for Anna. They exchange a gold watch for the wool. Next the wool must be spun, then dyed, then woven into cloth before a tailor can make the coat. All these steps take such a long time that Anna must wait a year before she wears her beautiful new coat. On Christmas Eve, Anna's mother, the farmer, the spinner, the weaver, and the tailor all agree that Anna looks very smart indeed! [Dragonfly Books]

1 IS ONE
written and illustrated by Tasha Tudor
"1 is one duckling swimming in a dish. 2 is two sisters making a wish." This book will teach you to count life's simple joys from one to twenty. [Simon & Schuster]

ONE MORNING IN MAINE
written and illustrated by Robert McCloskey

One morning Sal wakes up with a loose tooth, and she is worried that she won't be able to go with her father to Buck's Harbor to dig for clams. But when her mother explains about becoming a big girl, Sal is very excited. After her tooth falls out, Sal and her father row across the bay to the grocery store, and Sal tells everyone in the village all about it. [Viking]

> In May they planted potatoes, turnips, and cabbages, while apple blossoms bloomed and fell, while bees woke up, starting to make new honey, and geese squawked in the barnyard, dropping feathers as soft as clouds.

ONE WAS JOHNNY: A COUNTING BOOK
written and illustrated by Maurice Sendak

This book will teach you your numbers. It's a funny story about a lot of strange creatures who come to visit Johnny. [HarperCollins]

OVER THE RIVER AND THROUGH THE WOOD
written by Lydia Maria Child, illustrated by Christopher Manson

"Over the river and through the wood to Grandfather's house we go." This familiar poem about riding a sled to Grandfather's house for Thanksgiving Day is illustrated with beautiful woodcuts and includes the musical score at the end. [North-South Books]

THE OWL AND THE PUSSY-CAT
written by Edward Lear, illustrated by Hilary Knight

You will love the funny nonsense verse of the Owl and the Pussy-Cat who "set out to sea in a beautiful pea-green boat." [Simon & Schuster Children's]

OX-CART MAN
written by Donald Hall, illustrated by Barbara Cooney

Every year, the farmer fills his ox-cart with all the left-over things he and his family have made or grown all year long—shawls and mittens, candles and shingles, apples and turnips, and everything else imaginable. He takes his load to market where he sells everything for a fair price. He then buys the supplies his family needs to make all sorts of new things. All year long, they carve and stitch and weave and knit and plant on their happy little farm. [Penguin]

PETER AND THE WOLF, ADAPTATION
written by Sergei Prokofiev, illustrated by Ian Beck
Prokofiev wrote this short orchestral piece to introduce musical instruments to children, and this edition of the story helps you follow the music even better by illustrating each character with the instrument the orchestra plays for each one. Meet brave Peter, his grumpy grandfather, the little bird, saucy duck, slinky cat, and especially the big gray wolf! [Simon & Schuster]

PETUNIA
written and illustrated by Roger Duvoisin
Petunia is such a silly goose that she thinks that if she carries a book around with her everyone will think her wise. Petunia becomes prouder and prouder, and her neck stretches longer and longer. To make matters worse, all the animals who seek her advice suffer greatly from her most unwise counsel. Finally, Petunia realizes what she must do in order to become truly wise. [Knopf Books for Young Readers]

PIP CAMPS OUT
written by Myra Berry Brown, illustrated by Phyllis Graham
Pip decides to camp out in his backyard. The night becomes dark and menacing until he is joined by his dad. As they drink some hot chocolate, Pip decides that the backyard is not so scary after all. [Golden Gate Junior Books]

> Oh, now I was happy— as happy could be! For all of them—ALL OF THEM—were playing with me.

PLAY WITH ME
written and illustrated by Marie Hall Ets
A little girl tries to persuade different creatures to play with her, but they all run away. Then she sits in the meadow without making a sound, and all the creatures come out of their hiding places to play with her. [Penguin Putnam]

A QUILT FOR BABY
written and illustrated by Kim Lewis
As a mother sews a patchwork quilt for her baby, she tells the baby about each square. One shows a picture of their sheep, one is for Floss the dog, and one for each of the other farm animals. When she has finished, the mother wraps the baby snugly in the quilt that tells the story of his home. [Candlewick Press]

SAM THE MINUTEMAN
written by Nathaniel Benchley, illustrated by Arnold Lobel
Sam Brown's father is a minuteman in colonial America. That means he is part of the colonial militia and has to be ready to fight at a minute's notice. One day, British soldiers start marching from Boston to Concord. Sam and his dad leap into action to defend their town. And before anyone knows it, the American Revolution has begun. The next time the British march, Sam and the Minutemen are ready for them! [HarperCollins]

SNOW-WHITE AND ROSE-RED
written and illustrated by Barbara Cooney
This is a retelling of a Grimm's fairy tale. Even though Snow-White is quiet and gentle, and Rose-Red is merry and lively, the two sisters are inseparable friends. One day, a friendly black bear comes into their cottage to warm up during a winter storm. The girls are eager to make him comfortable, and the bear becomes a regular visitor to their happy home. Snow-White and Rose-Red are even kind to a mean little dwarf, helping him out of all sorts of fixes. Before long, their compassion is well rewarded in the most surprising way. [Delacorte Press]

THE SNOWY DAY
written and illustrated by Ezra Jack Keats
When Peter wakes one winter morning, he discovers a world covered with a blanket of snow. He scrambles into his snowsuit and runs outside to make crunchy tracks and snow angels, and he slides down snow mountains all the way to his house. The snowball he has saved in his pocket will never last the night, but in the morning the snow falls all over again. [Penguin Putnam]

SPRING IS A NEW BEGINNING

written and illustrated by Joan Walsh Anglund

A book about spring when everything is fresh and "leafy-tipped and new." It lists all the childhood pleasures of springtime—sailing boats, finding birds' eggs, planting things, and picking spring flowers. Look for other sweet stories by this author. [Harcourt Brace]

SPRINGTIME FOR JEANNE-MARIE

written and illustrated by Françoise Seignobosc

Jeanne-Marie has two pets—a duck called Madelon and a sheep called Patapon. Madelon loves to swim on the river while Jeanne-Marie and Patapon watch. One day, Madelon does not come back. Jeanne-Marie and Patapon cannot find her anywhere, and they are very sad—but not for long! You will love all the Jeanne-Marie books including *Noel for Jeanne-Marie*, *The Big Rain*, *What Time Is It?*, and *Jeanne-Marie Counts Her Sheep*. [Smithmark]

STONE SOUP

written and illustrated by Marcia Brown

Three hungry soldiers arrive at a country village, and none of the villagers will give them any food. So the ingenious men say they will make some soup out of a stone. They persuade the villagers to flavor the soup with vegetables and meat, and soon it is a delicious meal. The villagers are grateful to the soldiers for teaching them how to make soup from stones! [Simon & Schuster]

THE STORM BOOK

written by Charlotte Zolotow, illustrated by Margaret Bloy Graham

On a slow, dusty summer day, the flowers are wilting, and even the birds are too hot to sing. Dark clouds gather, and suddenly lightning flashes and thunder rolls. Far away in the city, rain pours onto the streets. In the countryside, rain streams down over the mountains into the lake. But inside one house, a little boy looks out of the windows watching the pit-a-pat slowly become sunny again. [Turtleback Books]

> Shooting through the sky like a streak of starlight comes a flash so beautiful, so fast, that the little boy barely has time to see the flowers straining into the storm wind.

THE STORY ABOUT PING
written by Marjorie Flack, illustrated by Kurt Wiese
Ping the duck lives with his mother and father and sisters and brothers and aunts and uncles and cousins on a boat on the Yangtze River. Each day, all the ducks leave the boat to find things to eat on the shore, and each night they return to the boat. The last duck on board always gets a spanking. So Ping is careful not to be last. One day, he is the last duck to return to the boat, so he hides on the riverbank. Ping has some exciting adventures on the shore of the Yangtze River. [Penguin Putnam]

> Ping was always very, very careful not to be last, because the last duck to cross over the bridge always got a spank on the back.

THE STORY OF BABAR
written and illustrated by Jean de Brunhoff
One day, Mrs. De Brunhoff makes up a story about an elephant to entertain her children. Their father writes the story down and illustrates it. And that's how the Babar stories got started. This first Babar story tells how Babar leaves the forest and comes to the city. He soon adapts happily to city life after he obtains a suit in a becoming shade of green. On his return to the forest, he is crowned King of the elephants, and Celeste is crowned Queen. This is the first of many other Babar adventures. [Random House]

> In the great forest a little elephant is born. His name is Babar.

THE STORY OF FERDINAND
written by Monro Leaf, illustrated by Robert Lawson
Most of the other bulls of Spain want to fight in the big bullfight, but Ferdinand likes to sit under a tree and smell the flowers. So when Ferdinand finds himself in the bullring with the Picadores and the Matador—well, all Ferdinand notices are the flowers in the ladies' hair! [Penguin Putnam]

THE STORY OF JOHNNY APPLESEED
written and illustrated by Aliki
Johnny Appleseed, the gentle pioneer, travels across America with a cooking pan on his head and a bag of apple seeds on his back. Wherever he goes, he makes friends and leaves behind him a gift of apple trees. [Simon & Schuster]

THE TALE OF CUSTARD THE DRAGON
written by Ogden Nash, illustrated by Lynn Munsinger
This is a funny nonsense poem. Belinda has four pets, Ink a kitten, Blink a mouse, Mustard a dog, and "a realio, trulio little pet dragon." Now the dragon has all the usual things—spikes and scales and fire and smoke coming out of his mouth and nose, but he's a coward, so Belinda calls him Custard. The others think they're the brave ones, but when a horrible someone breaks into Belinda's house, who do you think is the hero? [Little, Brown]

THE TALE OF PETER RABBIT
written and illustrated by Beatrix Potter

> *P*eter rushed into the tool shed and jumped into a can. It would have been a beautiful thing to hide in if it had not had so much water in it.

The adventure of naughty Peter Rabbit who attempts an excursion into Mr. McGregor's vegetable garden. The easy part of his adventure is getting into the garden. Peter's real problem is getting out again and safely home to his nice soft rabbit hole. You will love all of Beatrix Potter's classic animal tales such as *The Tale of Jemima Puddle-Duck*, *The Tale of Mrs. Tiggy-Winkle*, and *The Tale of Mr. Jeremy Fisher*. [Frederick Warne]

THE TALE OF THREE TREES
written by Angela Hunt, illustrated by Tim Jonke
Angela Hunt has retold this traditional American folktale about three little trees and what they dream of becoming when they grow up. One wants to be a beautiful treasure chest, one wants to be a sailing ship,

but the third tree just wants to grow tall and point people to God. [Lion Publishing]

THREE DUCKS WENT WANDERING
written by Ron Roy, illustrated by Paul Galdone
Three little ducks wander in and out of the most frightening situations, completely unaware of their danger. They encounter a bull, some foxes, a hawk, and a snake, and narrowly escape each time, until at last they come home to mother's wings. [Ticknor & Fields]

THE THREE RAILWAY ENGINES
written by the Rev. W. Awdry, illustrated by C. Reginald Dalby
Edward, Gordon, and Henry are three engines who can't seem to get along together. They are always bragging about what they can do and being impolite to one another. But they learn to be kind and helpful, and now they are good friends. Also look for *Henry the Green Engine, Thomas the Tank Engine,* and *Tank Engine Thomas Again.* [Heinemann]

TIME OF WONDER
written and illustrated by Robert McCloskey
On an island in Maine, two children watch the wildlife and explore the coastline where sometimes a cloud darkens the hills, sometimes the fog turns the trees into ghosts, and sometimes the blue water sparkles and is filled with boats and porpoises. And during a storm, the children are cozy and safe at home. [Puffin]

> You, on your island, are standing in the shadow, watching the rain begin to spill down way across the bay.

TIM MOUSE
written and illustrated by Judy Brook
Tim Mouse is enjoying a quiet, sunny nap one day when suddenly he hears that his friends the field mice are in great trouble. They are trapped in a cornfield that is being cut! Tim Mouse leaps into action and daringly saves his friends from a horrible fate. [Platt & Munk]

TOO MUCH NOISE

written by Ann McGovern, illustrated by Simms Taback
Old man Peter is unhappy about his noisy house, so the wise man of the village gives him some sage advice that teaches him to be content. [Houghton Mifflin]

A TREE IS NICE

written by Janice May Udry, illustrated by Marc Simont
Here are some good reasons why a child thinks a tree is nice. [HarperCollins]

THE UGLY DUCKLING

written by Hans Christian Andersen,
retold and illustrated by Troy Howell
A duck's newly hatched ducklings are all yellow and fluffy, except for one odd gray bird. The other ducks are unkind to the gray bird and call him an ugly duckling. Even his sisters and brothers ignore him. Finally, the ugly duckling runs away. How rejected he feels until one day he makes a wonderful discovery. [Putnam]

UMBRELLA

written and illustrated by
Taro Yashima

> The word Momo means "the peach" in Japan where her father and mother used to live.

A little girl called Momo is given two birthday presents: red rubber boots and an umbrella. While the sun shines brightly, Momo waits and waits for the rain. One day, the rain falls. Momo runs outside, and the raindrops make wonderful music on her umbrella. [Puffin]

THE VELVETEEN RABBIT

written by Margery Williams, illustrated by William Nicholson
This is a tale about a favorite toy rabbit who starts off life in a beautiful Christmas stocking and, through lots of years and loving, becomes quite tattered and old. Just as he thinks his days are numbered, he undergoes an amazing transformation. [Doubleday]

WARM AS WOOL
written by Scott Russell Sanders, illustrated by Helen Cogancherry

In 1803, three little children travel with their parents to the wilderness of Ohio. It is a very cold winter, and the children's teeth chatter as they try to get warm. What they need is wool for warm clothes, but they don't own any sheep. Their mother takes their savings to buy a few sheep, and although their hardships are not over, they are now happy to be warm as wool. [Simon & Schuster]

The clothes the children had worn since moving out here to the Ohio frontier were tattered and frayed. Betsy Ward sewed patches on their patches, and still the cold played music on the children's ribs, the wind whistled about their knees.

WHAT DO PEOPLE DO ALL DAY?
written and illustrated by Richard Scarry

Busytown is bustling with activity. There are dentists, taxi-drivers, firemen, barbers, and chimney sweeps, but everyone is a worker. These funny stories tell how people like Farmer Alfalfa and Stitches the tailor make their livings. You will learn how a letter is mailed, how a house is built, how the fire department works, with the help of Lowly Worm, and what it's like to visit the doctor. This book will answer questions you wouldn't think to ask! Other Richard Scarry titles include *Great Big Air Book* and *Great Big Schoolhouse*. [Random House]

WHEN WE WERE VERY YOUNG
written by A.A. Milne, illustrated by Ernest Shepard

These are poems that you will remember all your life. Some of our favorites are "Politeness" ("If people ask me, I always tell them, 'Quite well, thank you, I'm very glad to say.' . . . But SOMETIMES I wish that they wouldn't."), "Buckingham Palace," "The King's Breakfast," and "Disobedience" ("James James Morrison Morrison Weatherby George Dupree took great care of his Mother, Though he was only three"). You will also want to read the poems in A.A. Milne's *Now We Are Six*. [Dutton]

WHERE'S WALLACE?
written and illustrated by Hilary Knight
Wallace is an orange orangutan who lives at the zoo. Wallace is very happy, but he keeps escaping from his cage and doing the things that *people* do, like buying suits, visiting museums, and picnicking. See if you can spot Wallace in all the pictures before you turn each page! [Harper & Row]

WHISTLE FOR WILLIE
written and illustrated by Ezra Jack Keats
Peter wants to know how to whistle so that he can whistle for his dog Willie. He tries and tries. All of a sudden he can whistle, and Willie comes straight to him! [Puffin]

WHITE SNOW, BRIGHT SNOW
written by Alvin Tresselt, illustrated by Roger Duvoisin
Everyone in the town—the grown-ups, the farmer, the policeman, the children, even the rabbits—knows it is going to snow. The snow falls and covers the houses, trees, and roads with a soft white blanket. The children catch the snowflakes on their tongues. They make a snowman and a snow fort and have a snowball fight. Then the sun shines and melts the snow, and the children watch for the first robin to tell them that spring has come. [William Morrow]

> White snow, bright snow, smooth and deep.
> Light snow, night snow, quiet as sleep.
> Down, down, without a sound;
> Down, down to the frozen ground.

THE WORLD OF WINNIE-THE-POOH and THE HOUSE AT POOH CORNER
written by A.A. Milne, illustrated by Ernest Shepard
The adventures of Christopher Robin and his friends: Pooh, a very stout bear with no brain, little Piglet, Pooh's loyal friend whose ears stream out behind him when he runs, Tigger, who gets so bouncy that he has to be unbounced, Eeyore, a gray donkey who is always gloomy, and lots of other friends and relations. When Pooh visits Rabbit and eats

a large meal, he finds he can't squeeze through the front door. "The fact is," said Rabbit, "you're stuck." Pooh: "It all comes of not having front doors big enough." Rabbit: "It all comes of eating too much." [Dutton]

WYNKEN, BLYNKEN, AND NOD
written by Eugene Field, illustrated by Johanna Westerman
Three children make a magical voyage by moonlight. This poem is a special bedtime favorite. [North-South Books]

ILLUSTRATIONS
Cinderella, illustrated by Arthur Rackham
(London: William Heinemann, 1919), see page 75.

ELEMENTARY
SCHOOL FICTION

ABEL'S ISLAND
written and illustrated by William Steig
Abelard Hassam di Chirico Flint, or "Abel" for short, is a mouse who enjoys all of life's luxuries. One day, he and his new wife Amanda are eating a leisurely picnic when a terrible storm sweeps him away and deposits him on a deserted island. For a while, Abel amuses himself by imagining what he will say to everyone about his adventure. Then he begins to criticize his friends for being so slow about rescuing him. But when he realizes he's not going to be rescued any time soon, this ingenious mouse devises one scheme after another to get off the island and home to his dear wife. [Farrar, Straus & Giroux]

ADAM OF THE ROAD
written by Elizabeth Janet Gray, illustrated by Robert Lawson
Adam is eleven years old and lives in thirteenth-century England. He and his father are minstrels. They travel from castle to castle, entertaining lords and ladies by telling stories in song. One day, Adam's dog Nick is stolen, and, even worse, Adam is separated from his father. Now he is alone and must fend for himself against many dangers. At one point, he is pursued by robbers and must dodge the arrows whistling by his ears. Adam suffers many hardships on his long journey to find his father and his dog. This book gives you a great picture of medieval England. In it, you will meet palmers and chapmen, wassailers and Oxford clerks, and all the other colorful members of medieval society. [Puffin]

THE ADVENTURES OF PINOCCHIO
written by Carlo Collodi, translated by M.A. Murray,
illustrated by Charles Folkard

Once upon a time, an old man makes a wooden puppet called Pinocchio. Pinocchio is a very mischievous puppet, but he learns the hard way how foolish it is to tell lies and consort with bad companions. But Pinocchio simply cannot stay out of trouble. One day, Pinocchio discovers that his ears have grown long and hairy—he has turned into a donkey! Do you think this bad puppet will ever learn to be good? Pinocchio will have to reform if he is to get his wish and be transformed into a real human boy. [Penguin]

> At this third lie his nose grew to such an extraordinary length that poor Pinocchio could not move in any direction.

ADVENTURES OF THE GREEK HEROES
written by Mollie McLean and Anne Wiseman,
illustrated by Witold T. Mars

Two fine storytellers retell some classic Greek myths. This collection tells the exciting tale of Hercules doing battle with a nine-headed monster and a three-headed man. Also included are Perseus's encounter with Medusa, Orpheus's descent into the underworld, and Jason's search for the Golden Fleece. [Houghton Mifflin]

AESOP'S FABLES
written by Aesop, translated by S.A. Handford, illustrated by Brian Robb

Aesop's tales are short and funny and may even remind you of some foolish people you have met before. You will have fun reading about the boy who cried wolf too often, the dog in the manger, and the race between the tortoise and the hare. [Penguin]

ALICE'S ADVENTURES IN WONDERLAND
written by Lewis Carroll, illustrated by John Tenniel

Alice's extraordinary adventures begin when she falls down a very long rabbit hole into Wonderland. She experiences nerve-wracking changes in her size, once growing so small that she falls into a pool of her own tears. Her adventures are amazing: she comforts a baby who turns into a pig; meets a Cheshire cat who is able to disappear leaving behind only his grin; attends a tea party with a March Hare, a Mad Hatter, and a Dormouse who falls asleep in his teacup; and plays croquet with the Queen of Hearts. By this time, Alice

Curiouser and curiouser!" cried Alice (she was so much surprised, that for the moment she quite forgot how to speak good English).

is hardly surprised to find that the croquet players use live hedgehogs as balls and flamingoes as mallets. You will also enjoy the sequel, *Through the Looking Glass.* [HarperCollins]

AMAHL AND THE NIGHT VISITORS
written by Gian-Carlo Menotti, illustrated by Roger Duvoisin
This is an adaptation of Menotti's opera. It tells the story of a crippled shepherd boy visited one night by three kings as they journey towards Bethlehem and the baby Jesus. Amahl gives them a gift for Jesus; it is all he has to give—his crutch. In return he receives the most wonderful gift of all. [William Morrow]

AMERICA TRAVELS
written by Alice Dalgliesh, illustrated by Hildegard Woodward
This is a collection of stories about the many ways that American children traveled one hundred years ago. Deborah travels by stagecoach; David rides on the first train of the Mohawk and Hudson Railroad, and other children travel by canal boat, covered wagon, and buggy. Two children are the first boys in their town to ride in a horseless carriage. This fascinating book also includes a "Picture Story of Travel" with lots more information about travel in America during the last century. [Macmillan]

AMY'S GOOSE
written by Efner Tudor Holmes, illustrated by Tasha Tudor
Amy is an only child who lives on a farm. Every fall, a flock of geese comes to her lake to spend a night on their way south. They eat the corn that they know Amy will have ready for them. How Amy looks forward

to their arrival! This year, Amy sees them coming from far away. She and her father go down to the lake that night to spread out their feed. Just then, a fox darts into the flock and attacks one of the beautiful birds. What will happen to Amy's goose? [Thomas Y. Crowell]

ANAK, THE ESKIMO BOY
written by Piet Prins, translated by Alice Veenendaal,
illustrated by Annelies Kuiper
Anak lives with his father, mother, sister, grandfather, and grandmother in a snug little igloo in an Eskimo settlement in the far lands of the North. During the winters, the sun does not rise at all, and the days are cold and dark. But Anak and his friend Jako take advantage of the snow to learn how to drive sleds pulled by teams of dogs. Both boys are growing up so quickly. But they have much to learn—how to hunt seals, caribou, and walruses, and also how to stay out of trouble. One day, Anak's father takes him on a trading trip to the white man's settlement. Anak is introduced to many new things like guns, matches, and, best of all, the Gospel of Christ. [Inheritance Publications]

AND THEN WHAT HAPPENED, PAUL REVERE?
written by Jean Fritz, illustrated by Margot Tomes
Boston is a busy town, but one of the busiest men living there is Paul Revere. He is a silversmith, bell-ringer, soldier, portrait maker, dentist, and patriot. This great tale gives the details of Revere's role in the Boston Tea Party and his exciting "Big Ride" through the countryside alerting the colonies of the coming Red Coats. After that historical ride, Paul Revere entertains at least a dozen grandchildren with stories of his adventures. Whenever he pauses for a moment, they all ask, "And then what happened?" [Putnam]

There was a tax on tea, glass, printers' colors, and paper. The one tax England would never give up was the tax on tea. And what did Paul Revere do about it? He became a leader of the Sons of Libery, a secret club that found interesting ways to oppose the English.

ANNE OF GREEN GABLES

written by L.M. Montgomery

Matthew and Marilla Cuthbert have decided to adopt a boy from the agency to help with the farm work at Green Gables. When the boy turns out to be a girl, neither of them knows quite what to do with her. Anne Shirley has carrot-red pigtails and a fiery imagination to match. Despite her ceaseless chatter and mischievous mind, she soon charms Matthew and Marilla, and eventually even softens the gossipy Mrs. Lynde. Before long, Anne has transformed life at Green Gables. Her sharp tongue and love of adventure cause her many troubles. But soon the whole community is convinced that they could never imagine life without Anne of Green Gables. Other titles in this series: *Anne of Avonlea, Anne of the Island, Anne of Windy Poplars, Anne's House of Dreams, Anne of Ingleside, Chronicles of Avonlea, Further Chronicles of Avonlea.* [Bantam]

> Ann sighed. "I can't. I'm in the depths of despair. Can you eat when you are in the depths of despair?"
>
> "I've never been in the depths of despair, so I can't say," responded Marilla.

ANNIE HENRY AND THE REDCOATS

written by Susan Olasky

In the middle of the American War for Independence, Annie, the teenage daughter of Patrick Henry, has plenty of ideas of her own. The story opens as the whole Henry household is leaving Richmond to settle on the frontier. Life is busy for Annie as she teaches lessons to her mischievous brother and her fashion-conscious sister. But she longs for something "important" to do as the war rages on. When an opportunity arises for her to go to Richmond to stay with her aunt and cousins, she jumps at the chance to be close to the action. As she tends battle-weary soldiers and evades Redcoats, Annie finds her character tested and strengthened. Also look for *Annie Henry and the Birth of Liberty, Annie Henry and the Mysterious Stranger,* and *Annie Henry and the Secret Mission.* All four volumes are also available as a single volume, *Annie Henry: Adventures in the American Revolution.* [Crossway]

"B" IS FOR BETSY

written and illustrated by Carolyn Haywood

Betsy is six years old and facing her first day of school. She doesn't know what to expect, but she's pretty sure she won't like it. Betsy changes her mind after she meets her teacher, sweet Miss Grey, and a little girl named Ellen who sits near her. What with school projects like tadpoles, Thanksgiving baskets, and even a pretend circus, every day seems full of new surprises. [Odyssey]

BABE THE GALLANT PIG

written by Dick King-Smith, illustrated by Mary Rayner

You may have seen the movie *Babe,* but have you read the book on which the movie is based? When farmer Hogget and his wife first acquire Babe, all they think about are the hams they'll have for Christmas, but when Babe saves their sheep from sheep rustlers, they change their minds about this extraordinary pig. Babe proves that he's better at sheepherding than the sheepdog. [Crown]

BACK TO SCHOOL WITH BETSY

written and illustrated by Carolyn Haywood

This is the sequel to *"B" Is for Betsy.* How will Betsy raise enough money for a wedding present for her favorite teacher? When she decides to club together with her friends Ellen and Billy to buy a grand present, she discovers Billy has some strange gift ideas. In fact, he has his heart set on a monkey. Too bad they won't have enough money to make the purchase! [Odyssey]

> The two little girls stuck their heads through the window. There was Billy, up to his shoulders in the barrel of whitewash.

BAMBI

written by Felix Salten, illustrated by Barbara Cooney

Bambi is a happy little fawn. He has many playmates in the forest and a loving mother who answers his questions. But Bambi has much to learn. He must learn to be alone without his mother. He must learn about the danger of Man and the terrible thunder that shoots from his hand. [Aladdin]

THE BAT-POET

written by Randall Jarrell,
illustrated by Maurice Sendak

The little brown bat is not like all his brothers and sisters. Even though he snuggles up with the rest, he likes even better to sleep on the porch, where he can see the world around him. The other bats cannot understand why anyone would want to be awake in the daytime, but the brown bat enjoys looking out at the sunlight and its whir of bright activity. He watches the chipmunk and listens to the mockingbird. Then he begins to compose poems about the amazing world he sees. [HarperCollins]

> When he would wake up in the daytime and hang there looking out at the colors of the world, he would say the poems over to himself.

A BEAR CALLED PADDINGTON

written by Michael Bond, illustrated by Peggy Fortnum

Paddington is a stow-away bear who is found by the Brown family at a railway station. He is a gruff sort of bear, but he unbends when plied with generous servings of marmalade. The Brown family adopts him, loves him, and gives him pocket money, despite his annoying habit of getting lost and making messes. After all, "It's nice having a bear about the house." [Collins]

THE BEARS ON HEMLOCK MOUNTAIN

written by Alice Dalgliesh, illustrated by Helen Sewell

Jonathan lives in a farmhouse at the foot of Hemlock Mountain. When his mother sends him on an errand over the mountain, Jonathan is scared because he thinks there are bears on Hemlock Mountain. After all, one of his uncles had once seen a bear, hadn't he? All the way over the mountain, Jonathan says to himself, "There are no bears on Hemlock Mountain." But coming home again, Jonathan decides that there are! [Aladdin]

BEN AND ME

written and illustrated by Robert Lawson

Anyone who thinks that Benjamin Franklin thought up all his inventions must be greatly mistaken because this book tells us that Ben

Franklin really got his ideas from a mouse called Amos. For instance, when the two of them first meet, Amos notices that the doctor's fire is inefficient. That observation results in the Franklin stove. Amos makes a deal with Ben—the mouse's assistance with all Ben's experiments in return for a home and a regular supply of cheese. So you see Amos is the mind behind all Ben's inventions, and it's thanks to an ingenious mouse that America has its Declaration of Independence! [Little, Brown]

BENJAMIN WEST AND HIS CAT GRIMALKIN
written by Marguerite Henry, illustrated by Wesley Dennis
Benjamin West, who lives in eighteenth-century America, loves to draw. His main inspiration is Grimalkin, his cat. Because Benjamin's Quaker parents think that painting is foolish, Benjamin must find unusual ways to pursue his hobby. He makes colors from the earth and a paintbrush from hairs taken from his cat's tail. When he starts cutting hairs from all over Grimalkin's coat, his parents think the cat is sick! One day, his father receives a letter from the Philadelphia Academy suggesting that Benjamin go there to study painting. When he leaves for Philadelphia, Grimalkin—of course—goes with him. [Bradford Press]

THE BEST-LOVED DOLL
written by Rebecca Caudill, illustrated by Elliott Gilbert
Betsy is invited to a party, and she must bring one doll—a hard decision since prizes are to be awarded. Girls whose best playmates are their dolls will enjoy reading about Betsy's choice and its results. [Henry Holt and Co.]

BETSY-TACY
written by Maud Hart Lovelace, illustrated by Lois Lenski
Betsy longs for a girl just her age to move into the empty house across the street. To her delight, in moves Tacy, soon to be Betsy's best friend. Betsy and Tacy do everything together: they color Easter eggs, play dress up, and sit beside each other in school. Then into their lives comes Tib to share their wonderful games of make-believe. Other Betsy-Tacy books include *Betsy, Tacy and Tib; Betsy and Tacy Go Downtown;* and *Betsy and Tacy Go Over the Big Hill.* [HarperTrophy]

BIG RED

written by Jim Kjelgaard

When Danny Pickett is given charge of a wealthy neighbor's Irish Setter, he and the champion show dog become inseparable. Danny trains Red to become the best game dog ever, and the two of them have some hair-raising adventures. One time, Big Red saves Danny from being mangled to death by a lynx, and on another occasion he saves Mr. Pickett's life. Together Danny and his dog fight a wolverine that hurls itself down the chimney of their cabin! But their long-standing enemy is a huge brown bear. After the bear kills the Picketts' mule, three hound dogs, and almost Mr. Pickett himself, Danny and Big Red set off into the mountains to track down their enemy. You will also enjoy *Irish Red,* the story of Big Red's pup who proves himself to be the worthy son of Big Red. [Yearling]

> The rank odor of the great bear filled Danny's nostrils, and for a moment he looked steadily into the eyes of his ancient enemy.

THE BIRDS' CHRISTMAS CAROL

written by Kate Douglas Wiggin, illustrated by Jessie Gillespie

When a little baby girl is born on Christmas day, Mr. Bird, Mrs. Bird, and all the boys are delighted with their new child. She is named Carol—Christmas Carol. Carol is a happy, generous child. Before she is ten years old, however, Carol becomes very sick and is confined to bed. Carol makes the best of her situation and throws an elaborate Christmas feast for some neighborhood children. [Houghton Mifflin]

BLACK BEAUTY: THE AUTOBIOGRAPHY OF A HORSE

written by Anna Sewell

This is the life story of a horse told by Black Beauty himself. He begins life happily in the home of a good master where he is greatly loved. But because of one adverse circumstance after another, Black Beauty is sold to many different owners. He endures a harsh life as a cab horse

> If your Black Beauty had not been wiser than we were, we should all have been carried down the river at the wooden bridge.

and is subjected to such cruelty and abuse that he wishes he could drop dead in order to end his misery. You will be amazed and saddened to read how some of Black Beauty's owners mistreat him. His life is not all cheerless, however. A few of Black Beauty's owners love him, and some give him years of happiness and care. Black Beauty also makes life-long friends with his fellow horses Ginger and Merrylegs. [Yearling]

THE BLACK STALLION
written by Walter Farley
Alec Ramsay has always dreamed of horses; he loves their speed and beauty. On a ship traveling back to New York from India, Alec meets a magnificent, unbroken black stallion. One day, a storm arises, and the ship is struck by lightning. The ship goes down, but not before both the stallion and Alec are propelled into the ocean. For hours they fight the thrashing sea before they are cast on the shore of a deserted island. They soon learn that they need each other to survive. Alec is thrilled when he is able to tame the Black Stallion enough to ride him, and soon they become inseparable. When at last they are rescued, their adventures together have only just begun. You will also enjoy the other books in this series. [Yearling]

BLACKTHORN WINTER
written by Douglas Wilson, illustrated by Peter Bentley
This historical novel is set on the eastern seaboard in the eighteenth century when vicious pirates roamed the high seas. Fifteen-year-old Thomas Ingle finds a treasure map that has been hidden by some pirates; shortly afterwards, he sets sail on the *Prudent Hannah*. His ship is captured by pirates, one of whom is the very pirate that Thomas had seen burying the treasure map and murdering another man. A particularly brutal pirate shoots Thomas and leaves him

> He sat down on a log, with a pirate on either side of him . . . He felt like a goose twixt two foxes, as he told his mother later.

for dead. And this is only the beginning of an exciting series of adventures. If you like books with lots of fighting, pirates, and buried treasure, this is the book for you! Read the sequel to this novel, *Susan Creek*. [Veritas Press]

BLOSSOM COMES HOME
written by James Herriot, illustrated by Ruth Brown
Mr. Dakin's drooping mustache is even more droopy than usual because this is the day Blossom the cow leaves the farm. She is old and not producing enough milk to pay for her keep. There's no getting around the fact that Dakin's gentle friend has got to go. The cattle-drover comes to take her to market. He leads her slowly out of the farm and into the village to collect some other animals. All of a sudden, Blossom breaks off and makes a run for it. She legs it across the fields, and, before anyone can do anything about it—well, you can probably guess what happens to Blossom! [St. Martin's Griffin]

BLUEBONNETS FOR LUCINDA
written by Frances Clarke Sayers, illustrated by Helen Sewell
Lucinda lives on Oleander Island in the Gulf of Mexico. Her most precious possession is a silver music box given her by her dear German neighbors, Herr and Frau Geranium. One day, the Geraniums move away, to Lucinda's great despair. She is consoled by the thought of visiting them in Texas, and very soon Lucinda makes the trip to see her friends. There, together with her cat and her little music box, she charms some pesky geese and leads a parade into hills covered with bluebonnets. [Viking Press]

BLUE WILLOW
written by Doris Gates
Ever since Janey Larkin can remember, her family (her dad, mom, and herself) has had to move every month or so, to wherever work can be found. This time they have come to a shack in flat countryside. All Janey has to lift her spirits during a long, hot summer is her blue willow plate and her imagination. But when she finds a friend living in the house opposite, she hopes that her family will be able to stay a while. It is her dream to have a home to live in a long time, to go to school at a regular school, and to read as many books as she likes. The summer brings many surprises, both bad and good, for the Larkin family, but in the end Janey's spunk and curiosity save the day—with the help of her beautiful blue willow plate. [Puffin]

BONNY'S BIG DAY

written by James Herriot, illustrated by Ruth Brown
This is the tale of a Yorkshire farmer and his retired carthorses. The loyal animals have now finished their years of labor for Farmer Skipton, but the old farmer still loves them. In fact, he enters Bonny in a local Pet Contest. Bonny is definitely the most unusual pet entry, and, of all the pet owners, Farmer Skipton is certainly the proudest. [St. Martin's Griffin]

BOOK OF GREEK MYTHS

written and illustrated by Ingri and Edgar Parin D'Aulaire

> After a while Mother Earth bore three more sons. Uranus looked at them with disgust. Each of them had fifty heads and a hundred strong arms.

This is an exciting collection of the Greek myths, written and illustrated for young people. One story tells about Hermes, the mischievous messenger god. One day, Hermes steals some of Apollo's cows, and, to cover up his theft, he wraps the cows' hoofs with bark and ties brooms to their tails. This way, the cows wipe away their own tracks! Other stories in this book include tales about Poseidon the Earthshaker, and foolish people like King Midas, who wears donkey's ears, and Narcissus who falls in love with himself! [Delacorte]

CADDIE WOODLAWN

written by Carol Ryrie Brink
Caddie lives in Wisconsin during Civil War era pioneer days. She is a tomboy who always gets into scrapes. She would rather plow a field than stitch samplers. In fact, Caddie seems to fit in better with her brothers than her sisters. And Caddie has spunk enough to stick up for the Indians when the whites begin to spread rumors about an Indian massacre. Caddie is sure that good Indian John and his tribe will never attack them, so she rides to their camp in order to warn them that her

> Just do the best you can and don't let it worry you. In that way you'll have a clear conscience and a tranquil heart.

people plan an invasion. Because of her courage, Caddie helps to heal the tension between the whites and the Indians. This story is based on the experiences of the author's grandmother. [Aladdin]

CALICO BUSH
written by Rachel Field, illustrated by Allen Lewis
Marguerite Ledoux is a teenage French girl who sails to America as the slave of a pioneering family. Time and again, Marguerite demonstrates her courage. She saves the Sargents' livestock from drowning, their children from a bear, and the whole family from wild Indians. When the baby crawls into the fireplace and is badly burned, Marguerite gets help from neighbors by crossing the frozen sea. This exciting story tells about life in pioneering America: roof raising, corn-shelling bees, cloth weaving, and grafting apples onto thorn-bushes. It describes the dangers and heartache that accompany survival in a new land. [Aladdin]

THE CANADA GEESE QUILT
written by Natalie Kinsey-Warnock, illustrated by Leslie Bowman
Ten-year-old Ariel lives on a farm in Vermont with her father, mother, and grandmother who always knows what to do. Ariel loves to draw the beautiful things she sees around her, especially wildflowers and birds. When she finds out that her mother is going to have a baby, Ariel wants to give the baby a special gift. She and her grandmother plan to make a baby quilt, and Ariel draws the pattern from the Canada geese she has seen flying by the farm. But when her grandmother suddenly becomes ill and is laid up in bed, Ariel is heartbroken and wonders if she can ever finish the quilt by herself. [Puffin]

CAROLINA'S COURAGE
written by Elizabeth Yates, illustrated by Nora Spicer Unwin
When Carolina has to leave her New Hampshire home, it nearly breaks her heart, but her parents allow her to take along on the wagon the one thing she loves best, her doll Lyddy. Carolina and her parents make the long, dangerous trek west across the prairie, always on the lookout for hostile Indians. On the way, Carolina clutches her doll tightly in her arms, but then comes the terrible moment when she must give up her beloved Lyddy. [BJU Press]

CAUTIONARY VERSES
written by Hilaire Belloc, illustrated by Lisa M. Catalano-Bechtel
This is a hilarious collection of poems that tells what happens to children who are naughty and disobedient. One little boy has a nasty habit of chewing bits of string. "At last he swallowed some which tied itself in ugly knots inside." And a little girl named Sarah simply refuses to do her schoolwork and has a shocking surprise: unable to read a warning sign, she comes face-to-face with a very furious bull! [Templegate Publishers]

CHARLOTTE'S WEB
written by E.B. White, illustrated by Garth Williams
All the farmyard animals of Farmer Arable's farm, as well as Fern Arable, believe that the runt of the litter, Wilbur, is certainly "Some Pig." However, Fern must persuade her father that Wilbur should not be turned into bacon for the breakfast table. There seems to be no hope for little Wilbur until he finds a friend in a cunning spider, Charlotte. Aided by the filthy but useful rat Templeton, Charlotte spins a web above Wilbur that not only saves him from an untimely death, but also wins him the admiration and wonder of the entire county. [HarperTrophy]

> "He isn't dead," hollered Zuckerman. "He's fainted. He gets embarrassed easily."

A CHILD'S CHRISTMAS IN WALES
written by Dylan Thomas, illustrated by Trina Schart Hyman
One eventful Christmas Eve, the Prothero's house is filled with smoke. The fire brigade enters armed with a hose, and Mr. Prothero gets out just before they turn it on. Their task accomplished, the firemen stagger exhausted and dripping from the wreckage. Mrs. Prothero descends the stairs, peers at them and inquires, "Would you like anything to read?" So begins Dylan Thomas's amusing memory of Christmas. [Holiday House]

CINDERELLA
written by C.S. Evans, illustrated by Arthur Rackham
This is a beautiful retelling of the well-known fairy story. Cinderella's cruel stepsisters cause her much unhappiness by their mean and spiteful behavior. But it is Cinderella, not her horrid sisters, who marries the handsome Prince! [Everyman's Library]

THE COMPLETE FAIRY TALES OF
THE BROTHERS GRIMM
written by Jacob and Wilhelm Grimm, translated by Jack Zipes, illustrated by John B. Gruelle
This is a wonderful collection of old German fairy tales. Children everywhere love the story about some kind elves who make shoes every night for an impoverished shoemaker. Other stories include the tale of a young princess who makes a rash promise to an ugly frog and the story of Hansel and Gretel who get lost in a forest and stumble upon an amazing adventure. [Bantam]

THE COURAGE OF SARAH NOBLE
written by Alice Dalgliesh, illustrated by Leonard Weisgard
Based on a true story, this book tells of Sarah Noble's hard journey into the Connecticut wilderness in the early eighteenth century. While her father builds a home for his family, Sarah overcomes her fears of wolves and savage Indians. [Aladdin]

THE CRICKET IN TIMES SQUARE
written by George Selden, illustrated by Garth Williams
Chester is a Connecticut cricket who belongs to a boy named Mario Bellini. Mario's parents own a newsstand in New York City, at the subway station in Times Square. Chester has many adventures with his two friends, Tucker (a mouse) and Harry (a cat). Mario loves Chester, but his parents are not so thrilled with this unusual pet, until they discover that Chester can chirp opera. So begins the most remarkable week in the

> Although he thought that glory was very nice, Chester found that it made you tired.

life of this talented cricket. You will also enjoy *Chester Cricket's New Home*, which continues Chester's adventures. [Yearling]

DANCING SHOES
written by Noel Streatfeild
After Rachel's mother dies, she and her adopted sister Hilary go to live with Rachel's Aunt Cora. Aunt Cora runs a dancing school called "Mrs. Wintle's Little Wonders," and their spoiled cousin Dulcie has long been the star of the show. Hilary is a spunky little girl and shrugs off Dulcie's proud airs, but shy Rachel is daunted by the expectation that she must now learn to be a Little Wonder. Other books in Streatfeild's "Shoes" series include *Ballet Shoes* and *Theater Shoes*. [Random House]

> The School of Dancing was in North London. Outside it looked like just an ordinary house. . . . But it was anything but ordinary to the neighbors, who knew that in it were trained Mrs. Wintle's Little Wonders.

DAVID COPPERFIELD
written and abridged by Charles Dickens, illustrated by Alan Marks
We do not generally recommend abridged novels, but Dickens himself wrote this shortened version of his popular novel. The story is full of colorful characters such as David's dear old friend Mr. Peggotty, sweet Little Emily, conniving Steerforth, and pretty, silly Dora who marries David but cannot face the fact that he is poor. "Jip [her dog] must have a mutton chop every day at twelve, or he'll die!" Then there's happy-go-lucky Mr. Micawber who is unemployed and unemployable but prances around the punch bowl ever hopeful that something will turn up. [North-South Books]

DETECTIVES IN TOGAS
written by Henry Winterfeld, translated by Richard and Clara Winston, illustrated by Charlotte Kleinert
This historical novel is set in ancient Rome. It all starts with a harmless classroom prank, but when someone attacks their teacher leaving him bound and gagged, the students who attend the Xanthos School must get to the bottom of the strange crime. While they attempt to solve the

mystery, one boy is imprisoned on a false charge and may face the death sentence. The other boys and their teacher have to prove his innocence. This is a good mystery, and you will also learn a lot about life during the Roman Empire. [Odyssey]

THE DOLL'S HOUSE
written by Rumer Godden, illustrated by Tasha Tudor
Tottie Plantagenet is a sweet little wooden doll, and all she wants is a dollhouse—a real home for her family. It finally arrives, but along with the dollhouse comes a conceited china doll, and Tottie must learn how to promote peace in her little home. [Puffin]

THE DOOR IN THE WALL
written and illustrated by Marguerite de Angeli
This story is set in medieval England. Robin is left at home alone when his parents go to serve the king and queen. He becomes very ill, and a kind monk rescues him. Robin becomes a cripple, but the monk teaches him to read and write and even to swim. Robin serves as a page at the castle of Sir Peter de Lindsay, but, because he is crippled, he worries that he will never be a good page or a brave knight in the service of the king. However, Robin's courage is soon put to the test. [Bantam Doubleday Dell]

DRUMS OF WAR: INDEPENDENCE
written by Peter Reese Doyle
Early on an April morning in 1775 while the citizens of Williamsburg, Virginia, sleep, British marines steal the colonists' gunpowder, making resistance to the British impossible. Two young boys, Andrew and his friend Nathan, are caught up in the pre-Revolutionary turmoil as they carry important letters to the Sons of Liberty, but when they run into men who spy for the governor, their lives are in danger. The two boys and their sisters play a vital role in America's fight for freedom. This is the first book in the exciting Drums of War series. [Providence Foundation]

EMIL AND THE DETECTIVES
written by Erich Kastner, illustrated by Walter Trier
Emil travels by train to Berlin, and in his pocket is money for his grandmother. At the end of his journey, it's gone! In Berlin, Emil meets a lot

of other children, and they excitedly form a gang of detectives to catch the thief. [Scholastic]

FIVE LITTLE PEPPERS AND HOW THEY GREW
written by Margaret Sidney

Mrs. Pepper and her children—Ben, Polly, Joel, Davie, and Phronsie—all live together in the Little Brown House. Ever since Mr. Pepper died, Mrs. Pepper has struggled to feed and clothe her little Peppers. But even though they have a daily breakfast of mush and molasses, and the old black stove has a hole that simply will not be plugged, and there never seems to be quite enough of anything to go around—except measles—the Little Brown House is always filled with laughter. [Aladdin]

> She had met life too bravely to be beaten down now. So with a stout heart and a cheery face, she had worked away day after day at making coats and tailoring and mending of all descriptions.

FRIGHTFUL'S MOUNTAIN
written by Jean Craighead George

This is the third book in the series about Sam Gribley and his peregrine falcon, and it's told mainly from the perspective of the bird herself. When a conservation officer confiscates Frightful, Sam and his beloved falcon are separated, and she has to learn to survive in the Catskill Mountains away from the boy who raised her. As Frightful learns to adapt to the wilderness, she encounters many dangers such as poachers' traps and electric utility lines. Frightful constantly returns to Sam, and when she mates and makes a nest for her eggs, Sam comes to her rescue. She has built her nest on a bridge that's being repaired, so Sam climbs up to her. He persuades her to stay on her nest and feeds her while the deafening construction work goes on. The baby chicks are safely hatched. Then the days grow shorter and colder, and it's time again for the birds to migrate to warmer climates. Frightful is faced with a wrenching decision: should she fly south or stay with Sam? In spite of the definite environmental bias, this is an exciting story about a noble and courageous bird. [Puffin]

GENTLE BEN
written by Walt Morey, illustrated by John Schoenherr
Mark Anderson's best friend is a tame brown bear called Ben that Fog Benson keeps chained up and starving in a shed. Every day on the way home from school, Mark unchains Ben and sits with his pet in the sunshine feeding him his lunch. When Mark hears that Fog Benson plans to sell the bear, he tries to help Ben escape into the Alaskan mountains, but the bear is too fond of Mark to leave him. When Mr. Anderson finds the pair of them asleep in a field, he understands the love between them and buys Ben for his son. All seems well until one day the Andersons must face the possibility that Ben might not always be a gentle bear. [Puffin]

GEORGE WASHINGTON'S BREAKFAST
written by Jean Fritz, illustrated by Paul Galdone
Because George shares the same birthday as George Washington, he wants to find out all he can about the first President. He even wants to know what Washington had for breakfast. He reads lots of books, but none of them mention Washington's breakfast. He visits Washington's home in Mount Vernon, but he is still no wiser about what Washington ate in the morning. Then one day, George's perseverance is rewarded, and his grandmother cooks him a big breakfast—just like Washington's! [Putnam]

THE GIFTS OF THE CHILD CHRIST
AND OTHER STORIES AND FAIRY TALES
written by George MacDonald, edited by Glenn Edward Sadler
A collection of wonderful fairy tales such as "The Giant's Heart," "The Carasoyn," and "The Cruel Painter." In "The Carasoyn," Colin is a happy lad whose great delight is a bubbling stream. He loves this water so much that he tunnels a path so that it flows through his house. This is a splendid arrangement until he discovers that the water carries with it a host of fairies—mischievous, evil fairies that like to steal children. With the help of a wise old woman and the amazing set of creatures that do her bidding, Colin outsmarts the evil fairy queen. [Eerdmans]

For there is no friend
like a sister
In calm or stormy
weather;
To cheer one on the
tedious way.
To fetch one if one
goes astray.

GOBLIN MARKET
written by Christina Rossetti
You will enjoy the rhythm of Christina Rossetti's mysterious and mesmerizing poem. Its plot is intriguing, and its moral is timeless. [Dover]

THE GOLDEN KEY
written by George MacDonald,
illustrated by Maurice Sendak
One day, a boy makes an amazing discovery: he finds a golden key at the end of the rainbow. He knows that it is a wonderful key and that it will unlock amazing mysteries, but he doesn't yet know what they are. That is when he begins his quest. Together with a girl named Tangle, Mossy begins his journey that will take years and years to complete. They come across strange creatures such as flying fish, and they meet people like the Old Man of the Sea and the Old Man of the Earth. But in the end, they make the strangest and most wonderful discovery of all as they unlock the mystery of the golden key. [Farrar, Straus & Giroux]

GONE-AWAY LAKE
written by Elizabeth Enright, illustrated by Beth and Joe Krush
Portia and her cousin Julian make some interesting discoveries during their summer vacation. During their wanderings through the woods near their summer home, they discover a swamp that was once a lake. Gone-Away Lake is surrounded by abandoned homes, and a kind but eccentric old couple live in two of the houses. Aunt Minnehaha and Uncle Pin warn the children about the Gulper, a dangerous quicksand in the middle of the swamp. Portia and Julian keep their discoveries to themselves until one awful day when Portia's small brother follows them and gets sucked into the Gulper. Then Gone-Away Lake and its strange inhabitants are a secret no longer. [Harcourt Brace]

THE GOOD MASTER
written by Kate Seredy
Jancsi is a Hungarian boy who lives on a farm. When his cousin Kate comes to visit, Jancsi quickly finds out that she is a real tomboy and "when she looks like an angel, she's contemplating something

disastrous." While Jancsi and his father are driving Kate home, she manages to get them both out of the wagon and takes off with the four horses at full gallop. Another time at a fair, she exposes a fake sideshow by smashing the glass cage. However, Kate's strong will sometimes comes in handy, such as the time she corrals a herd of stampeding cattle. The sequel to this book is *The Singing Tree*. [Puffin]

GRANDMA REMEMBERS
written and illustrated by Ben Shecter
Grandma and her grandson take a last look around a home full of happy memories. Each room yields its own particular remembrance, but finally Grandma locks the front door and leaves "to see and do and hear new things." [HarperCollins]

THE GREEN FAIRY BOOK
edited by Andrew Lang, illustrated by H.J. Ford
Andrew Lang's fairy stories are great favorites. This collection consists of forty-two stories from the folklore of England, Germany, France, Russia, and other countries. It includes such tales as "The Twelve Huntsmen," "The Golden Mermaid," and "The Three Musicians." Andrew Lang has gathered twelve books of folk tales; the first is *The Blue Fairy Book*. Other titles include *The Red Fairy Book* and *The Yellow Fairy Book*. [Dover]

THE GRIFFIN AND THE MINOR CANON
written by Frank Stockton, illustrated by Maurice Sendak
A hideous Griffin comes to a little village to see a stone likeness of himself hanging over a church door. He frightens the entire village, except a patient and mild-mannered clergyman, the Minor Canon. The Griffin and the Minor Canon become constant companions, so the townspeople soon banish the Minor Canon in order to get the Griffin to leave. However, they soon find out that the Griffin is a difficult pest to be rid of. [Michael Di Capua]

HANNAH
written by Gloria Whelan, illustrated by Leslie Bowman
When the new teacher comes to live with Hannah's family, the little girl's dull life changes forever. Hannah would give just about anything

to go to school, but instead she has to stay at home on the farm with her mother. No one lets her do anything for herself, and everyone calls her "poor Hannah" because she is blind. But the new teacher persuades her stern mother to let Hannah attend school, and there she learns to read, write, and do arithmetic, and the school bully becomes her good friend. [Random House]

HANS BRINKER, OR, THE SILVER SKATES
written by Mary Mapes Dodge, illustrated by Alice Carsey
Hans Brinker and his sister Gretel live in a shabby little house with their crippled father and hard-working mother. This story is set in the middle of a Dutch winter when all the canals are frozen and everyone travels on ice skates. The story begins as a competition has just been announced—an open ice-skating race—and the prize is a beautiful pair of silver skates. Both Hans and Gretel long to enter the race, but neither of them owns good skates. Hans and Gretel must be content with patched clothing, meager food, and wooden skates. The children have more on their minds than the race, however. They desperately want their crippled father to be restored to health. The amazing events that follow explain some fascinating mysteries and bring joy to the Brinker household. [Cosimo Classics]

> The judges lean forward without seeming to lift their eyes from their watches. Cheer after cheer fills the air; the very columns seem rocking.

THE HAPPY PRINCE
written by Oscar Wilde, illustrated by Harriet Golden
A heartwarming story about the statue of a prince who, despite his name, grieves at the misery he sees in the lives of the people around him. With the help of a swallow, the Happy Prince sacrifices everything in order to bring joy to those in need. [Dover]

HEIDI
written by Johanna Spyri, illustrated by Jessie Willcox Smith
The Alm Uncle is the gruff old man who lives at the top of the mountain and is feared throughout the valley. He never speaks to the village

people, and you can be sure that few people talk to him! Imagine how little Heidi feels to discover suddenly that she must go to live with this curious man. But Heidi is not afraid. In fact, she quickly begins to love her new home and is soon prancing about with the goats on the mountain and listening to the whistling of the pines. Heidi and her "grandfather" become fast friends. When Heidi is taken away from him to be a companion for Klara, a sick little girl in Frankfort, she finds that even though the city holds new friends, she longs for the mountains, the goats, and most of all her dear grandfather. [HarperCollins]

HERE'S A PENNY
written and illustrated by Carolyn Haywood
This is the first book in the series of stories about Penny whose real name is William. When his mother and father adopted him as a baby, they nicknamed him "Penny" because of his shiny copper hair. Penny and his friend Patsy have some fun adventures, like the day they eat a picnic lunch on top of a sticky tar barrel, or the day Patsy decides to dress up Penny's feisty kittens in her doll clothes. Penny adopted those kittens as his very own, but what he most wants to adopt is an older brother! There are three other books in this series. [Harcourt]

HIAWATHA
written by Henry Wadsworth Longfellow, illustrated by Susan Jeffers
Longfellow's poem tells about a legendary Indian boy and his wise old nurse, Nokomis, who teaches him all about the world around him. [Puffin]

HUGUENOT GARDEN
written by Douglas M. Jones
Renée and Albret Martineau are young twin sisters whose parents are Protestant Huguenots living in seventeenth-century France. Renée and Albret look after their gardens they have each started as well as their pet lamb. But gradually the French king's soldiers threaten their safety, even demanding housing. Then the king destroys their church, and the family flees to the peace of a country farm. Even there, they are not safe. Soon they must take to the ocean. The faith of these brave souls is inspiring. [Canon Press]

THE HUNDRED DRESSES
written by Eleanor Estes, illustrated by Louis Slobodkin
Wanda's family is poor, so she always comes to school in the same old blue dress. One day, she tells the other girls that she has a hundred dresses in her closet. From then on, Peggy and Maddie tease Wanda about her dresses, but they learn a hard lesson about their unkindness to Wanda when it's too late to make amends. [Harcourt Brace]

THE INCREDIBLE JOURNEY
written by Sheila Burnford, illustrated by Carl Burger
The amazing story of two dogs and a Siamese cat who make their way across 250 miles of Canadian wilderness. The three animals band together to protect and encourage one another. They overcome great dangers, such as bears, rushing rapids, and thunderstorms. Their devotion and courage never fail as they make their incredible journey. [Yearling]

IN GRANDMA'S ATTIC
written by Arleta Richardson, illustrated by Dora Leder
Grandma remembers all sorts of funny things that happened to her when she was a little girl, and she tells story after story to her granddaughter. Most of her stories are funny, and they also show how things like pride and foolishness can get little girls into big trouble—like the time Mabel wears a hoop skirt to church without her parents' permission. She learns the hard way that pride always comes before a fall! Also read *More Stories from Grandma's Attic*. [Chariot Victor]

> No one had ever told us the hazards of sitting down in a hoop skirt without careful practice! The gasps we heard were not of admiration as we had anticipated—far from it! For when we sat down, those dreadful hoops flew straight up in the air!

IRON SCOUTS OF THE CONFEDERACY
written by Lee McGiffin
When Ben Fane's older brother, Gant, leaves their farm in Alabama to become an Iron Scout for General Hampton, Ben runs away to Virginia

to join him. Fourteen-year-old Ben gets tossed into the war with a vengeance: he narrowly escapes being shot by deserters, is captured by Yankee troopers, and saves his brother from being ambushed by Union men. Riding through the night dodging bullets and Yankees, Ben becomes a first-rate scout. He memorizes every trail and carries his reports in his head. The last time Ben is captured, he is placed in manacles on a Yankee prison barge. This is a fast-paced novel about two boys who play a vital part in the War Between the States. [Christian Liberty Press]

IVANHOE
written by Marianna Mayer, illustrated by John Rush
This is a gorgeously illustrated retelling of Sir Walter Scott's classic novel. The story, which is faithful to the original, takes place after the Norman conquest of England when Norman and Saxon knights battle one another to the death. Knights of old were valiant indeed, but none more courageous than Wilfred of Ivanhoe, and never is Ivanhoe braver than when, badly wounded, he must save a beautiful young woman from burning at the stake. This is a great tale for any young person who loves jousting, romance, and adventure. [Chronicle Books]

JARED'S ISLAND
written and illustrated by Marguerite de Angeli
When a ship sailing from England to America sinks in a storm, Jared is separated from his brother and rescued by some New Jersey Quakers. However, life in this quiet household is far too tame for this adventurous lad, especially when he is made to do "girl's work." Jared runs away in search of Captain Kidd's treasure and ends up living for a time with some Indians. Little does he know that, when he returns to the home of his kind Quaker friends, he is in for the biggest surprise of all. [Doubleday]

JEM'S ISLAND
written by Kathryn Lasky, illustrated by Ronald Himler
Jem goes kayaking with his dad on a camping trip to the island of his choice. He learns how to use a compass and chart a course. Realistic illustrations throughout this story will show you exactly how Jem prepares for the camping trip of a lifetime. [Scribner]

A JOURNEY TO THE NEW WORLD: THE DIARY OF REMEMBER PATIENCE WHIPPLE
written by Kathryn Lasky

Remember Whipple is one of the children on board the *Mayflower*—the ship that took the Pilgrims to the New World—and this is her journal. Remember paints a vivid picture of her grueling journey across the stormy ocean. She writes about seasickness, horrible smells, loathsome food (horse meat and hardtack), and the crush of people jammed together at close quarters. "If one wants to change a petticoat with any modesty one must practically crawl into a barrel." When the main beam cracks, the passengers are in danger of drowning or being eaten by sharks. She mentions a young man blown overboard and a woman giving birth during a raging gale. But Remember is a plucky little girl and makes light of her appalling situation. Her record of this amazing journey is an inspiring testimony to the Pilgrims' courage and faith in God. Although this is a fictional account, it is accurate in many details. This is just one book in the Dear America series. [Scholastic]

> I'm twelve years old. Maybe by the time I am full grown, say fifteen, I shall be patient.

THE JUNGLE BOOK
written by Rudyard Kipling,
illustrated by Kurt Wiese and William Henry Drake

This is the story of Mowgli, the boy brought up by wolves in the Indian jungle. Mowgli has some unlikely friends: Bagheera, a cunning black panther, and Baloo, a sleepy old brown bear who teaches him the lore of the jungle. But he also has a deadly enemy: Shere Khan the tiger, who is determined to kill Mowgli. Mowgli has many exciting adventures. Once he is carried off by a tribe of monkeys and escapes with the help of Kaa the python. Another time, Mowgli traps Shere Khan in a ravine and, with the

> So Mowgli went away and hunted with the four cubs in the jungle from that day on.

help of his wolf friends, charges at him with a stampeding herd of buffalo. [Everyman's Library]

JUST-SO STORIES
written and illustrated by Rudyard Kipling
Young people have loved these animal stories ever since Kipling wrote them one hundred years ago. You will learn how the Camel got his hump, which will teach you not to be lazy; how the Rhinoceros got his skin, which will teach you not to be selfish; how the Whale got his throat, which will teach you not to be greedy; and how the Elephant got his trunk, which will teach you not to be too curious. [Puffin]

THE KING'S DAUGHTER
AND OTHER STORIES FOR GIRLS
written by J.E. White
This is an enjoyable collection of old fashioned stories that are fascinating to read; in fact, as you read, you won't even realize that each one is teaching an important lesson about growing up to become a godly young woman. [A.B. Publishing]

THE KING OF THE GOLDEN RIVER
written by John Ruskin, illustrated by Juan Wijngaard
This is the story of three brothers. The two older brothers are very ugly (they have bushy eyebrows and squinty eyes) and so mean that they work their servants until they won't work any more and then get rid of them without paying them any wages. The youngest brother is very handsome and kind. Because of the meanness of the two brothers, all three of them become impoverished and set off independently to find the treasures of the Golden River. As you might imagine, they achieve varying degrees of success. [Candlewick]

LAD: A DOG
written by Albert Payson Terhune
Lad is a thoroughbred collie who loves his family, the Master and the Mistress of The Place. He is as courageous a dog as you'll ever meet. No other dog would so valiantly hurl himself between a baby and a copperhead so that the snake's deadly fangs sink deep into the dog and

not the child. And when Lad is accidentally thrown out of a car and lost in dense traffic in the middle of New York City, his incredible instinct saves his life and brings him home after a terrifying thirty-mile journey. You will enjoy all the adventures of this "thoroughbred in spirit as well as in blood." [Penguin Putnam]

LASSIE COME HOME
written by Eric Knight, illustrated by Marguerite Kirmse
Lassie is a beautiful collie whose unemployed owner Joe has to sell her to put food on his table. Time and time again, Lassie escapes from his new owner, the Duke of Rudley, to return to his original master. The duke gets angry and takes Lassie off to the Scottish Highlands, four hundred miles away from Joe. One day, however, Lassie escapes and begins what turns out to be a thousand-mile trek home. During this desperate trip, Lassie must face such terrible dangers as gun shots, wild animals, and—perhaps worst of all—dogcatchers! [Henry Holt]

THE LIGHT PRINCESS
AND OTHER FANTASY STORIES
written by George MacDonald, illustrated by Craig Yoe
From her birth, Princess Makemnoit has had a weight problem: she has no gravity. Imagine how frustrating it would be for a baby to be continually bobbing around the ceiling and floating away from nurses.

> With one push of her foot, she would be floating in the air above his head; or she would go dancing backwards and forwards and sideways.

Well, this is the situation of the Light Princess. The Princess herself doesn't seem to mind her condition in the least. On the contrary, she is the most joyful baby; in fact, it is because she cannot cry that she weighs so little. She is entirely too light-hearted. The baby princess soon grows into a lady princess, very beautiful except that she can't stand on her own two feet. It is only through a set of extraordinary circumstances that she comes down to reality, hitting the earth with a loud thump! The other fairy stories in this book are just as fun. [Eerdmans]

THE LION, THE WITCH, AND THE WARDROBE

written by C.S. Lewis, illustrated by Pauline Baynes

When Peter, Susan, Edmund, and Lucy go to spend their holidays in the old house of a peculiar Professor, they make an amazing discovery, a wardrobe that becomes the doorway to Narnia. This mystical land has been under a long-standing curse, the spell of the evil White Witch. She has usurped control of Narnia and placed the land in everlasting winter. The forces of the White Witch are strong and fearsome. She is determined to destroy Aslan the great Lion as well as the children and to establish her evil empire forever. But, in fact, Aslan has called the four children to do battle between good and evil and to assume their thrones in the great castle, Cair Paravel. The other Chronicles of Narnia are *Prince Caspian, The Voyage of the Dawn Treader, The Silver Chair, The Horse and His Boy, The Magician's Nephew,* and *The Last Battle.* Having read all seven of the Narnia books, an eight-year-old American boy wrote to Lewis begging him to write another one soon because, "If you don't, what am I going to read when I am nine, ten, eleven, and twelve?" [HarperCollins]

THE LION AND THE PUPPY
AND OTHER STORIES FOR CHILDREN

written by Leo Tolstoy, translated by James Riordan, illustrated by Claus Sievert

Leo Tolstoy was a great writer who loved children so much that he invited them to his mansion and taught them to read and write. He also taught them games like croquet in the summer and skating in the winter. This famous author wrote stories for children that are fun to read and contain many great lessons. Many of the twenty-four short stories in this collection are based on Russian folklore or Aesop's fables. [Henry Holt]

THE LITTLE BOOKROOM

written by Eleanor Farjeon, illustrated by Edward Ardizzone

This is a collection of the author's favorites among her own stories for children. The stories are about kings and shepherds, animals and peacocks, boys and girls, and a king's daughter who wants the moon. [Oxford]

LITTLE EDDIE
written and illustrated by Carolyn Haywood
Eddie collects so much "valuable property" that soon his house is filled with accumulated trash. His father finally puts his foot down firmly, but he has not reckoned on the ingenuity of his son. [William Morrow]

LITTLE FARM IN THE OZARKS
written by Roger Lea MacBride, illustrated by David Gilleece
This book was written as a continuation of the life of Laura Ingalls Wilder, and it features Laura's daughter, Rose Wilder, a spunky little girl much like her mother was at her age. Rose's parents, Laura and Almanzo, have moved to the Rocky Ridge Farm in the Missouri Ozarks, away from all Rose's friends. At first, Rose finds it very hard to adjust, but she soon makes new friends and finds new adventures. Swiney, a neighborhood boy, teaches her how to fish, shows her how to play tree-topping, and once helps Rose put out a house fire. When Rose goes to a new school, she finds it difficult to fit in. Many of the town girls are snobbish, and she doesn't know anyone. Eventually, she earns the respect of the other students, once and for all. The sequel to this book is *Little House on Rocky Ridge*. [HarperTrophy]

> While she fed the chickens and poured their warmed water into a pan, she took deep breaths of the spicy autumn air. Everywhere Rose looked there were spiderwebs in the grass, sparkling with dewdrops. Puffy white clouds floated in a deep blue sky.

LITTLE HOUSE IN THE BIG WOODS
written by Laura Ingalls Wilder, illustrated by Garth Williams
Laura lives in a little log house on the edge of the Big Woods with Pa, Ma, Mary, and baby Carrie. They all work hard in the little house churning butter and smoking meat, but there is always time to laugh and play. One of the jolliest memories of all is the dance at Grandpa's house, where everyone talks, eats, and dances, down to the smallest cousin. Even when all is quiet, the Little House is happy. Bears and black panthers prowl outside, but Laura snuggles safe in her trundle

bed and listens to Pa quietly fiddling and Ma gently rocking as she sews.

You will also love other books in this series: *Little House on the Prairie, Farmer Boy, On the Banks of Plum Creek, By the Shores of Silver Lake, The Long Winter, Little Town on the Prairie, These Happy Golden Years,* and *The First Four Years.* [HarperCollins]

LITTLE LORD FAUNTLEROY
written by Frances Hodgson Burnett

Cedric Errol was born in America. His father, the youngest son of an English earl, died when Cedric was very young. Cedric and his mother live by themselves, poor but happy that they have each other, and the little boy cheers his mother a great deal. One day, a man comes to tell them that Cedric is the only heir to a great fortune and that he is to be the next Earl of Dorincourt. Cedric and his mother are whisked away to England. His grandfather, the grand Earl, is a fierce old man who sends the boy's mother away. But Cedric, now little Lord Fauntleroy, eventually charms everyone, including his stern grandfather. [Everyman's Library]

A LITTLE PRINCESS
written by Frances Hodgson Burnett, illustrated by Barbara McClintock

Captain Crewe and his daughter Sara, the best of friends, have always lived and played together. But because India is not the best climate for little girls, Sara must go to a boarding school in England. At school, Sara quickly becomes the envy of all the other girls; she has so many pretty dresses and playthings. However, Sara has something much more valuable than toys—imagination. When Sara's father tragically dies, leaving her penniless, she is left in the hands of a cruel teacher. She must leave her beautiful room to live in a cold attic.

> She was always dreaming and thinking odd things and could not remember any time when she had not been thinking things about grown up people and the world they belonged to. She felt as if she had lived a long, long time.

Sara's trials bring her near to starvation, and she must rely upon a few faithful friends and the world of her imagination. [HarperCollins]

THE LITTLE WHITE HORSE
written by Elizabeth Goudge

The mystery begins on the night Maria arrives at Moonacre Manor. When the carriage drives the young girl and her governess up to the manor house, Maria catches sight of the little white horse. At her new home in Silverydew, Maria discovers that her family has long been involved in a bitter feud and that her new home lies under a sort of spell. With the help of her friend Robin, a dwarf cook called Marmaduke, her guardian Sir Merriweather, the village preacher, and an amazing group of animals, Maria is able to heal the hatred and bring happiness to Silverydew. [Puffin]

> In mid-gallop she was halted by a strange and terrible sound, a thin high screaming that came threading through the happy sounds of the wind . . . pushing into her heart like a sharp needle.

THE LOST PRINCESS
written by George MacDonald, edited by Rolland Hein

Rosamond is a spoiled princess. She has been given everything in the world except what she really needs—discipline. As a result, Rosamond has turned into a hateful little girl. One day, a wise woman takes her away from the foolish king and queen to her magical cottage. There she begins to mold Rosamond's character by giving her work and responsibility. The wise woman has another subject: a poor little girl named Agnes. Even though she is only the daughter of a shepherd, Agnes is conceited and rude. Because of a strange set of circumstances, Rosamond and Agnes find their places in life reversed, with amazing results. [Chariot Books]

MAGICAL MELONS:
MORE STORIES ABOUT CADDIE WOODLAWN
written by Carol Ryrie Brink, illustrated by Marguerite Davis

Caddie and her two rascally brothers, Tom and Warren, are at it again, scooping up fun, getting into mischief, and doing a very poor job of keeping their clothes clean. Imagine their delight when they find a secret hoard of delicious watermelons in their barn. Do you think they tell anyone about their mysterious find or quietly dispose of the treasure?

This episode begins a series of escapades involving the seven Woodlawn children who live in Wisconsin in 1860. [Collier/Macmillan]

THE MAGIC FISHBONE
written by Charles Dickens, illustrated by F.D. Bedford
One of Dickens' little known fairy tales. The good fairy Grandmarina gives Princess Alicia a magic fishbone that can be used only once but will bring her whatever she wants, provided that she wishes for it at the right time. Princess Alicia can think of a lot of things to wish for. Not only is the King poor and the Queen sick, but Alicia has lots of work to do looking after her eighteen brothers and sisters. But Alicia is a wise little girl, and she chooses to make her wish after her impatient father the King has learned some important lessons of his own. [Frederick Warne]

THE MAGIC WALKING STICK
written by John Buchan
Imagine being given a magic stick that can take you anywhere you want to go! That's what happens to an English schoolboy named Bill. The magic stick takes him all over the world, sometimes with horrifying results. In the Solomon Islands, Bill narrowly escapes being attacked by fierce savages. Another time, he comes face-to-face with a dangerous kidnapper. One day, Bill hears about the story of a Balkan prince whose life is threatened by evil men. With the help of his stick, Bill rushes off to rescue Prince Anatole from his dreadful fate. [Canongate]

THE MATCHLOCK GUN
written by Walter D. Edmonds, illustrated by Paul Lantz
Edward Van Alstyne is fascinated by his great-grandfather's matchlock gun that hangs over the fireplace. It is a magnificent gun with beautiful brass bindings, but when Edward's father leaves for militia duty, he always takes his musket and leaves the matchlock. Mr. Van Alstyne explains to Edward that the musket is easier to handle and to fire, but Edward still admires the old matchlock gun. One day, Mr. Van Alstyne gets into his blue militia coat and goes to ward off the French and Indians who are fighting the Dutch settlers. He leaves his wife, Edward, and little Trudy alone in the house. That night, Edward gets his chance to use the old matchlock gun. [Putnam]

MILLY-MOLLY-MANDY
written and illustrated by Joyce Lankester Brisley

> Well, Milly-Molly-Mandy's legs were short, as I've told you, but they were very lively, just right for running errands.

In a nice white cottage with a thatched roof live Mother, Father, Grandpa, Grandma, Uncle, Auntie, and, of course, Milly-Molly-Mandy. With errands to run for the family, teas to be planned with little-friend-Susan, blackberries to be picked, and three-legged-races to be won, Milly-Molly-Mandy has hardly enough time to explore her new little attic bedroom, which is her very own. [Kingfisher]

MISTY OF CHINCOTEAGUE
written by Marguerite Henry, illustrated by Wesley Dennis

Every spring, there is a roundup of wild ponies from Chincoteague Island, and this year Paul and Maureen Beebe have their hearts set on the legendary horse, Phantom. Their grandpa doesn't hold out much hope that Paul or anyone else will be able to capture the horse who is really "just a piece of wind and sky." Amazingly, Paul does round up Phantom and her newborn colt, Misty. When the day comes for the big horse sale, Paul and Maureen are determined to buy both Phantom and Misty. Will their hopes be dashed when a man beats them to the sale? [Aladdin]

> The Phantom was wild with happiness when she raced. She showed it in the arching of her neck, in the upward pluming of her tail, in the flaring of her nostrils.

THE MOST WONDERFUL DOLL IN THE WORLD
written by Phyllis McGinley, illustrated by Helen Stone

Dulcy, a little girl with indulgent parents and lots of dolls, is very discontent. She always wants things to be better or more beautiful. One day, Dulcy loses an old doll, and she dreams about a more and more beautiful wardrobe for the missing toy. All this wishful thinking results in Dulcy's ignoring her friends and becoming even more discontented. Imagine what happens when Dulcy discovers her doll again. [Scholastic]

MOTHER CAREY'S CHICKENS
written by Kate Douglas Wiggin
When their father dies, the Carey children are left very poor, but they are happy together and change many lives for the better. Their mother even finds room in her home and heart for selfish cousin Julia who's a snobbish prig. All the children have hard lessons to learn. Gilbert, for example, has to abandon his dream of going away to college, and Julia realizes that true happiness is not based on wealth. This is a very giving family that finds great happiness in loving and caring for others. [Foundation for American Christian Education]

MOUNTAIN BORN
written by Elizabeth Yates, illustrated by Nora Spicer Unwin
Peter's family lives in the mountains where they tend sheep and grow vegetables. One evening, Peter's mother and an old shepherd bring a little black lamb into the cottage. The lamb is cold and almost dead, but Peter's mother nurses him until he is well. Biddy becomes Peter's pet, following him as he would his own mother. Peter finds joy in the hard work and simplicity of a shepherd's life, and his black lamb soon becomes the leader of the whole flock. Her fleece is the thickest and softest and makes Peter a beautiful coat. One day, Biddy displays her intelligence and loyalty by saving the entire flock from a pack of wolves. [BJU Press]

> Words were whispering within him, but so softly were they uttered that only Biddy could have heard them; and yet there was no sound in the barn but stillness and the movement of shadows as night came in the place of day.

MR. BLISS
written and illustrated by J.R.R. Tolkien
This story tells the antics of some very curious creatures: Mr. Bliss, an assortment of neighbors, a Girabbit (a rabbit-giraffe), and some greedy bears. They all end up visiting the Dorkinses in Mr. Bliss's new car and arrive unannounced by crashing into the garden wall and landing on top of the Dorkinses' picnic lunch. They continue to forget their party manners and move on to further comical exploits. [Houghton Mifflin]

MR. POPPER'S PENGUINS
written by Richard and Florence Atwater, illustrated by Robert Lawson
Mr. Popper is a house painter who is very interested in the South Pole and especially the penguins that live there, so you can imagine how pleased he is when he gets one. His children think the bird is cute even when he eats their goldfish and sleeps in the refrigerator. Soon Mr. Popper has to hire a repairman to drill holes in the icebox door and put a handle on the inside. Before long, Mr. Popper has a second penguin, then another and another. . . . How is he to feed his own family and a family of twelve penguins? [Little, Brown]

MRS. FRISBY AND THE RATS OF NIMH
written by Robert C. O'Brien, illustrated by Zena Bernstein
Mrs. Frisby, a field mouse, is very worried because her son Timothy is sick and too weak to be moved. But the Frisby family must move because soon the field where they live will be plowed up, and they'll be killed by Farmer Fitzgibbon's tractor. Mrs. Frisby gets help from the Rats of Nimh, who are very intelligent, good rats. Is it possible that these extraordinary rats will solve the poor mother's problem? [Aladdin]

MY FATHER'S DRAGON
written by Ruth Stiles Gannett, illustrated by Ruth Chrisman Gannett
Elmer wants to fly more than anything else in the world. So when he hears that there's a flying dragon held captive on Wild Island, he is determined to find him and go for a ride. This is no easy mission, but Elmer is not afraid. He faces wild animals equipped with all the essentials—including toothbrush, chewing gum, and lollipops. Elmer's careful planning pays off, and before long he is on the back of his wonderful winged dragon. [Yearling]

> "Did you see him? How big is he?"
> "Oh, yes, indeed I saw the dragon. In fact we became great friends," said the cat.

MY FRIEND FLICKA
written by Mary O'Hara
Ken constantly frustrates his dad because he is irresponsible, he daydreams, he flunks fifth grade, and all he can think about is owning his

own colt. So his father makes a bargain with him: Ken gets his colt, but he must learn responsibility. Ken chooses a wild yearling filly, much against his father's better judgment, and names her Flicka. The spirited horse is finally caught, but when she attempts to escape, she becomes entangled in twenty yards of barbed wire. [HarperCollins]

MY SIDE OF THE MOUNTAIN
written by Jean Craighead George
Sam Gribley runs away from his New York City home to survive in the Catskill Mountains. Sam learns to make fire with flint and steel and catches animals in homemade traps for his meat supply; he also eats frogs' legs and crows' eggs boiled in leaves. He seasons his food with salt made from hickory sticks boiled dry. In fact, there's no end to this boy's resourcefulness. He trains a baby falcon to hunt, sews a deerskin suit when his clothes get worn out, and makes friends with Jessie Coon James (a raccoon) and the Baron (a weasel).

In the sequel, *On the Far Side of the Mountain,* Sam's sister Alice joins him and his friends Jessie Coon James, Baron Weasel, and Frightful the falcon. When Sam is forced to give up his falcon, he finds out something strange about the man who confiscated Frightful. [Puffin]

OLD POSSUM'S BOOK OF PRACTICAL CATS
written by T.S. Eliot,
illustrated by Edward Gorey
A fun collection of nonsense verse by a great poet. One of our favorite poems about a particularly fierce feline is "Growltiger's Last Stand." A wretched fate awaits this bad cat! [Harcourt Brace]

> Growltiger was a Brave Cat, who traveled on a barge;
> In fact, he was the roughest cat that ever roamed at large.
> From Gravesend up to Oxford he pursued his evil aims,
> Rejoicing in his title of "The Terror of the Thames."

OLD YELLER
written by Fred Gipson
When his dad leaves fourteen-year-old Travis in charge of his mom and little brother, as well as all the farming and hunting, Travis feels mighty big. In his dad's absence, Travis is called upon to act like a grown man. Thankfully, he is not alone. He has the fellowship of his faithful dog,

Old Yeller, and the two of them face many hair-raising incidents. Travis's little brother is almost mangled by a bear, Travis is savagely attacked by killer hogs, and their mother is attacked by a wolf. Each time, Old Yeller is there to protect them. But the love between the family and this faithful dog is never more tested than when Old Yeller must sacrifice his life for theirs. [Harper Perennial Modern Classics]

ONCE ON THIS ISLAND
written by Gloria Whelan
When war breaks out in 1812 between England and America, British soldiers take over Mackinac Island off Lake Michigan, and twelve-year-old Mary O'Shea's father leaves home to join the army. Feisty red-headed Mary is left with her refined older sister, Angelique, and her impatient brother, Jacques, to keep the family's farm going. They endure the British occupation and protect their home through sheer hard work and pluckiness, occasionally resorting to strange tactics such as the time they hide the cow inside the house all night. [HarperTrophy]

THE 101 DALMATIANS
written by Dodie Smith, illustrated by Michael Dooling
Although you've probably seen the movie, do read the book that describes the kidnapping of fifteen Dalmatian puppies and their parents' daring journey across England to rescue them in the nick of time before Cruella de Vil turns them into fur coats! [Puffin]
    This book has a sequel, *The Starlight Barking*. [Egmont Books]

ON TO OREGON!
written by Honoré Morrow
John Sager is one tough lad. At age thirteen, he thinks that he is ready to face just about any danger that comes his way as the Sager family makes the journey west to Oregon and pioneer country. But John quickly learns that he has a lot of growing up to do. He resents adults, especially his parents, giving him orders, but he soon learns that angry feelings get him nowhere. Very soon, John faces more responsibility than he ever dreamed of. His father contracts a serious illness, and the boy must assume the role of head of the household. Continuing the journey west, the Sager family faces hardship after hardship—Indians,

illness, and starvation—but John faces each new danger with renewed commitment to his father's dream of settling in Oregon. This novel was later republished by Scholastic as *Seven Alone* and inspired an exciting movie. [HarperTrophy]

OSCAR, CAT-ABOUT-TOWN
written by James Herriot, illustrated by Ruth Brown

One day, a starving waif of a cat comes to the Herriot home. The Herriots nurse him back to health and, because he seems to be such a friendly cat, they decide to keep him. Oscar turns out to be more than friendly. They discover that their new cat will disappear for hours at a time to visit people at various social functions. He is truly a cat-about-town. When his real owners come to take him home, Oscar will never forget his newfound friends. You will also enjoy James Herriot's other animal stories such as *Only One Woof* and *Market Square Dog*. [St. Martin's Griffin]

> "This cat you lost," I asked, "what did he look like?"
> "Sort of tabby but with gingery stripes. He was very handsome."
> My heart thumped.
> That sounded very like Oscar.

OWLS IN THE FAMILY
written by Farley Mowat

A group of boys in Saskatoon, Saskatchewan, are the proud owners of some very strange pets—rats, snakes, gophers, pigeons, and best of all, Wol (an owl). Wol doesn't get on too well with the other pets and is very lonely until the boys come home with a second owl, Weeps (he whimpers a lot). The two owls have some crazy adventures. Wol learns how to fly accidentally—he falls out of a tree, and when the family laughs at him, he is very hurt and retires in a huff to his cage. Then he wades into a river and nearly drowns. Wol just doesn't seem to understand that he's not a human being. One day, the boys enter their pets in a Pet Parade. They dress the owls in dolls clothes and enter a surprise pet—a rattlesnake—that creates the biggest ruckus Saskatoon has seen in one hundred years. [Yearling]

PANDORA'S BOX: THE PARADISE OF CHILDREN
written by Nathaniel Hawthorne, illustrated by Paul Galdone
This is Hawthorne's retelling of the Greek myth of Pandora, her play-mate, Epimetheus, and the mysterious box which must never be opened because it contains—but that is what foolish Pandora must find out. [McGraw-Hill]

PAUL REVERE'S RIDE
written by Henry Wadsworth Longfellow, illustrated by Ted Rand
Brave patriot Paul Revere waits impatiently for news of the arrival of the British armies. As soon as he receives word, Revere leaps on his horse and thunders off to alert all the colonists to defend their land and freedom. The beautiful paintings and map in this edition bring to life one of history's most exciting moments. [Puffin]

THE PERILOUS JOURNEY
written by Humphrey Johnson
Conrad is a twelve-year-old boy living in medieval Germany. His father is a merchant who travels with Conrad up the Rhine River to the great fair. They hope they can bring prosperous trade to their battle-torn vil-lage of Coblenz. Conrad, his father, and the other merchants are joined by a knight and his squire in the service of the king, Emperor Frederick. At the fair everyone, especially Conrad, is overwhelmed by the wealth of goods from around the world. However, they are surrounded by en-emies, and their journey home is filled with danger. This tale includes exciting details of the medieval world—merchants, robbers, castles, and secret tunnels. [Henry Holt]

No words of mine can tell you how Wendy despised those pirates. To the boys there was at least some glamour in the pirate calling; but all that she saw was that the ship had not been scrubbed for years.

PETER PAN
written by J.M. Barrie, illustrated by F.D. Bedford
Never-Never Land is the amaz-ing land where the Lost Boys live. Led by their fearless and happy-go-lucky leader, Peter Pan, the Lost Boys have all sorts of larks, but they desperately want a mother. That's

why Peter pleads with Wendy to take care of them and read them bed-time stories. Wendy and her two brothers take an amazing journey, but little do they know what dangers lie ahead—worst of all, Captain Hook! [Everyman's Library]

THE PHANTOM TOLLBOOTH
written by Norton Juster, illustrated by Jules Feiffer
It's a very sad thing, but Milo is not much interested in anything. He doesn't see the point of learning about words or numbers. However, when he steps through a mysterious tollbooth that suddenly appears in his bedroom, he finds himself in a land full of unusual places and people. Milo and his companion, a watchdog called Tock, travel to Dictionopolis, where the letters and words are all mixed up and confusion reigns. Their travels take them to the Island of Conclusions (they jump there), and Digitopolis, where they meet Dodecahedron, a man with twelve faces who is passionate about numbers. They eat subtraction stew and find that the more they eat the hungrier they get. After navigating through the dangerous Mountains of Ignorance, Milo finds himself back at home and realizes he has no more time to be bored because there are so many things to learn all around him! [Random House]

THE PIED PIPER OF HAMELIN
written by Robert Browning, illustrated by Kate Greenaway
Hamelin Town is a pleasant, prosperous town with one major problem: rats. The rodents bother the Hamelin babies, squeak through the Hamelin houses, and eat the Hamelin cheeses. The well-fed Mayor and his councilors wring their hands, but they cannot get rid of the pests. The Pied Piper promises to get rid of the rats and is as good as his word. But after the town is rid of the rats, the

> And I chiefly use my charm
> On creatures that do people harm,
> The mole and toad and newt and viper;
> And people call me the Pied Piper.

Mayor refuses to pay up. The Piper then leads all the children of Hamelin in a dance, all the way out of town. [Everyman's Library]

THE PLAIN PRINCESS
written by Phyllis McGinley, illustrated by Helen Stone
Princess Esmeralda has everything in the world except one thing: beauty.
She is also horribly spoilt and selfish. But in a wonderful way, Esmeralda changes. She grows into a pretty girl and, more importantly, someone who is unselfish. [J.B. Lippincott]

PRAIRIE SCHOOL
written and illustrated by Lois Lenski
Prairie school in the 1940s was very different from schools today. The
children ride to school on horseback, and the teacher lives at the schoolhouse. There are all kinds of things for the teacher to worry about,
such as prairie fires, a dwindling coal supply, and blizzards. One year,
teacher and children live through the worst winter in the history of the
Great Plains when they are marooned in a freezing schoolhouse without any coal. Some of Lois Lenski's other regional stories include *Blue
Ridge Billy, Cotton in My Sack, Strawberry Girl,* and *Texas Tomboy.*
[Lippincott]

PRINCE RABBIT and
THE PRINCESS WHO COULD NOT LAUGH
written by A.A. Milne, illustrated by Mary Shepard
Here are two little-known stories by the creator of Winnie the Pooh
and friends. One day, a king conducts a series of tests to see who will
succeed to his throne. Among the competitors is a rabbit who is very
fast and very clever and outwits all the others. That's not the end of the
story, however, because the rabbit is turned into—but you will have to
find out for yourself how this story ends. Another king has a daughter who never laughs in spite of her father's many attempts to amuse
her. How this solemn princess learns to laugh is a very funny story.
[E.P. Dutton]

THE PRINCESS AND THE GOBLIN
written by George MacDonald, illustrated by Arthur Hughes
The story begins as Princess Irene gets lost in her enormous castle and
stumbles upon a little room at the very top where a beautiful old woman sits spinning. She is her great-great-grandmother Irene. The princess
then meets another new friend, a brave young miner named Curdie.

Irene is fortunate to have such wise and loyal friends because all sorts of evil Goblins and other Uglies threaten her very life. Her great-great-grandmother gives her a magic ring and an invisible ball of thread that will always lead her home. The sequel to this book, *The Princess and Curdie,* completes the adventures of Irene and her brave miner friend. [Puffin]

RABBIT HILL
written and illustrated by Robert Lawson
The creatures on Rabbit Hill are excited that new folks are moving into the Big House—hopefully farming folks who will plant all sorts of vegetables for the animals to eat. Mother Rabbit worries that the new family might bring new dangers such as dogs, cats, shotguns, traps, and boys. But the new folks turn out to be kind and generous and very fond of animals. One day, however, a tragic accident occurs: the new folks' car runs over one of the most popular of the younger animals, Little Georgie. The animals are grief-stricken until Willie Fieldmouse brings wonderful news to Father and Mother Rabbit, and good days return to Rabbit Hill. [Puffin]

> Suddenly the night air was rent by that hideous sound that brings a chill of dread to the hearts of all country dwellers—the long, rising shriek of car brakes, the whine of slithering tires.

RAIDERS FROM THE SEA
written by Louis Walfrid Johnson
Briana O'Toole is a strong, capable Irish lass—strong enough to rescue a strange boy from drowning and drag him to safety. Little does she know that this stranger will turn out to be her most dreaded enemy—a Viking raider. Briana has long heard rumors of ruthless pagan invaders from the north, but she never thought she would become a victim of their cruel raids. Briana (or "Bree" as she is called) and her brother Devin face dangers that test their faith as it's never been tested before. This stirring adventure story will keep you looking for more books in the Viking Quest series. The other titles are *Mystery of the Silver Coins, The Invisible Friend, Heart of Courage,* and *The Raider's Promise.* [Moody Publishers]

THE RAILWAY CHILDREN
written by E. Nesbit, illustrated by Shirley Hughes
Roberta, Peter, and Phyllis live in a grand house with two fun-loving parents. One day, however, a mysterious disaster strikes. Father must leave suddenly, and Mother becomes very sad and worried. She and the children move to a dark little country cottage. But the cottage isn't so gloomy after their things are unpacked, and the children find all sorts of interesting places to explore in the countryside—best of all, the railway station. The trains rush back and forth, bringing the most interesting types of people into the children's lives: Perks the Porter, the Station Master, the famous (but lost) Russian writer, and the kind old gentleman who helps them solve the sad mystery of Father. The children get into all sorts of adventures and grow to love their new life as the Railway Children. [Henry Holt]

> Holding his bottle with both hands and feet he drank as fast as a little raccoon can.

RASCAL
written by Sterling North
Sterling has all kinds of pets including skunks that stink up the local Methodist church, a pet bird called Poe the Crow who yells "What fun!" down the church belfry during services, Wowser the dog, and a pet raccoon named Rascal. Sterling and Rascal eat and sleep together, go to school together, and take fishing trips together. However, not everyone shares Sterling's love for this unusual pet. When Rascal develops a taste for sweet corn, the neighbors whose corn has been raided demand that he be caged. Then Rascal breaks out of his cage to raid the minister's hen house, and Sterling must make a tough decision about his mischievous little friend. [Puffin]

REBECCA OF SUNNYBROOK FARM
written by Kate Douglas Wiggin, illustrated by Helen Mason Grose
Miranda and Jane Sawyer are rather shocked to learn that their niece Rebecca is coming to live with them, for Rebecca is anything but the

docile, quiet kind of girl whom elderly aunts like to invite into their parlors. Rebecca has an active imagination and a restless, impulsive nature, but she soon feels quite at home with her aunts. She loves her new school, where she quickly persuades all the children that her games are the best. She charms old Mr. and Mrs. Cobb with her elaborate poems, and she even persuades a complete stranger to buy three hundred bars of soap! [Houghton Mifflin]

> Going to Aunt Mirandy's is like going down the cellar in the dark. There might be ogres and giants under the stairs, but . . . there might be elves and fairies and enchanted frogs!

THE RELUCTANT DRAGON

written by Kenneth Grahame, illustrated by Michael Hague

This is the story of a very different sort of dragon—a poetry-writing beast who is unwilling to fight even when faced with his old antagonist, St. George. "In the old days," says the dragon, "I always let the other fellows do all the fighting." In fact, when he first meets his archrival, the dragon talks about the weather! Only the clever schemes of an ingenious boy finally persuade this lazy animal to agree to a fight. [Henry Holt]

THE RESCUERS

written by Margery Sharp, illustrated by Garth Williams

The mice of the Prisoners' Aid Society have decided to rescue a Norwegian poet imprisoned in the Black Castle. Once the decision has been made, however, the question is, How? It is not an easy proposition to be sure. A ferocious cat of enormous size guards the castle, and, to make matters worse, the prisoner in question does not know he is being rescued, nor does he speak English. They must find a mouse who can speak Norwegian. The obvious answer is the amazing Miss Bianca. Miss Bianca is a white mouse who lives a pampered life in a Porcelain Pagoda. Honest Bernard persuades her to undertake the mission, and seafaring Nils joins them on this daring adventure. Sequel: *Miss Bianca.* [Little, Brown]

RHYMES AND VERSES: COLLECTED POEMS FOR CHILDREN

written by Walter de la Mare, illustrated by Elinore Blaisdell
A collection of Walter de la Mare's wonderful poetry arranged under topics such as "All Creatures Great and Small" and "Soldiers, Sailors, Far Countries, and the Sea." [Henry Holt]

RIDING THE PONY EXPRESS

written by Clyde Robert Bulla
The time is the 1860s. Dick Park's dad lives in Owl Creek, Nebraska, and is a rider for the Pony Express. He carries the mail from east to west on horseback. Dick hardly sees his father because Mr. Park is always away carrying the mail. One day, when Dick is left alone at Owl Creek Station, Indians steal the horses and burn the house down. Even worse, Mr. Park is wounded, and Dick must carry the mail on a perilous journey. Another good book by Clyde Bulla is *A Ranch for Danny*. [Sonlight]

> People will never forget the Pony Express and all it did to hold the East and West together.

RIKKI-TIKKI-TAVI

written by Rudyard Kipling, illustrated by Monique Felix
This is one of the stories in Kipling's *Jungle Book*, and it tells the adventures of a brave mongoose who must prevent two evil black cobras from killing the family with whom he lives. Says Kipling, "This is the story of the great war that Rikki-Tikki-Tavi fought single-handed." [Creative Education]

ROBIN HOOD OF SHERWOOD FOREST

written by Ann McGovern, illustrated by Tracy Sugarman
This book retells the daring adventures of Robin Hood and his merry band of outlaws and describes his encounters with the Sheriff of Nottingham, who is determined to capture this brave champion of the poor. [Scholastic]

RUN, KEVIN, RUN!

written by Piet Prins, translated by James C. van Oosterom,
illustrated by Jaap Kramer
Kevin is an unhappy, friendless boy who lives with foster parents, but
he dislikes being dragged to church twice on Sundays so he runs away.
That's when his troubles start. He foolishly becomes involved with two
criminals and is wanted by the police. The further Kevin runs, the more
his difficulties increase. [Paideia Press]

SAINT GEORGE AND THE DRAGON

written by Margaret Hodges, illustrated by Trina Schart Hyman
an adaptation of part of Edmund Spenser's Faerie Queene
The Red Cross Knight has been sent
by the Queen of the Fairies to slay the
most deadly of dragons. This dreadful creature has devastated the land,
and only Princess Una has courage
enough to seek out the knight and
guide him to the dragon. The encounter is hideous to behold, but the
Red Cross Knight is valiant and con-

> In the days when monsters
> and giants and fairy folk
> lived in England, a noble
> knight was riding across a
> plain.

fronts his foe each time with renewed vigor. After he slays the dragon,
all the people rejoice and flock around the knight admiringly, including
the beautiful Princess Una. [Little, Brown]

SARAH, PLAIN AND TALL

written by Patricia MacLachlan
Jacob Witting wants a wife and a mother for Anna and Caleb, so he
places an advertisement in the newspaper! Into their lives strides Sarah,
plain and tall. Jacob and the children
like Sarah, but they keep reminding
themselves that Sarah will not stay
because she is from Maine, and she
misses the sea. One day, Sarah hitch-
es the horses to the wagon and drives
away. The children wonder if she'll
ever come back. [HarperTrophy]

> Sarah loved the chickens.
> She clucked back to
> them and fed them grain.
> They followed her, shuffling
> and scratching primly in the
> dirt. I knew they would not
> be for eating.

THE SATURDAYS
written by Elizabeth Enright
The four Melendy children—Mona, Rush, Miranda, and Oliver—are
tired of unexciting Saturdays, so they form the Independent Saturday
Afternoon Adventure Club and pool their pocket money to spend as
they like. Rush goes to a concert, Randy to an art gallery, and Mona visits a theater, but little Oliver, who is only six, slips away from the house to a circus. The Club is an unqualified success and the start of many other adventures. Also read *Thimble Summer.* [Henry Holt]

> Now it's going to be Saturday every day all summer long," said Randy, and yawned a wide, peaceful, happy yawn.

SCOUT: THE SECRET OF THE SWAMP
written by Piet Prins, illustrated by Jaap Kramer
Scout is a fantastic German shepherd dog. His keen insight and loyalty
to his owner, Tom, save the boy-dog team from many narrow escapes.
Once, Scout and Tom track down a band of thieves who have just stolen
some valuable property from Tom's house. But the robbers catch them
outside their hideout, and both Tom and Scout face a sad end, unless
Scout can escape and bring help. But this escapade is nothing compared
to the life-threatening dangers Tom, Scout, and their Dutch community
experience when the Nazis come and control their whole country. During the dangerous days ahead, Tom and his intelligent dog risk their lives
for the cause. [Inheritance Publications]

THE SECRET GARDEN
written by Frances Hodgson Burnett,
illustrated by Charles Robinson
When pampered Mary Lennox—Mistress Mary Quite Contrary,
as some call her—comes to Misselthwaite Manor, her face is yellow
and her expression sour. Her misery is understandable because her father has just died, leaving her quite alone, and she must now live with
strangers in the country. Her new home is an old English manor on
the Yorkshire moors. The mystery begins when Mary hears strange
cries coming from somewhere in the house. She soon discovers that the

house and gardens, and one garden in particular, hold a deep mystery. Through the friendship of a good-hearted Yorkshire boy, Mary unearths the secret of the garden. [Everyman's Library]

SHADRACH
written by Meindert DeJong, illustrated by Maurice Sendak
Davie wants a rabbit so badly, and he has even picked out a name: Shadrach. He already has a hutch and three big bags of clover, even though his brother Jem tells him that rabbits swell up, burst, and die from eating too much clover! The week that Davie has to wait for Shadrach seems like forever. But as soon as Shadrach arrives, Davie has plenty of other things to worry about, especially when his pet disappears. [HarperTrophy]

> Shadrach was gone! The hutch was empty! Shadrach wasn't in his hutch. He stood there in his horrible scare, the forgotten bun squeezing to pieces in his hand.

SHH! WE'RE WRITING THE CONSTITUTION
written by Jean Fritz, illustrated by Tomie dePaola
This is a fun-filled and information-packed account of America's founding era. After the Revolutionary War, most Americans consider themselves to be citizens of their individual states. They have little concept of national citizenship. Pretty soon, however, some state representatives decide that the states need more national unity, and they hold a Continental Congress to decide what can be done. Throughout their meetings, their discussions are kept secret—locked doors and closed windows—for four months! Read all about it in this entertaining book. Look for other books by Jean Fritz such as *Where Do You Think You're Going, Christopher Columbus?* and *What's the Big Idea, Ben Franklin?* [Putnam]

SHILOH
written by Phyllis Reynolds Naylor, illustrated by Barry Moser
When Marty Preston finds a beagle in the hills behind his home, he and the dog become instant friends. Marty realizes that Shiloh has been

brutally treated, so he hides him in the woods near his home. Soon the beagle's cruel owner shows up, angry and demanding the dog back. [Aladdin]

THE SIGN OF THE BEAVER
written by Elizabeth George Speare
When Matt's father leaves him in the wilderness to guard the log cabin they have just built, Matt feels lonesome and helpless, especially after a passing stranger steals his gun. Now he is unable to hunt or even protect himself. Before long, however, he is saved by an Indian boy named Attean who teaches Matt how to survive in the forest in exchange for reading lessons. Together Matt and Attean read *Robinson Crusoe* and stories from the Bible, and they join forces against a formidable foe: a huge brown bear. The months pass as Matt anxiously waits for his family to return. [Yearling]

SNOW TREASURE
written by Marie McSwigan
Peter and the other children who live in a small Norwegian village love sledding down the hills in the thick snow. It is one year after the start of World War II, and Nazi soldiers have invaded Norway. They want to get their hands on Norway's treasure—her gold bullion. So the children are enlisted in a dangerous scheme to carry the gold to safety—on their sleds—right past the watching eyes of the Nazi guards. It's a race against time, and the children's lives are in constant danger. [Scholastic]

> ig boy like you, playing with a sled!" he taunted. "In Germany, you'd be one of Hitler's Youth. You'd learn to march. You'd be on your way to being a soldier!"

SQUANTO: FRIEND OF THE PILGRIMS
written by Clyde Robert Bulla, illustrated by Peter Buchard
When white men land in the New World, a Patuxet Indian called Squanto befriends them. He sails with them to England, where he meets Captain John Smith, and to Spain, where he is sold as a slave. When Squanto is eventually able to return to his village near Cape Cod, he makes a heartbreaking discovery. [Scholastic]

STORIES FROM THE ARABIAN NIGHTS

written by Laurence Housman, illustrated by Girard Goodenow
The heart of Arabia is the perfect setting for tales of mystery and magic. One day, a fisherman uncorks an ancient vessel hoping to find treasure inside. But instead of finding jewels or gold coins, he is astonished to see a thick column of black smoke fill the air and form an enormous human shape. It is the Genie who has been imprisoned there for two thousand years. Even though the Genie vows he will take revenge for his imprisonment on anyone who releases him from the bottle, the fisherman is a quick thinker. He tricks the Genie into leading him to a great fortune. This is just one of many amazing stories from Arabia. [Junior Deluxe Editions/Nelson Doubleday]

STORMY, MISTY'S FOAL

written by Marguerite Henry, illustrated by Wesley Dennis
This is the true story of a terrible storm that hit two islands off the coast of Virginia and almost wiped out the wild ponies that live there. Paul and Maureen Beebe's family, who own a pony ranch on one island, are evacuated when the storm strikes, and their island is flooded. But what worries the children most is that they must leave behind their beloved pony who is about to give birth in Grandma's kitchen. Thanks to the efforts of hundreds of people, the island of Chincoteague is rebuilt after the storm, and the wild ponies of Assateague are replenished. [Aladdin]

THE STORY OF DOCTOR DOLITTLE

written by Hugh Lofting, illustrated by Michael Hague
Dr. Dolittle is a fine animal doctor, and, with the help of Polynesia the parrot, he learns the animals' language so that he can easily cure their aches and pains. His sister leaves in disgust one day when he takes in a crocodile, which, she says, is "a nasty thing to find under the bed." Dr. Dolittle has many adventures, including a trip to Africa where he is pursued by the mean King of the

Oh, we parrots can talk in two languages . . . If I say, 'Polly wants a cracker,' you understand me. But hear this: Ka-ka oi-ee, fee-fee?"
"Good Gracious!" cried the Doctor. "What does that mean?"
"That means, 'Is the porridge hot yet?'—in bird-language."

Jolliginki and thrown into a dungeon. The kind old doctor is accompanied by Dab-Dab the duck, Chee-Chee the monkey, and his other animal friends, including the rarest of rare animals—an animal that can talk and eat at the same time without being rude, the pushmi-pullyu. There are eleven other Dr. Dolittle books. [William Morrow]

THE STORY OF HOLLY AND IVY
written by Rumer Godden, illustrated by Barbara Cooney
It is Christmas Eve, and all the dolls in Mr. Blossom's toyshop, including a doll in a red dress named Holly, want desperately to be sold in time for Christmas. And of course there are many girls—especially Ivy—who would love a new doll. Ivy lives in an orphanage and longs for a doll of her own, but when she is sent far away to live at another orphanage in the country, it seems that Holly and Ivy will never find each other. [Viking]

THE STORY OF ROLF AND THE VIKING BOW
written by Allen French
This is an ancient Icelandic tale of a man named Hiarandi who lives high above treacherous cliffs. One night, Hiarandi decides to light a fire to signal an oncoming ship instead of accepting the salvage of the shipwreck according to pagan custom. Because of a strange twist of irony, however, the life he saves that night eventually causes his own death and the unjust outlawing of his sixteen-year-old son, Rolf. The boy sets out to avenge his father's death and prove his innocence. To achieve his quest, Rolf must seek out strange alliances and learn to master the mighty Viking bow, a nigh impossible task even for a lad who is one of the most skilled bowmen in all of Iceland. [Bethlehem Books]

THE STORY OF THE FOUR LITTLE CHILDREN
WHO WENT ROUND THE WORLD
written by Edward Lear, illustrated by Stanley Mack
This is the very funny story of Violet, Slingsby, Guy, and Lionel who travel around the world with a cat to steer their boat and a Quangle-Wangle to cook dinner and make tea. They have all sorts of adventures. For instance, they land on an island full of veal cutlets and chocolate drops;

they are almost thumped to death when a high wind blows millions of oranges onto their heads; they are very offended when a multitude of white mice refuse to share their custard pudding; and they are amazed to visit a land entirely populated by blue-bottle flies who live—of course— in blue bottles. But their worst adventure occurs when their boat is bitten to pieces by a most unfriendly Seeze Pyder. [Harlin Quist/Crown]

THE STORY OF THE OTHER WISE MAN
written by Henry Van Dyke
This is the story about a fourth Wise Man who longs to join the other Magi on their journey to see the Christ Child. This Wise Man is providentially delayed by several people who need his help, and, time after time, he gives away the gifts he had hoped to give to the King of Kings. At the end of his life, he has no gifts left, but in one transcendent moment, he realizes that his journey has not been in vain. Younger children will enjoy a retelling of this story, *The Fourth Wise Man* by Susan Summers, which is reviewed in the Preschool section. [Ballantine Books]

THE STORY OF THE TREASURE SEEKERS
written by E. Nesbit, illustrated by Cecil Leslie
The Bastable children consist of six brothers and sisters all thirsting for adventure. They live with their father in a large house which has gotten shabbier and shabbier ever since their mother died. The children watch the silver spoons and the servants go and realize that their family's fortunes have dwindled. It's up to them to restore the family to wealth, and they conclude that the best way to achieve this end is to find treasure. Their search for fortune brings them many surprises and even a little success! Although wretched things happen to

> *C*ome and dig! Then you shall share the treasure when we've found it."
> But he said, "I shan't—I don't like digging—and I'm just going in to my tea."

them like falling into pits and starting questionable business ventures, they also befriend princesses, poets, and a Generous Benefactor. The sequel to this book is *The Wouldbegoods*. [Puffin]

STRANDED AT PLIMOTH PLANTATION 1626

written and illustrated by Gary Bowen

Thirteen-year-old Christopher Sears sails for Jamestown, Virginia, in 1626 but is shipwrecked and stranded at Plimoth Plantation. While he waits for a passage to Jamestown, Christopher records details of everyday life in a journal. He writes about the food—cold eel pie and beet tarts!—visits from Indians, planting vegetables, digging for clams, Sabbath worship, and discipline—two men are put in the stocks, one for fighting with his wife in a public place and another for smoking in public! This story is illustrated with colorful woodcuts of life at Plimoth Plantation and is a fascinating account of early American life. [HarperCollins]

Note: *The book does contain some inaccuracies; for example, Squanto could not have visited the community because he died in 1622.*

STUART LITTLE

written by E.B. White,
illustrated by Garth Williams

> Every morning . . . Mrs. Little went into his room and weighed him on a small scale which was really meant for weighing letters. At birth Stuart could have been sent by first class mail for three cents.

Stuart is a most unusual mouse. He has been born into a human family, and because he is only two inches high, he wears small clothes and carries miniature dimes made out of foil. It is sometimes useful to be so small because Stuart is able to rescue a ring that has slipped down a drain, unjam piano keys, and navigate a toy sailboat during a boat race. But sometimes Stuart gets into terrible scrapes. One time he gets locked inside the refrigerator overnight and catches bronchitis! [HarperTrophy]

THE SUMMER OF THE SWANS

written by Betsy Byars

Sara just tolerates her bossy aunt and her beautiful sister, Wanda, but, above all, Sara loves her little brother, Charlie, who is mentally retarded. Sara and Charlie spend a lot of time together watching the swans on the lake. At first, Sara is absorbed with her own concerns, especially her appearance, but when Charlie disappears in the middle of the night, Sara starts to think about someone else instead. [Puffin]

THE TALE OF TROY
written by Roger Lancelyn Green, illustrated by Pauline Baynes
In this companion volume to *Tales of the Greek Heroes,* you will read about the story of Paris's love for Helen and their elopement that starts the Trojan War. In the ensuing battle between the Greeks and the Trojans, the Greeks lay siege to Troy, and, through a clever ploy—the Trojan horse—they conquer the city. After the war, Odysseus has many adventures before he finally arrives home in Ithaca. [Puffin]

TALES OF THE GREEK HEROES
written by Roger Lancelyn Green,
illustrated by Alan Langford
These legends of ancient Greece provide a fascinating look into the ancient world. Here are tales of hideous monsters, brilliant heroes, and squabbling gods. The gods—Olympians, they call themselves—never tire of meddling in the lives of mortals, and the adventures that result are very entertaining. Roger Lancelyn Green also wrote about ancient Egyptian myths in *Tales of Ancient Egypt.* [Puffin]

> Heracles . . . grasped a snake in either hand, gripping them by their necks and keeping the poisoned fangs away from him.

TANGLEWOOD TALES
written by Nathaniel Hawthorne
This book includes six classic legends of Greek mythology. Read about the exploits of Theseus as he wrestles with a fearful monster, Jason's pursuit of the Golden Fleece, and Ulysses's encounter with an evil enchantress who changes men into pigs. [Tor Classics]

Another excellent book of Greek mythology is Nathaniel Hawthorne's *A Wonder Book.* [Everyman's Library]

THE THANKSGIVING STORY

written by Alice Dalgliesh, illustrated by Helen Sewell

Giles Constance, Damaris Hopkins, and their parents sail on the *Mayflower* to the New World. You will learn how these brave Pilgrims survive during their first winter in Plymouth. They befriend Indians, plant corn, build homes, and have a Thanksgiving feast with their Indian friends that lasts for three days. [Atheneum]

THAT WILD BERRIES SHOULD GROW

written by Gloria Whelan

Elsa loves life in the busy city of Detroit, so she dreads spending a whole summer marooned at her grandparents' cottage in the country. She's an only child recovering from a recent illness, and her parents smother her with their concern; however, her grandparents get on with their work, leaving Elsa to her own devices. She learns to enjoy simple pleasures such as fishing in the lake and picking wild berries. Surprisingly, when the summer ends, she is sad to say goodbye to her grandparents and the beautiful countryside. [Eerdmans]

> The doctor feels you need fresh air." She was trying to look happy, but it wasn't working.
> I began to worry. I knew the only place you find fresh air is where there is nothing else.

THREE YOUNG PILGRIMS

written and illustrated by Cheryl Harness

Mary, Remember, and Bartholomew Allerton are three of the Pilgrims who sail across the Atlantic Ocean to America. When they drop anchor off Cape Cod, the mothers and children continue to live crowded together on the ship while the men find good land and build houses for their families at Plymouth Colony. Many Pilgrims fall sick and die that first winter, including Mrs. Allerton and her newborn baby. But life becomes happier for the settlers when Samoset and Squanto show them how to grow corn, and the Pilgrims share their first Thanksgiving meal with their Indian friends. [Aladdin]

THURSDAY'S CHILD

written by Noel Streatfeild

When she was a small baby, Margaret Thursday was found in a basket with a note stating that money for her care would be supplied each year. After several years, however, another note arrives: "No More Money for Margaret." She must be shipped off to an orphanage miles away. Even for stouthearted Margaret, leaving all the people she has ever known is a horrid change. She finds life harsh at St. Luke's Orphanage, but she also finds friends—Lavinia, Peter, and Horatio Beresford. Margaret is certain that her mysterious origins will someday be revealed and that she will turn out to be "someone." The quest to discover her identity leads her and her new-found friends into some amazing adventures. [Collins]

> What nobody understands is what wearing boots does to me—they humiliate my legs.

THE TINKER'S DAUGHTER

written by Wendy Lawton

This novel is based on the life of Mary Bunyan, John Bunyan's little blind daughter who brings her father a bowl of soup each day he spends in Bedford prison. Bunyan is imprisoned for preaching God's Word without a license. Although Mary is a loving daughter, she is very proud. She dislikes offers of help and relies on her own ability to overcome her disability. She has to learn that she can overcome her blindness only when she trusts in Jesus to strengthen her. Look for other books in the Daughters of Faith series by this author. [Moody Publishers]

TITUS IN TROUBLE

written by James Reeves, illustrated by Edward Ardizzone

Titus has always wanted to go to sea, but an unfortunate mishap is the beginning of so many troubles that Titus thinks he will never make enough money to fulfill his dream. The harder he works, the more scrapes he gets into, and then, after the worst accident of all, he makes an amazing discovery. [Henry Z. Walck]

TREASURES OF THE SNOW
written by Patricia St. John
Annette lives in the Swiss Alps. One day, her little brother, Dani, has a terrible accident and is crippled because he is teased by the village bully, Lucien. After the accident, Annette hates Lucien, and so does the whole village. Utterly miserable, Lucien runs off to the woods and, with the help of an old woodsman, learns to carve wooden animals. He takes a beautiful hand-carved Noah's ark to Dani, but Annette throws it away in fury, along with a horse Lucien has carved for the village handicraft competition. Now Annette must come to terms with her bitterness toward Lucien while every day she prays for a miracle to heal Dani's crippled leg. Also look for *Rainbow Garden* and other books by Patricia St. John. [Moody Publishers]

THE TRUMPET OF THE SWAN
written by E.B. White, illustrated by Fred Marcellino
While Sam is camping in Canada with his father, he meets a family of trumpeter swans. Sam makes friends with the entire swan family and in particular with one of the young swans named Louis. Louis is different from the rest because he is unable to make any sound at all. When Sam goes back home, he takes Louis to school with him. There Louis learns to communicate through some amazing ways. Soon Louis is no longer a defective bird but a swan of great distinction. [HarperCollins]

> He decided that since he was unable to use his voice, he should learn to read and write. "If I'm defective in one respect," he said to himself, "I should try and develop myself along other lines."

TURN HOMEWARD, HANNALEE
written by Patricia Beatty
This exciting story is based on an historical event. Hannalee lives in Roswell, Georgia, a southern mill town, during the War Between the States. Her father has been killed, and her brother is fighting for the Confederacy. The Union Army invades Georgia, burning the mills and shipping the mill workers, including Hannalee and her brother, to Kentucky where they work for Northern mill owners. Before she leaves her

home, Hannalee tells her mother that she will come back. To fulfill that promise, Hannalee must escape and, disguised as a boy, make a long, dangerous journey. [William Morrow]

TWO LITTLE CONFEDERATES
written by Thomas Nelson Page

Frank and Willy live on a plantation in Virginia during the War Between the States. Their mother is devoted to the Southern cause and provides food and shelter for the Confederate soldiers. Their home is looted by Union men who steal everything they can carry away. The family is

> Frank thought his hour had come. . . . Then he thought of his father and of how proud he would be of his son's bravery. . . . This gave him strength.

left with nothing to eat and almost starve until Frank and Willy save the day by catching some hogs. One day, their soldier brother and a Southern general visit them and have to hide when Union solders arrive at the house to search for them. When the boys take food to the fugitives, Union men catch them and order them to lead the way to the two men in hiding or face being shot. Sequel: *Among the Camps.* [Pelican]

UNDERSTOOD BETSY
written by Dorothy Canfield Fisher, illustrated by Kimberly Bulcken Root

Elizabeth Ann's life turns upside down when she leaves the city and her overprotective Aunt Frances and goes to live with her adult cousins in New England. Aunt Frances has always spoilt her, so Elizabeth Ann doesn't know how to wash dishes, cook, or set the table. She is pale, thin, and afraid of just about everything. However, after a year on the farm with her hard-working cousins, she overcomes her timid ways. When Aunt Frances comes to visit, she hardly recognizes her frail little niece. [Henry Holt]

WE LIVE BY THE RIVER
written and illustrated by Lois Lenski

This is one of the Roundabout America stories that are set in different parts of the country. This book is filled with authentic details about life on and around the Mississippi, Ohio, and Pearl Rivers. A map gives the locations of these stories of three children and their families. Other Roundabout America Titles are *Little Sioux Girl, Peanuts for Billy Ben, Project Boy, We Live in the City,* and *We Live in the South.* [J.B. Lippincott]

WE WERE THERE WITH THE MAYFLOWER PILGRIMS
written by Robert Webb, illustrated by Charles J. Andres
When Dickon and Patience's parents make plans to leave Holland and travel to the New World, they decide to leave the children behind because the journey will be too dangerous. However, before the *Speedwell* can take off, the children get caught on board and end up traveling as stowaways! They overhear a nasty plot by some of the sailors to spring a leak in the ship, and, sure enough, the *Speedwell* doesn't make the trip. The whole Whitcomb family climbs aboard a second ship, the *Mayflower.* On board with them are fiery Captain Myles Standish, dependable William Bradford, and others all on their way to the New World. This story of their amazing adventure makes history come alive. [Grosset & Dunlap]

WHAT KATY DID
written by Susan Coolidge
Katy Carr is the oldest of the six Carr children who come in all sizes and personalities. They share wonderful adventures, and Katy's schemes are behind them all. Her mind is full of delightful stories and surprises. Once Katy "adopts" a little Irish girl for a day, brings her home to the other children, and feeds her scraps of old bread and biscuits. They all delight in the grand secret of owning a baby, until the child's crying gives them away. One gloomy morning, Katy wakes up on the wrong side of everything. She has a horrible accident that confines her to bed. With the help of her family and her wise cousin Helen, Katy finds happiness even in affliction. Sequel: *What Katy Did Next.* [Dover]

> They always got up on Monday full of life and mischief, and ready to fizz over at any minute, like champagne bottles with the wires just cut.

THE WHEEL ON THE SCHOOL
written by Meindert DeJong, illustrated by Maurice Sendak
Six children who go to school in a tiny Dutch fishing village begin to wonder why no storks ever come and build nests in their village. It doesn't seem right—a seaside village without storks. So the children begin to think the way storks think; maybe, for instance, it's because there are no trees, or maybe it's because the roofs are too sharp. Storks nest in trees and roofs, but the village roofs need wheels for storks to build their nests on. So each child sets off to find a wheel. During their searches, they face many difficulties and make new friends. Soon the whole community is working together to make the children's dream come true. [HarperTrophy]

> Storks do not sing. They make a noise like you do when you clap your hands.

A WHITE HERON: A STORY OF MAINE
written by Sarah Orne Jewett, illustrated by Douglas Alvord
Sylvy lives with her grandmother on an isolated farm, and her only companion is an old cow. She knows the woods very well, and when a friendly bird lover asks Sylvy to lead him to the nest of the rare white heron, she must decide whether to keep the heron's secret or give its life away. [David R. Godine]

WILLIAM TELL
written and illustrated by Margaret Early
This is an exciting retelling of an old Swiss legend. When William Tell refuses to bow to the symbol of an oppressive ruler—a hat perched high on a pole—he is captured and forced to perform an impossible feat: he must shoot an arrow through an apple placed on his son's head. When the moment for the test comes, Walter stands bravely, waiting for his father to release his arrow. If William Tell misses his mark, they will both die! [Harry N. Abrams]

> "What dust-clouds shall spring up behind me as I speed on my reckless way!" . . .
> "What are we to do with him?" asked the Mole of the Water Rat.
> "Nothing at all," replied the Rat firmly.

THE WIND IN THE WILLOWS
written by Kenneth Grahame, illustrated by Ernest Shepard

Toad of Toad Hall is the most conceited and opinionated creature in the animal kingdom. He is attracted to all the latest fads—especially shiny motor cars! His reckless driving habits land him in such terrible scrapes that his loyal friends Ratty and Mole despair over his riotous living. Eventually, the two of them, together with wise old Badger, determine to reform the incorrigible Toad. [Atheneum]

WISE WORDS: FAMILY STORIES THAT BRING THE PROVERBS TO LIFE
written by Peter Leithart

This is a collection of stories about proud kings, lazy sons, discontented wives, and jealous neighbors, all of whom certainly get what they deserve. The stories are filled with monsters and dragons and all the other things you expect to find in fairy tales, but, unlike most fairy tales, they illustrate the wisdom of the Book of Proverbs, so you will learn a lot about God's Word while you have fun reading these wise words. [Canon Press]

THE WIZARD OF OZ
written by L. Frank Baum, illustrated by W.W. Denslow

> While Dorothy was looking earnestly into the queer, painted face of the Scarecrow, she was surprised to see one of the eyes slowly wink at her.

A fierce cyclone whisks Dorothy's house right out of Kansas to the Land of Oz where it flattens and kills the Wicked Witch of the East! Everyone's glad about that, but Dorothy just wants to get home again. Some Munchkins tell her to follow the yellow brick road so that she can get help from the Wizard. Along the way, she and her little dog Toto have lots of adventures with a Scarecrow, a Tin Woodman, and a Cowardly Lion. [Everyman's Library]

ILLUSTRATIONS
Men of Iron, illustrated by Howard Pyle
(New York: Harper & Brothers, 1919), see page 148
for an unillustrated edition.

3

MIDDLE
SCHOOL FICTION

THE ADVENTURES OF ROBINSON CRUSOE
written by Daniel Defoe, illustrated by J.J. Granville
Robinson Crusoe is shipwrecked and lives as a castaway on a desert island for nearly thirty years. He survives because of his courage, ingenuity, and faith in God. In spite of loneliness and fears for his safety, he looks to his Savior for help and comfort and interprets his misfortunes as the will of God. After many years, he saves the life of a man named Friday who is about to be devoured by cannibals, and Friday becomes Crusoe's devoted servant. Together, Crusoe and Friday experience many hair-raising adventures and make plans to escape the island. [Trident Press International]

THE ADVENTURES OF TOM SAWYER
written by Mark Twain
Tom Sawyer is a mischievous young boy raised by his formidable Aunt Polly. Tom's creativity sometimes works to his advantage, such as when he tricks his friends into doing his chores, and sometimes it doesn't. Tom gets himself into a heap of trouble when he saves Becky Thatcher from punishment by confessing to the crime she has committed. In another episode, Tom faces the wrath of brutal Injun Joe when he attends the trial of Muff Potter. Muff has been wrongly convicted of murder, and Tom reveals that Injun Joe is the real criminal. Tom has lots of other adventures—he gets lost in a cave with Injun Joe, he finds pirates' treasure, and he even manages to attend his own funeral! [Bantam Classics]

AROUND THE WORLD IN EIGHTY DAYS

written by Jules Verne

Eccentric Phileas Fogg bets £20,000 that he can travel around the world in eighty days. Accompanied by a faithful servant, Fogg travels by all sorts of unconventional means, including an elephant, a sled, and a balloon. To make the journey even more lively, an English detective trails him everywhere he goes because he suspects that Fogg is a bank robber on the run. In addition to the detective, other obstacles—including savage Indians and the threat of human sacrifice—threaten to thwart Fogg as he races against the clock to complete his extraordinary journey around the world. [Bantam Classics]

> Having made a tour of the world, he was behind-hand five minutes.

AUGUSTINE CAME TO KENT

written by Barbara Willard, illustrated by Hans Guggenheim

Wolf is an Italian boy who travels with his father and St. Augustine from Rome to Kent in order to christianize pagan Britain. Their mission is successful. Augustine baptizes the once pagan king, and he becomes the first Archbishop of Canterbury. Meanwhile, Wolf makes friends with Fritha, an English peasant girl who, along with her father, become Augustine's first converts. But Fritha pays a terrible price. Her home is burned by those who hate Christians. This story of two brave young people is set during an exciting period of early English history. [Doubleday]

BANNER IN THE SKY

written by James Ramsey Ullman

Rudi Matt longs to climb the Citadel, the last unconquered summit of the Alps. However, Uncle Franz forbids him to attempt the climb because Rudi's father was killed on this mountain. So Rudi washes dishes in a Swiss hotel. One day, he hears that a great mountaineer, Captain Winter, is preparing to climb the Citadel. Rudi sneaks away from home to join him. Four men inch toward the top, but one of the guides has a bad accident, and Rudi must make an agonizing decision. Should he climb on to the summit alone and fulfill his dream, or should he help the injured man down the mountain to safety? [HarperTeen]

BEOWULF THE WARRIOR
translated by Ian Serraillier, illustrated by Mark Severin
We do not know who composed Beowulf, but it is a great Anglo-Saxon poem about man-eating monsters, probably written four centuries before the Norman Conquest. The first half of the poem deals with a hideous monster, Grendel, who lurks around the meadhall where Hrothgar, King of the Danes, celebrates his victories. While Hrothgar's thanes sleep, Grendel snatches up thirty at a time and drags them away to devour them in his dark lair. The hero, Beowulf, is summoned to destroy both Grendel and his fiend-like mother. Much later in his life, Beowulf faces his most terrible antagonist: a fire-breathing dragon. To kill him, Beowulf must make the ultimate sacrifice. [Bethlehem Books]

BLACK FALCON
written and illustrated by Armstrong Sperry
A historical novel set during the War of 1812. Sixteen-year-old Wade Thayer and his father run a British blockade and become marooned off the Louisiana coast. Captain Thayer is killed, and Wade is taken prisoner, but he escapes to become a messenger for the pirate Jean Lafitte, the Black Falcon. Wade must persuade first the governor of Louisiana and then General Andrew Jackson to accept Lafitte's help in defending New Orleans against British attack. This exciting tale describes the bloody Battle of New Orleans. During this battle, Wade comes face-to-face with an old enemy who intends to bludgeon him to death with a bayonet. [Holt, Rinehart & Winston]

THE BLACK PEARL
written by Scott O'Dell
As Ramon and his father search for pearls in the waters of Baja, California, Ramon dreams of finding a great black pearl. Ramon's dreams are clouded by stories of the Manta

There followed a groan, a rending of timbers, and the canoe rose crazily and tipped and I was pitching slowly sideways into the sea.

Diablo, which, according to the legend, is a monstrous creature of the deep that owns the great black pearl. When Ramon at last finds the black pearl, he is warned to throw it back into the sea, or the monster will take both the pearl and his life. By now Ramon has another deadly enemy, Sevellano, an arrogant diver of his father's fleet. Ramon must eventually confront both adversaries, the man and the monster. [Yearling]

THE BRONZE BOW
written by Elizabeth George Speare
Daniel is a Jewish boy who lives in Palestine during the time of Christ. His one consuming passion is his hatred of the Romans because they killed his mother and father. Daniel is motivated by his desire for revenge until he meets Jesus and hears the Savior preach about victory achieved not by force but by love. Daniel remains skeptical for a long time and has to suffer greatly and experience much danger and heartbreak before he realizes that his real enemy is not the Romans but the hatred festering in his own heart. [Houghton Mifflin]

CALICO CAPTIVE
written by Elizabeth George Speare
This book is based on a diary that recorded events during the French and Indian War. Miriam's head is full of romantic thoughts about her young man when suddenly Indians raid her brother-in-law's cabin in Charlestown. Miriam and the rest of the family are forced to march through the wilderness with little sleep and meager food, perhaps to be sold as slaves to the French, perhaps to face the dreaded gauntlet. On the trail, her sister Susanna gives birth to baby Captive, then the rest of the family are forced to leave Susanna behind in the wilderness with their brutal captors. In Montreal, Miriam becomes a servant in a wealthy French household, and the direction of her life again changes dramatically. Will she ever get back to her home and marry her handsome sweetheart? [Houghton Mifflin]

CALL IT COURAGE
written and illustrated by Armstrong Sperry
This is the legend of Mafatu, the Polynesian boy who is afraid of the sea. In response to other boys' taunts, Mafatu sets out to sea in a canoe

to conquer his fear and prove that he is not a coward. When a storm breaks up his canoe and lands him on a desert island, Mafatu is very resourceful. He builds another canoe, and, with a handmade whalebone knife and a spear, he kills a hammerhead shark and a wild boar. Then he must battle for his life against the most dreadful

> Mafatu saw that the savages were armed with ironwood war clubs—clubs studded with sharks' teeth or barbed with the sting-ray's spike.

of all sea monsters, the octopus. Mafatu gradually learns that the sea is only another element for man to subdue. [Aladdin]

CANTERBURY TALES
written by Geoffrey Chaucer, adapted by Barbara Cohen,
illustrated by Trina Schart Hyman
The year is 1386, and Geoffrey Chaucer is riding away on a pilgrimage from London to Canterbury to visit the shrine of the martyred Thomas à Becket. He stays at an inn where he meets other pilgrims traveling to the same place. The innkeeper has a good idea: He suggests that they all tell stories, and the best storyteller will win a free meal at the inn. One of the tales in this collection is about a proud rooster and a wily fox who plans to have the rooster for his dinner. Another describes the adventures of three greedy young men who come to a very sad end. There is also a tale about a knight's impossible

> Now gentlemen," the old man replied, "if you're so anxious to find Death, turn up this crooked road."

quest. Chaucer's *Canterbury Tales* perhaps have never been more lavishly illustrated or more charmingly retold. [Lothrop, Lee & Shepard]

Another excellent retelling of Chaucer's *Canterbury Tales* is *A Taste of Chaucer: Selections from "The Canterbury Tales,"* which is selected and edited by Anne Malcolmson. [Harcourt Brace Jovanovich]

CAPTAIN, MY CAPTAIN
written by Deborah Meroff
This romance, based on a true story, is a page turner. Mary Patten is barely married before she sets out with her sailor husband on a clipper

race from New York to San Francisco. Mary insists on learning how to navigate the ship, but when her husband falls desperately ill, she discovers that she is the only other person on board who can navigate. During this ordeal, Mary relies on God as she steers the ship round Cape Horn, "the graveyard of ships." [Inheritance Publications]

CAPTAIN BLOOD
written by Rafael Sabatini
Spectacular adventure and hairbreadth escapes on the high seas. This is the tale of an audacious pirate, Captain Blood, whose daring and courage are the talk of the Caribbean. Time and again, he dupes his enemies with his resourceful schemes. During the affair at Maracaybo, Captain Blood's genius reaches its zenith. Trapped on the high seas off Maracaybo without hope of escape, Spaniards bent on his capture, and outnumbered two to one, Blood carries out a brilliant ruse and once again outwits his enemies. [Penguin Classics]

> My name is Blood—Captain Peter Blood." "Blood!" shrilled the little man. "A pirate!"

CAPTAINS COURAGEOUS
written by Rudyard Kipling
An exciting sea adventure about a spoiled, rich teenager, Harvey Cheyne, who considers himself too good for manual labor until he falls overboard and is rescued by a fisherman. On board the fishing boat, Harvey must earn his keep and cooperate with his rescuers. During the course of his adventures with the fishing crew, he is transformed from a snob to an enterprising boy who values others for themselves rather than for their wealth. [Oxford]

> Look's if your line was fast to somethin'. Haul!" shouted Dan, but the shout ended in a shrill double shriek of horror, for out of the sea came—the body of the dead Frenchman buried two days before!

THE CHALLENGE OF THE GREEN KNIGHT
written by Ian Serraillier, illustrated by Victor G. Ambrus
King Arthur and all his knights are feasting on New Year's Day, when into their midst strides a most unusual knight. He is the Green Knight, and he comes to Arthur's court to issue a strange challenge: He invites one of Arthur's knights to behead him, but he warns his opponent that in a year and a day the Green Knight will exchange the deadly blow. Sir Gawain accepts the challenge and beheads their visitor. Unperturbed, the Green Knight rides away with his head under his arm. This is a lively retelling of the medieval poem *Sir Gawain and the Green Knight*. [Henry Z. Walck]

THE CHILDREN'S HOMER: THE ADVENTURES OF ODYSSEUS AND THE TALE OF TROY
written by Padraic Colum, illustrated by Willy Pogany
In this retelling of Homer's *Odyssey* and *Iliad*, Telemachus, Odysseus's son, goes on a voyage in search of his father who is away fighting the Trojan War. After defeating the Trojans, Odysseus wanders for ten years, experiencing amazing adventures, before he finally returns to Ithaca. The Greek hero must subdue a one-eyed Cyclops, evade Circe the Enchantress, and sail precariously between a fierce whirlpool called Charybdis and a six-headed monster called Scylla who eats passing sailors for snacks. [Aladdin]

A CHRISTMAS CAROL
written by Charles Dickens
Dickens calls this "a ghostly little book." You probably know the story from television specials and movies, but read the real thing for yourself—the marvelous tale of Ebenezer Scrooge, that "squeezing, wrenching, grasping, scraping, clutching, covetous old sinner!" You remember how badly Scrooge treats poor Bob Cratchit and how three spirits transport him to his past, present, and future lives, until Scrooge stands gaping in horror at the edge of his own grave. But, as you know, the story ends happily with a raise for Mr. Cratchit, health for Tiny Tim, and a merry Christmas for everyone! [Aladdin]

A CHRISTMAS MEMORY
written by Truman Capote, illustrated by Beth Peck
Buddy's great friend is his eccentric elderly cousin who wears tennis shoes and an old sweater. Every November, when "fruitcake weather" begins, she and Buddy collect pecans in an old baby carriage and bake cakes for all sorts of people—the knife grinder, Baptist missionaries, the bus driver, and President Roosevelt. Another time, they chop down and decorate their Christmas tree and make each other kites, which they immediately put to flight. Says the old woman, "I could leave the world with today in my eyes." [Knopf Books for Young Readers]

A CONNECTICUT YANKEE IN KING ARTHUR'S COURT
written by Mark Twain, illustrated by Trina Schart Hyman
A Yankee from Connecticut is knocked out in a fight and awakes to find himself at King Arthur's court in Camelot where he is promptly sentenced to death. Recovering from this discouraging reception, the ingenious Yankee escapes by posing as a magician and correctly foretelling an eclipse. The rest of the book concerns his humorous adventures as "Sir Boss," Arthur's right-hand man, much to the annoyance of Arthur's other magician, Merlin. The Yankee has Merlin imprisoned, and after eliminating his rival, he then decides to modernize medieval England. [William Morrow]

> Friend, do me a kindness. Do you belong to the asylum, or are you just here on a visit or something like that?"
> He looked me over stupidly. and said: "Marry, fair sir, me seemeth—"
> "That will do," I said. "I reckon you are a patient."

THE CORAL ISLAND
written by R.M. Ballantyne
This is one of the best shipwreck novels of all time. Ralph, Jack, and Peterkin meet one another on a ship heading for the South Seas and great adventure. Little do they expect the dangers that lie ahead. The ship is suddenly thrown into a tropical storm, and the three boys narrowly escape by hanging desperately onto one of the ship's oars. The rest of the crew are lost, but Ralph, Jack, and Peterkin survive and are

cast onto a deserted island. All they now possess is the remaining oar, the clothes on their backs, and the few items they happened to have in their pockets when the disaster struck. The boys quickly put their heads together and discover that, with some ingenuity and courage, they can actually live quite splendidly off the fruit of this wonderful Coral Island. [Puffin]

CORONATION OF GLORY
written by Deborah Meroff
A moving fictionalized story of Lady Jane Grey. The book spans Jane's life from the death of Henry VIII to her own tragic death. Jane's short life is filled with tragedy. Her ambitious parents betroth her to a boy she despises, but when she falls in love with him, her wicked parents reverse themselves, beat her, and order her to marry another man. Only God's love sustains Jane during the terrifying events of her brief reign as the nine-day Queen of England. [Inheritance Publications]

You will also enjoy *The Nine Day Queen of England: Lady Jane Grey* by Faith Cook. [Evangelical Press]

THE COUNT OF MONTE CRISTO
written by Alexandre Dumas, translated and abridged by Lowell Blair
Set in the Napoleonic era, this is the story of Count Edmond Dantes, condemned to life imprisonment on a false charge. After fourteen years of incarceration, Dantes makes a spectacular escape, finds hidden treasure, and becomes fabulously wealthy. The story then unfolds as he sets out to plot the ruin of his old enemies. This is a dramatic tale full of intrigue and suspense. [Bantam Classics]

One! Two! Three!" With the last word he felt himself flung into space. Fear clutched at his heart as he fell. . . . He was being swiftly dragged to the bottom by a cannon ball tied to his feet.

CRESS DELAHANTY
written by Jessamyn West, illustrated by Joe Krush
The story of a teenage girl growing up on a California ranch with all the insecurity and heartache that accompanies adolescence. Cress is imaginative and resilient. She writes poetry, makes a list of "Useful Traits for

> **I** think I might just stick my head in that bucket of fish and end everything.

School," and dreams about Edwin. Edwin defends her when she inadvertently drops her brightly colored hat into an aquarium and poisons all the fish. In order to become popular at school, Cress puts on her shoes in the bus so that she will be talked about, and when an older friend is dying, she unsuccessfully petitions God to take her in her friend's place. Cress Delahanty is funny, passionate, and very like many young teenage girls. [Harcourt Brace]

DR. JEKYLL AND MR. HYDE
written by Robert Louis Stevenson
This is a short horror story that involves a doctor who is plagued by a dual nature and the horrible conflict between the good and evil sides of his personality. Dr. Jekyll is a respectable London physician, but he leads a double life. He concocts a drug that causes his evil nature to dominate, and from time to time he is transformed into the diabolical Mr. Hyde. [Signet Classics]

THE DRAGON AND THE RAVEN
written by G.A. Henty
Edmund is a Saxon boy who lives in the ninth century during the days of King Alfred and the Danish invasions of England. He becomes Alfred's thane and with him fights the heathen Northmen who steadily ravage the land. Peasants' homes are burned and destroyed; churches and monasteries are savagely slaughtered. The cruel Danes seem invincible until Edmund builds a massive ship, equipped with oars as well as sails, in order to fight the Danes as they invade England's coastal cities. Edmund then engages the enemy in fierce combat until his ship is blown off course, and he is taken prisoner and in danger of being sacrificed to the Norse god Odin. [Preston Speed]

DREAM THIEF
written by Stephen Lawhead
This is a complex sci-fi novel. Spencer Reston is a scientist on a space station researching sleep in space. While trying to discover the meaning

of his unnatural nightmares, he realizes that an alien presence is attacking his dream life. This enemy, the Dream Thief, has acquired some alien technology and wants to link the technology with Reston's research in order to control men's minds. Reston travels between Earth and Mars in order to thwart his enemy's diabolical plans. Together with some Christian friends, he must track down the Dream Thief and fight for his own life as well as the lives of all mankind. [Lion UK]

DUNCAN'S WAR
written by Douglas Bond, illustrated by Matthew Bird
Duncan M'Kethe is a feisty Scottish lad who has one consuming desire—to fight English soldiers. He despises the way the English have invaded Scotland and are trying to force the Scots to worship in the Anglican way. Duncan watches some of his neighbors being persecuted and losing their homes. The Covenanters are loyal to the reformed faith, and Duncan is one son of Scotland who would rather fight and die. Duncan's father teaches him that they must not respond in prideful violence, but even great patience has a limit. Duncan must learn how to serve God in his fight for freedom's cause. Also look for the other two books in this Crown and Covenant series, *King's Arrow* and *Rebel's Keep*. [P&R Publishing]

DUTCH COLOR
written by Douglas M. Jones
Set in the golden age of art in Holland, this novel tells the tale of Clara Zoelen, a teenage girl who, for all her oddities, passionately loves her family and painting. Clara is concerned about the wellbeing of her father, who has traveled to Italy to pursue his trade as a color merchant, but the family hasn't heard from him for months. When Clara finds out that his letters are being withheld for mysterious reasons, she will do almost anything to find out the truth of her father's whereabouts. Together with her younger brother, two unusual uncles, and three-year-old cousin, Clara undertakes to solve the mystery. [Canon Press]

THE EAGLE OF THE NINTH
written by Rosemary Sutcliff
This is the first in a series of books about Roman Britain. It tells the story of a young Roman named Marcus whose father commanded the

Ninth Legion fighting northern tribes in Britain when the whole legion disappeared. Marcus' great desire is to honor his father by recovering the legion's lost standard, an eagle, which might mean the legion could be reformed. During a battle between the Romans and Celtic tribesmen, Marcus is badly wounded. His military career is over, but he is given the chance to fulfill his dream. Marcus sets out into the wilds of Scotland on a long and dangerous journey to bring back his father's Eagle. The other two books in the series are *The Silver Branch* and *The Lantern Bearers*. [Farrar, Straus & Giroux]

EIGHT COUSINS
written by Louisa May Alcott
After Rose's father dies, she finds herself orphaned and alone. She must go to live in the enormous house of Aunt Plenty and Aunt Peace. Rose has just about resigned herself to a lonely life when she meets the serving maid, Phoebe, who whistles the songs of birds. Rose also discovers that her days will be anything but lonely when seven cousins, all boys, suddenly tumble into her life. At first Rose is horrified at having to cope with so many horrid boys, but she quickly learns to love their jolly ways. Sequel: *Rose in Bloom*. [Puffin]

THE ESCAPE
written by A. Van der Jagt
Because of his faith, John and Manette's Huguenot father is condemned to serve as a slave on a galley ship for the rest of his life. Their family is slowly split up. First, Manette is taken from her mother and sent away to be brought up by a Roman Catholic lady in Paris. Then their mother dies, and John is left all alone. When a priest tries to send him away to a cloister, John decides to escape, rescue Manette, and run away to Holland and freedom. [Inheritance Publications]

ESCAPE FROM WARSAW
written by Ian Serraillier
Ruth, Edek, and Bronia are separated from their parents when they escape from war-torn Warsaw moments after their house is bombed by Nazi soldiers during World War II. Disaster escalates when Edek

is captured by the secret police and contracts tuberculosis. Joined by a mischievous street urchin, the children make the long journey to Switzerland hoping to find and rejoin their parents. Edek travels part of the way hanging on to the axles of a train. With them they carry a little silver sword, which becomes a symbol of hope that their parents are still alive. [Scholastic]

> Edek collapsed. There were beads of sweat on his brow, and he kept muttering, "I can't go on. I can't go on."

ESCAPE TO KING ALFRED
written by Geoffrey Trease
A story set in the England of Alfred the Great. Two children, Elfwyn and Judith, travel from Mercia to Wessex in order to warn King Alfred of the Danes' plan to attack Wessex. The land of Mercia has already been conquered by the Vikings, and Wessex is the last kingdom in all England to hold out against the Northmen. Elfwyn and Judith's journey is filled with danger. They are pursued by hungry wolves and in constant fear of discovery, but England's freedom hangs in the balance as they travel toward Wessex and Alfred. [Vanguard Press]

Also look for Trease's *Bows Against the Barons*, which takes place in medieval England during the time of Robin Hood. [Elliot & Thompson]

EXPLOITS OF DON QUIXOTE
written by James Reeves, illustrated by Edward Ardizzone
This is a retelling of Miguel de Cervantes's classic story. Don Quixote is a would-be knight-errant inspired by books on chivalry to undertake knightly quests. He decks himself out in rusty armor and a cardboard helmet and rides forth on a bony nag. Sancho Panza, an uncouth rustic, is his squire, and Dulcinea, a rough peasant girl, is the lady to whom he dedicates his valiant deeds. Don Quixote has some hilarious adventures. He attacks two flocks of sheep, believing they are warring armies, he steals a barber's basin for a helmet after his cardboard hat falls apart, and he accosts a caged lion. Fortunately, the lion is too lazy to accept the challenge. Don Quixote wanders through the Spanish

countryside in search of wrongs to right, leaving behind him confusion and laughter. [Henry Z. Walck]

Also look for Leighton Barret's retelling of Cervantes' masterpiece. Barret's book is called *The Adventures of Don Quixote de la Mancha.* [Alfred A. Knopf]

FAIR WIND TO VIRGINIA
written by Cornelia Meigs

The setting of this suspenseful novel is the early 1770s in pre-revolutionary Virginia. Hal and Peggy Morrow sail from England to America because their father is falsely accused of writing articles against King George III and faces imprisonment. Their father's "treason" causes the Governor of Virginia to refuse to help the destitute children. But kind Mr. Aldgate takes them into his household and helps Hal get a job as an errand boy to a young lawyer, Thomas Jefferson. Hal manages to expose the fraudulent schemes of a powerful enemy and makes a discovery that reverses his family's declining fortunes. You will also enjoy *The Two Arrows* by Cornelia Meigs. [Macmillan]

> The searchers were close behind. He was weary and panting, but the letter was safe in his pocket and the knowledge gave him strength.

THE FELLOWSHIP OF THE RING,
THE TWO TOWERS, and THE RETURN OF THE KING
written by J.R.R. Tolkien

These three books comprise a trilogy of exciting fantasy that continues the adventures begun in *The Hobbit.* Frodo Baggins, Bilbo's cousin, carries out the work Bilbo has begun by assuming the role of Ring-Bearer. Frodo's task is to return the Ring of Power whence it came, the land of Mordor, so that it and its evil Power may be destroyed in the fire in which it was forged. The journey of Frodo and his companions is full of great danger as the Black Riders and other servants of the Dark Lord of Mordor swoop around them to claim the Ring and its power. Follow Frodo and his clan as evil battles with good in these exciting tales. [Houghton Mifflin]

THE FLOWER O' THE HEATHER
written by Robert W. Mackenna
This historical novel is set in 1685 during "the killing times," the era of the Scottish Covenanters who suffered torture and death rather than give up their faith. Walter Bryden starts out serving King James II by hunting down and shooting people because they will not swear allegiance to the king. However, when Bryden is forced to stand by and watch two women die by drowning, he escapes and becomes a deserter with a price on his head. He is constantly on the run, pursued by the king's soldiers. One of the most horrifying moments of Bryden's life is when he finds a blackened, gutted house and makes a horrifying discovery about the girl he loves. Many other adventures await this brave friend of the Covenanters as he continues his dangerous work. [T.C. Farries]

FOR THE TEMPLE
written by G.A. Henty
Set in Israel in A.D. 70, just before the fall of Jerusalem, this is the exciting story of a brave Jewish boy, John of Gamala. John is determined to defend his homeland against the invading Roman legions. When the Romans capture the Jewish stronghold of Jotapata, forty thousand Jews are slaughtered, and only John and his friend Jonas escape. The Romans then lay siege to Gamala, during which the Jews are reduced to eating garbage, and huge numbers throw themselves, their wives, and children over cliffs to escape their cruel captors. Tens of thousands are massacred. Lawlessness and carnage spread throughout Judea. John organizes a small band of followers, and from the mountains around Jerusalem, he prepares to defend the Holy City and its Temple. [Preston Speed]

THE GIFT OF THE MAGI
written by O. Henry, illustrated by Lisbeth Zwerger
A young couple scrimp and save to buy each other gifts for Christmas. They want to surprise each other with a special present, even if it means that they have to give up something they love more than all other possessions. [Aladdin]

A GIRL OF THE LIMBERLOST
written by Gene Stratton Porter

Elnora Comstock lives near a swampy forest in Indiana called the Limberlost. When her father falls into the swamp and dies, her mother grieves for years and ignores her clever daughter. Elnora is determined to get an education, but because her mother will not pay for her schooling, Elnora finds the money for her books and tuition by selling rare moths she finds in the Limberlost. Eventually, Elnora discovers a terrible secret about her dead father, and then she meets handsome Philip Ammon who is engaged to Edith Carr, a pampered socialite from Chicago. Philip must decide which girl he truly loves, Edith or the girl of the Limberlost. [HarperCollins Children's]

GODS, HEROES AND MEN OF ANCIENT GREECE
written by W.H.D. Rouse

Here is a book full of incredible creatures—a god who swallows his children whole, one-eyed monsters, and heroes who slay roving beasts. These Greek myths are about larger-than-life heroes—such as Hercules, Perseus, and Odysseus—who face horrible adversaries such as Medusa with her head full of snakes and Polyphemus, the one-eyed monster. This book also contains tales that teach wisdom about life, such as the story of Phaethon who begs his father to allow him to drive the sun god's great chariot. Phaethon's foolishness ends in disaster as he falls from the sky into the sea. [New American Library]

THE HIGH KING
written by Lloyd Alexander

This is the fifth and last of the Chronicles of Prydain, a great fantasy cycle. All five books can be read independently, and this book describes the final clash of good versus evil and the greatest quest of Taran and his friends. The excitement begins when Arawn Death-Lord, who is King of Annuwin, the Land of the Dead, captures the powerful sword of Drnwyn. The land of Prydain is threatened with destruction. Taran and Gwydion, the High King of Prydain, must raise an army and travel to Annuvin in order to defeat their evil enemy and his cohorts. Their journey is dangerous and the odds against them enormous as they battle human and inhuman foes. The other books in this series are *The*

Book of Three, The Black Cauldron, The Castle of Llyr, and *Taran Wanderer.* [Henry Holt]

HINDS' FEET ON HIGH PLACES
written by Hannah Hurnard
Much-Afraid, who works for the Chief Shepherd, has two terrible handicaps: She is lame and full of fears. Her family, the Fearings, are enemies of the Chief Shepherd and try to force her to marry Craven-Fear. Then the Chief Shepherd tells Much-Afraid to travel to the High Places, but in order to make such a journey, she must develop hinds' feet and change her timid ways. The story describes her travels and the dangerous places she must journey through and the enemies she must overcome before she arrives at her destination. [Tyndale House]

THE HOBBIT
written by J.R.R. Tolkien
This is the first of Tolkien's adventure fantasies set in Middle-earth and is a prelude to The Lord of the Rings trilogy. *The Hobbit* tells the story of Bilbo Baggins, who loves nothing more than to curl up after a delicious meal and go to sleep. Despite his sedentary inclinations, however, Bilbo is bustled off against his will by thirteen grubby dwarfs and a wizard on a grand adventure. Their journeys take them into great danger, including the menace of orcs, wolves, and dragons. Bilbo discovers the Ring of Power, which belongs to an evil force and corrupts anyone who attempts to utilize its power. In bringing the Ring back to his country, Bilbo precipitates the wrath of the Enemy. Thus begins the War of the Rings chronicled in The Lord of the Rings trilogy. [Houghton Mifflin]

> One morning long ago in the quiet of the world, when there was less noise and more green, and the hobbits were still numerous and prosperous, Bilbo Baggins was standing at his door after breakfast smoking an enormous long wooden pipe that reached nearly down to his woolen toes.

THE HORN OF ROLAND
written by Jay Williams, illustrated by Sean Morrison
As a young boy, Roland fells a great ox with his axe and acquires his famous war-horn. When he daringly seizes the Emperor Charlemagne's

meat from under his very nose in order to feed his starving parents, the astonished Emperor makes Roland his page. At age thirteen, Roland saves Charlemagne's war banner from the invading Saracens, and he is rewarded with knighthood. Roland proves to be a worthy knight. He valiantly fights the giant Ferragus, a descendant of Goliath, and, in another fight, he wins from a powerful Saracen warrior the sword Durandal that no armor in the world can withstand. This book contains the many other heroic and thrilling adventures of Charlemagne's courageous knight. [Thomas Y. Crowell]

I AM DAVID [formerly NORTH TO FREEDOM]

written by Anne Holm, translated by L.W. Kingsland

David is a twelve-year-old boy who has spent his whole life in a concentration camp in Eastern Europe. With the help of a guard, he escapes and heads south to Italy, then north to Denmark. He remembers nothing of his family and is fearful, withdrawn, and distrustful of everyone, even the guard who switches off the current on the electric fence for exactly half a minute so that David can climb over. Escaping the prison gates, David begins a painful journey by foot, always expecting to be caught and returned to the camp. [Harcourt Paperbacks]

THE ILIAD OF HOMER

written by Barbara Leonie Picard, illustrated by Joan Kiddell-Monroe

> Achilles rose and armed himself in the armour which Hephaestus had made for him. . . and beneath the flashing, crested helmet, his young face was grim and set, and his eyes were without pity.

This is a retelling of an epic poem that Homer wrote three thousand years ago. The Trojan War has been going on for nine years when the Greek's bravest warrior, Achilles, refuses to fight any longer because of a foolish quarrel he has with King Agamemnon. The fighting continues, and the Greeks are almost defeated by the mighty Trojans. But when the most valiant Trojan warrior, Hector, kills Achilles' best friend Patroclus, Achilles gets good and mad—mad enough to come out of his tent where he's been sulking and reenter the battle in order to avenge his friend. You will also enjoy Picard's *Odyssey of Homer*. [Oxford]

INDIAN CAPTIVE: THE STORY OF MARY JEMISON
written and illustrated by Lois Lenski

The true story of a twelve-year-old girl who is captured by Indians during the French and Indian War. Molly's family is cooking breakfast when Indians break into their Philadelphia farmhouse and capture the whole family. They take Molly to an Indian village, paint her face, and dress her in deerskin. She tries to run away several times, but each time she is caught. Eventually, Molly overcomes her grief and learns the Indian way of life; she plants corn with a stick, collects sugar sap, makes clay pots, and carries babies on her back. Gradually, she learns to love her captors, and they love her as dearly as a daughter. When white men come to bring her back to civilization, Molly must make a hard decision. Lois Lenski's other historical fiction includes *Puritan Adventure* and *Ocean-Born Mary*. [HarperTrophy]

IN FREEDOM'S CAUSE
written by G.A. Henty

This is the exciting story of Scotland's brave struggle for independence. It seems a hopeless cause: Scottish patriots are few, the English army is vast, and the English king's treatment of Scottish rebels is brutal. Archie Forbes dreams of freeing his country from England's cruel yoke. He joins forces with a band of patriots led by one of Scotland's bravest heroes, William Wallace. Wallace's followers are willing to die for freedom. Eventually, after Wallace is betrayed into English hands by some base Scots and brutally executed, Archie persuades Robert the Bruce to become Scotland's new leader and king. Together, Archie and Bruce experience bloody battles and the constant threat of capture and certain death. [Preston Speed]

IN THE HALL OF THE DRAGON KING
written by Stephen Lawhead

The evil sorcerer Nimrod holds King Eskevar captive in a far-off dungeon. Nimrod makes his evil plans with Eskevar's treacherous brother Prince Jaspin, who plots to become King of Mensandor. Meanwhile, brave young Quentin and his friends set out on a dangerous mission to free the king. This is a suspenseful fantasy set in a world of magic and hair-raising adventure. Throughout Quentin's quest, you will sense the timeless conflict of good versus evil. The question is, Who will be the victor? This is the first book in The Dragon King Trilogy. The other two books in the series are *The Warlords of Nin* and *The Sword and the Flame*. [Zondervan]

THE INVISIBLE MAN
written by H.G. Wells
A spine-chilling mystery. When a curious stranger arrives at an English inn, his head covered in bandages, odd things begin to happen in the village. The innkeeper issues a warrant for his arrest, and the stranger finally tears off his bandages to reveal what is underneath—nothing! He is invisible. From then on, the situation deteriorates rapidly. A series of mysterious thefts is followed by a desperate fight during which the Invisible Man terrorizes the entire village. Then the murders begin. [Penguin Classic]

JOHNNY TREMAIN
written by Esther Forbes, illustrated by Lynd Ward
This is an exciting historical novel about a young man who lives in Boston and gets caught up in the stirring events prior to the Revolutionary War.

> We give all we have . . . we fight, we die, for a simple thing. Only that a man can stand up.

Johnny Tremain is apprenticed to a silversmith when a tragic accident changes his life forever and causes him to become a dispatch rider for the committee of public safety, a job that brings him into contact with men such as Samuel Adams, John Hancock, and other Boston patriots. He witnesses the tense events that lead to the Boston Tea Party and the Battle of Lexington. But Johnny has a personal battle of his own to fight as well. [Laurel Leaf]

JOURNEY TO AMERICA
written by Sonia Levitin, illustrated by Charles Robinson
Lisa's family is Jewish. They live in Germany when most Jews suffer great persecution, and it's a sad day when her father leaves Berlin in order to make a new home in America for his wife and children. Lisa is

terrified that the Nazis will discover their plan to escape when the rest of the family leaves for Switzerland, eventually to join their father in America. They pretend they're only going on a short vacation, but Nazi officers inspect their suitcases, subject Lisa's mother to a strip search, and confiscate her sister's violin with the precious money Lisa has hidden in the lining of the case. That is only the beginning of months of separation and grim hardship for Lisa's family. [Aladdin]

KIDNAPPED
written by Robert Louis Stevenson
An exciting historical novel set in the 1700s. David Balfour's Uncle Ebenezer wants to steal his nephew's inheritance and won't even stop at murder. Ebenezer kidnaps David and stows him away on a ship where he is bound for slavery in America. David lives in wretched conditions and hears about a gruesome murder before he befriends Alan Breck Stewart, a Scottish Highlander and anti-royalist with a price on his head. Together, David and Alan experience shipwreck and another mysterious murder. They hide out in the Highlands, knowing that if they are caught, they both will hang. [Penguin Classic]

THE LARK AND THE LAUREL
written by Barbara Willard, illustrated by Gareth Floyd
When Henry Tudor is crowned king of England, all noblemen who question his succession must flee for their lives. This is the fate of Cecily's father. He escapes to France and leaves his daughter Cecily in the capable hands of his widowed sister, Dame Elizabeth. At first, Cecily finds the countrified living of her aunt's home distasteful, especially compared to her fine home where she was thoroughly pampered. However, she soon discovers that her former life was full of empty pleasures. She is free to explore her new world, and she finds joy in mastering tasks such as churning, shearing, and brewing. She also makes friends with a young neighbor. Her only fear now is that her father will take her away from

> Cecily knew little enough of the world, but at least she knew that when men invited the name of traitor, they must watch out for their heads.

her beloved new home. Look for other titles in this series: *The Sprig of Broom* and *A Cold Wind Blowing.* [Harcourt, Brace & World]

THE LEGEND OF SLEEPY HOLLOW
written by Washington Irving, illustrated by Will Moses
Ichabod Crane is the lanky schoolteacher of Sleepy Hollow in love with blooming Katrina Van Tassel. But he has a rival, a prankster named Brom Bones. This formidable adversary carries out all kinds of pranks on Ichabod, which culminate in the strange affair of the Headless Horseman. [Putnam Juvenile]

LEOPARD'S PREY
written by Leonard Wibberley
Before the start of the War of 1812, an astounding event occurs. A British ship, the *Leopard*, fires on an American frigate, the *Chesapeake*, in American waters. Three American sailors are captured and taken aboard the *Leopard*. Shortly thereafter, young Manly Treegate is accused of aiding a deserter and is also taken aboard the ship. Manly leads a miserable life on the British frigate. His first introduction to life on this ship is to witness a deserter being flogged to death. He is forced to eat weevil-infested biscuits and is brutally beaten by a cruel midshipman. As powder-boy to one of the ship's guns, Manly takes part in several exciting sea battles. During one of these, he gets his chance to escape by jumping into a sea infested with sharks! [Farrar, Straus & Giroux]

LIEUTENANT HORNBLOWER
written by C.S. Forester
A seafaring adventure set during the Napoleonic Wars. This second book in Forester's Horatio Hornblower series begins when Hornblower is promoted to Acting Lieutenant under the command of a mad, tyrannical captain. An exciting series of events involves the ship in a desperate and unsuccessful attack upon a Spanish fort, during which the *Renown* runs aground under heavy artillery fire. Hornblower gallantly saves the day by executing a brilliant plan. He captures the fort, forces the Spaniards to surrender, and finally, risking his life, recaptures his ship by putting down an attack upon it by Spanish prisoners. A first-rate sea adventure. You will enjoy the entire Hornblower saga of eleven

volumes about this naval hero. Other titles include *Hornblower and the Hotspur, Hornblower and the Atropos, Beat to Quarters,* and *Ship of the Line.* [Back Bay Books]

THE LIGHT BEYOND THE FOREST: THE QUEST FOR THE HOLY GRAIL
written by Rosemary Sutcliff
King Arthur's peerless knights—among them Sir Lancelot, Sir Percival, and Sir Galahad—depart on the quest for the Holy Grail, and the fellowship of the Round Table is broken up forever. Arthur's knights know well that their journey may end in failure or death. The gallant knights have many adventures, and many never return to Camelot. Sir Percival, Sir Bors, and Sir Galahad together achieve the quest for the Holy Grail, but it is the world's most perfect knight who alone can approach the holy vessel and heal the maimed king. This second book in Sutcliff's Arthurian trilogy is an exciting retelling of the Grail myth. [Puffin]

THE LIGHT IN THE FOREST
written by Conrad Richter
True Son is a white boy captured by Indians and raised by a great Indian warrior. He grows up to think, feel, and act like an Indian. Then True Son's real father captures him and takes him home, where True Son is forced to live with people who think that Indians are brutal savages. All True Son can think about is escaping back to the mountains and his Indian friends. When war breaks out, True Son must take sides and decide where his loyalty lies. [Vintage]

LITTLE WOMEN
written by Louisa May Alcott
While Mr. March is away fighting in the Civil War, the March women—four sisters and their mother—must fend for themselves. Even though they are poor, they never lack laughter. Energetic and inventive, Meg, Jo, Amy, and Beth get into all sorts of scrapes and adventures. The family's poverty teaches the girls to fight temptation and envy, and everyone pitches in to do her part. Jo even sells her hair in order to make money for her beloved family. Sequels: *Good Wives, Little Men,* and *Jo's Boys.* [Puffin]

THE MEMOIRS OF SHERLOCK HOLMES
written by Sir Arthur Conan Doyle
A collection of murder mysteries recounted by Holmes's invaluable colleague, Dr. Watson. Each episode draws the reader into a baffling set of circumstances as Holmes's brilliant reasoning methodically unravels the crimes. [House of Stratus]

Look for other collections of Sherlock Holmes mysteries such as *The Adventures of Sherlock Holmes.* [Scholastic]

MEN OF IRON
written by Howard Pyle
Miles Falworth lives in fourteenth-century England when all true men are men of iron. His father is unjustly accused of treason, so his family has to flee into hiding. Miles becomes a squire of the great Earl of Mackworth. He proves to be a brave fighter and a loyal friend; in fact, Miles wins the respect of all around him, including Lord Mackworth, and he soon rises to knighthood. His courage sees him through some amazing adventures and equips him for his grimmest battle of all, a struggle between death or victory. [Dover]

THE MERRY ADVENTURES OF ROBIN HOOD
written and illustrated by Howard Pyle
This is an entertaining and beautifully illustrated collection of tales about Robin Hood and his merrymen—Little John, Allan a Dale, Friar Tuck, Will Scarlet, and the rest of his stout yeomen. Over and over again, the Sheriff of Nottingham tries to capture the bold outlaw, but Robin always outwits him, often to the Sheriff's acute embarrassment. Robin and his men get the best of the villains and administer their own brand of justice. Robin's fame attracts the admiration of the queen and the wrath of the king. Now all of the king's men, aided and abetted by Robin's old enemy, the Sheriff of Nottingham, pursue the merry outlaw. [Dover]

> Then bitterly the Sheriff rued the day that first he meddled with Robin Hood, for all men laughed at him and many ballads were sung by folk throughout the country, of how the Sheriff went to shear and came home shorn to the very quick.

MY LIFE AND HARD TIMES
written by James Thurber
A hilarious collection of some of Thurber's funniest short stories. "The Dog That Bit People" describes the antics of a family pet. Moggs bites everyone, but instead of getting rid of the dog, Mother sends Moggs's victims a box of candy every Christmas. One of the funniest tales, "The Night the Bed Fell on Father," recounts the nocturnal chaos for which this family seems to have a peculiar genius. On this particular occasion, Mother is convinced that Father is gasping his last breath underneath a collapsed bed while other family members—all, to varying degrees, crazy—believe that they, not Father, are the center of everyone's attention. [Harper Perennial Modern Classics]

> He never bit anyone more than once at a time. Mother always mentioned that as an argument in his favor; she said he had a quick temper but that he didn't hold a grudge.

ONE CORPSE TOO MANY
written by Ellis Peters
This mystery is set in twelfth-century England, close to the abbey of the Benedictine monk Brother Cadfael. King Stephen of England is engaged in a civil war as his cousin, the Empress Maud, vies with him for the throne. The king's forces attack Shrewsbury Castle, and when the castle falls into the king's hands, its ninety-four defenders loyal to Maud are hanged. As Brother Cadfael buries the dead, he discovers ninety-five bodies—one corpse too many. Thus begins a series of suspenseful and bizarre events that lead the clever monk ever closer to the ruthless killer. You will also enjoy *St. Peter's Fair* and the other Brother Cadfael medieval mysteries. [Little, Brown]

OTTO OF THE SILVER HAND
written and illustrated by Howard Pyle
Otto is brought up in a monastery during the days of the savage robber barons. His father is involved in a long-standing, bitter feud with another baron, and their conflict finally causes Otto to be cruelly and permanently injured. The boy is imprisoned and left to die in a dank

dungeon, but his father's faithful servant, one-eyed Hans, attempts a daring rescue. This is an exciting story about a young boy who suffers greatly and learns that men are conquered not by force but by mercy and love. [Dover]

OUT OF THE SILENT PLANET, PERELANDRA, and THAT HIDEOUS STRENGTH
written by C.S. Lewis

Lewis's famous space trilogy will open up new worlds to you. In this exciting series of stories, Dr. Ransom visits faraway planets, where he encounters incredible geological formations and space creatures that snap vicious jaws. Here Ransom experiences worlds free from sin and creatures tempted to rebel against their Creator. All the books in this trilogy emphasize the intense spiritual battles waged between the Bent (or Evil) One and the Lord and Ruler of all. [Scribner]

> "Stranger," he said, "I have been sent to your world through the Heaven by the servants of Maleldil. Do you give me welcome?"

PATRIOT'S DAUGHTER
written by Gladys Malvern

This is the story of a courageous French family, the Lafayettes. Lafayette becomes a hero of America's War for Independence, but when he returns to France, his family is soon caught up in the turmoil of the Reign of Terror. With growing horror, the Lafayettes hear of the storming of the Bastille and the deaths of the king and queen. Lafayette is arrested and imprisoned, Madame Lafayette and their daughter Anastasia are arrested, and family members are ruthlessly guillotined. The family is impoverished as they wait endlessly for news of Lafayette. When Anastasia and her mother are finally released, they make a dangerous journey to the prison fortress where Lafayette is being held. Reunited with her father in prison, Anastasia realizes that even though the world has forgotten her family, God will never forsake them. [Macrae Smith]

PEARLS OF LUTRA

written by Brian Jacques

The ninth novel in the Redwall series, this is another of the author's exciting fantasies. Ublaz Mad Eyes, an evil pirate emperor, can't wait to steal the six pearls of Lutra for his crown. The pearls are hidden inside Redwall Abbey, and hedgehog Tansy and her friends are determined to

> *M*artin found himself surrounded by lizards. With battle light blazing in his eyes and a warcry on his lips, the Warriormouse swung his mighty blade on the crowded staircase.

thwart the evil Ublaz. They set out on a treasure hunt to find and solve the clues to each pearl's whereabouts. Meanwhile, Warriormouse Martin and hare Clecky join forces with Grath Longfletch—whose family has been massacred by Mad Eyes' pirate rats—and set off on a daring mission to rescue the kidnapped Abbot of Redwall. [Puffin]

THE PILGRIM'S PROGRESS

written by John Bunyan

This is the story of Christian's journey through life, from the City of Destruction to the Celestial City. He has to deal with the kinds of temptations all Christians face as he travels through the Slough of Despond, Vanity Fair, Doubting Castle, and the Dark River. Christian must overcome these and other obstacles before he arrives at his heavenly home, but he is encouraged along the way by two friends, Faithful and Hopeful. This story is filled with unforgettable characters like Worldly Wiseman, Talkative, and Ignorance. During his greatest battle, Christian faces the foul fiend Apollyon. Make certain you read an unabridged edition of this book. You may also enjoy reading Nathaniel Hawthorne's amusing story based on *The Pilgrim's Progress* called *The Celestial Railroad* (see High School Fiction). [Signet Classic]

THE PRINCE AND THE PAUPER

written by Mark Twain, illustrated by William Hatherell

Two look-alikes, Prince Edward (later King Edward VI) and the son of a beggar, Tom Cantry, exchange clothes and roles in life with amusing results. Tom as prince commits many social blunders, such as eating with his fingers and greedily filling his pockets with nuts. However,

Tom does a great deal to help the English poor by ending harsh punishments—for instance, boiling criminals in oil. The Prince masquerading as a pauper does not fare so well. He is tormented, beaten, jailed, and almost stabbed to death. Both boys find it difficult to reveal their true identities because everyone they confide in thinks they are crazy! [Bantam Classics]

THE RANSOM OF RED CHIEF
written by O. Henry

"Hey little boy!" says Bill. "Would you like to have a bag of candy and a nice ride?" The boy catches Bill neatly in the eye with a piece of brick. "That will cost the old man an extra five hundred dollars," says Bill, climbing over the wheel.

The hilarious tale of a kidnapping scheme gone awry. When two scoundrels kidnap the only child of wealthy Ebenezer Dorset, they figure they're on to a good thing. In fact, they're not. "Red Chief" likes being kidnapped so much that he doesn't want to go home again. And his dad is only too glad to be rid of this redheaded terror. It turns out that the kidnappers must pay Mr. Dorset to take back his son and heir! [Oxford University Press]

REDWALL
written by Brian Jacques, illustrated by Gary Chalk
This is the first book of the Redwall series. When a hideous, evil rat called Cluny the Scourge attacks Redwall Abbey, its mice inhabitants must fight or die. Their only hope of defeating this villain is a young mouse named Matthias. He must find the ancient sword of Martin the Warrior so that he can battle the rat and save Redwall. If you love epic quests, battles, and suspense, you will love this book. Read it first, then all the others in the series. [Puffin]

RIFLES FOR WATIE
written by Keith Harold
Jeff Bussey is sixteen at the beginning of the War Between the States. When proslavery bushwhackers from Missouri attack his family, he can't wait to enlist with the Kansas volunteers and defend the Union. Jeff's unit marches south into the Cherokee Indian nation and fights

men led by Stand Watie, a warlike Cherokee Indian whose fierce cavalry unit fights for the South and raids the homes of Union sympathizers. As the conflict drags on, Jeff watches friends die, he sees horribly injured men held down to submit to the surgeon's knife, and he learns what it's like to march day after day hungry and exhausted. Then he has the misfortune to fall in love with a pretty girl who's "a rebel to the backbone." [HarperTeen]

RIP VAN WINKLE AND OTHER STORIES
written by Washington Irving
Read the curious tale of a henpecked husband who escapes the scolding of his shrewish wife by wandering into the Catskill Mountains. There he encounters some strange little men playing ninepins. He drinks their intoxicating beverage and falls asleep. Upon awaking, Rip is amazed to discover that he has slept for twenty years. [Puffin]

SARAH BISHOP
written by Scott O'Dell
During the Revolutionary War, Sarah Bishop's father is a royalist in an area where almost everyone is a patriot. To make matters worse, her brother Chad enlists in the patriots' army. The Bishops' farm is burned to the ground by patriots, Mr. Bishop is tarred and feathered, and Sarah must learn to survive in the wilderness. She sets off for New York in search of her brother, but more misfortune awaits her. In New York, she is falsely accused of arson and imprisoned. She escapes and is on the run with a "Brown Bess" (a musket), the King's Men in pursuit. Based on a historical character, Sarah Bishop is an exciting survival story. [Scholastic]

THE SCARLET PIMPERNEL
written by Baroness Emmuska Orczy
When the French peasantry rise up against the aristocrats during the French Revolution, they demand blood revenge. Under the evil hands of Monsieur Chauvelin, many innocent French noblemen fall to the guillotine. But hope appears in the form of a mysterious stranger known only as the Scarlet Pimpernel. Soon everyone in France and England has heard of this elusive crusader as he and his faithful band smuggle the innocent away from their executioners. The Pimpernel's daring escapes

and ingenious disguises earn him the hatred of his enemies and the admiration of all of Europe. Baroness Orczy's other titles about the escapades of the Scarlet Pimpernel include *The Triumph of the Scarlet Pimpernel* and *The Way of the Scarlet Pimpernel*. [Bantam Classics]

SCOTTISH SEAS
written by Douglas M. Jones
Mac Ayton, his father, mother, brothers, sister, and grandfather all live together in a little cottage in a fishing village on the east coast of Scotland. In the evenings, they often gather around as Grandfather tells hair-raising stories of battles and strange tales. These story times usually end with either poetry readings or wrestling matches. Mac has many fears—the crashing ocean, witches, echoing caves—but he learns to overcome them with the help of his family, his growing faith, and some extraordinary adventures. [Canon Press]

SON OF CHARLEMAGNE
written by Barbara Willard, illustrated by Emil Weiss
Gobbo and Carl are sons of Charles the Great. Gobbo is the elder and should inherit his father's title, but because he is a hunchback, the king names Carl his heir. Only Carl knows about his father's ambition to become the Holy Roman Emperor, and together Carl and Charlemagne ride into battle, defeating pagan tribes and spreading Christianity throughout the Frankish king's vast kingdom. Eventually, Charlemagne defeats the Saxon king and baptizes him into the Christian church. Charlemagne suffers great personal tragedy. His beloved wife dies, and a plot is afoot to murder him and seize the throne. [Bethlehem Books]

> Carl had heard the King called stern and implacable, but no man ever questioned his wisdom. Now his face in the starlight was so full of pain that Carl could hardly bear to look at it.

SOUNDER
written by William H. Armstrong, illustrated by James Barkley
Sounder is a coon dog that belongs to a sharecropper's family. It's been a hard winter, and crops are few. The family eats corn mush, and at

night the mother tells them stories about Joseph or King David. When the father steals meat for the family, he is arrested by cruel sheriff's men who shoot Sounder, shattering his shoulder and half his head. The boy visits his father in jail and tries to "act perkish" like his mother told him, but he is so grief-stricken that he can't go back. Then the father is sent far away to do hard labor. The boy is determined to find him, and he reminds his mother, "in Bible-story journeys, ain't no journey hopeless. Everybody finds what they suppose to find." [HarperTrophy]

ST. BARTHOLOMEW'S EVE: A TALE OF THE HUGUENOT WARS
written by G.A. Henty
St. Bartholomew's Eve is a gripping tale of perseverance through persecution. The story is set in the 1500s when the Protestant Christians of France are suffering under oppressive Catholic rulers. Philip Fletcher is the son of a French Huguenot mother and an English father. He is an intelligent, serious boy of sixteen when he travels from his home to France in order to serve in the Huguenot military. Philip's mission is to defend the Protestant faith—even if it means losing his life. In France, he travels to the home of his aunt, the Countess de Laville, and joins forces with his cousin, François. The two boys become fast friends and excellent soldiers, and they quickly earn the respect of their peers and their leaders. Their adventures lead them into great danger, however, and many people die for the cause of freedom. There are many other fine Henty novels currently in print. [Preston Speed]

THE STORY OF KING ARTHUR AND HIS KNIGHTS
written and illustrated by Howard Pyle
This is the story of Arthur Pendragon and the Knights of the Round Table who achieve fame by their knightly valor. After Arthur miraculously draws the sword out of the stone, he is proclaimed king of Britain. The story also relates how Merlin the Magician saves Arthur from certain death in a battle with King Pellinore, and how Arthur gains Excalibur from the Lady of the Lake. Although Arthur wins Guinevere for his queen and is victorious in his encounters with many knights, he is cruelly betrayed by his evil half-sister, Morgana le Fay. More stories of Arthur and his knights are contained in Pyle's *The Story of the Champions of the Round Table.* [Dover]

SWALLOWS AND AMAZONS
written by Arthur Ransome

The four Walker children—John, Susan, Titty, and Roger—want more than anything else in the world to strike out to sea and look for adventure. At last, their father gives them permission for their voyage. Stacked up to the scuppers with all sorts of tents, rugs, pots, pans, and tins of food, they begin their voyage on their sailboat, the *Swallow*. Navigating and steering a ship is no easy matter, but by pulling together they manage to dodge the treacherous rocks. They set up camp on an island, fish for food, dive for pearls, and encounter "pirates" who command a ship called the *Amazon*. The real battle of wills comes when the Amazons claim the island as their own. The Swallows must decide whether to fight, forfeit, or join forces with the Amazon crew. Other books by Arthur Ransome include *Swallowdale, Peter Duck, Winter Holiday, Coot Club, Pigeon Post, We Didn't Mean to Go to Sea, Secret Water, The Big Six, Missee Lee, The Picts and the Martyrs*, and *Great Northern*. [David R. Godine]

> Daddy thinks we shall none of us get drowned and that if any of us do get drowned it's a good riddance.

THE SWISS FAMILY ROBINSON
written by Johann R. Wyss

The Robinson family—husband, wife, four sons, and two dogs—are shipwrecked and cast ashore on a desert island near New Guinea. They build a treehouse for protection from wild animals and survive by eating penguin and worms! Instead of despairing about their hopeless situation, the Robinsons make the best of it. They make candles from berries, bread from roots, and a canoe out of a tree. They face many dangers including a boa constrictor, wolves, bears, and a lion, but the Robinsons gradually learn to view their wilderness hideaway as their home. [Bantam Classics]

> Then the voice of the captain was heard above the tumult shouting, "Lower away the boats! We are lost!"

THE SWORD AND THE CIRCLE
written by Rosemary Sutcliff
Another of Rosemary Sutcliff's retold Arthurian legends, this book describes how King Arthur came to power and tells some of the adventures of his famed Knights of the Round Table. With Merlin to advise him, Arthur becomes a great king, but he is constantly threatened by the schemes of his evil sister, Morgan La Fay. The noblest of the knights is Lancelot, loved by all the ladies including Queen Guinevere. Also famous is Sir Gawain whose encounter with the Green Knight is strange indeed. This book also includes the quests and romances of Tristan, Percival, and the rest of the famous knights of Camelot. [Puffin]

THE SWORD IN THE STONE
written by T.H. White
This is an amusing fantasy about young Arthur who is brought up by Sir Ector and tutored by Merlin. Merlin believes that "education is experience," so he teaches Arthur to fish by turning him into one—a fish, that is. The magician adopts the same principle when teaching Arthur about other animals. Merlin also travels backwards not forwards through life— which has the advantage of always knowing what's going to happen next—and he likes to knit. Since Arthur will one day become king of Britain, Merlin also teaches him the usual knightly things. [Bantam Doubleday Dell]

THE THREE MUSKETEERS
written by Alexandre Dumas, translated by Lowell Blair
Dumas's most famous novel is fast-paced and exciting. It narrates the adventures of D'Artagnan and three Musketeers employed in the service of Louis XIII of France. The four cavaliers band together on many escapades; they rescue the Queen's seamstress from her abductors, and they defend the Queen from the evil schemes of Richelieu and the Cardinal's agent, Lady de Winter. D'Artagnan has many brushes with death, but the flamboyant guardsman is more than a match for his nefarious enemies. [Bantam Classics]

THROUGH FLOOD AND FIRE
written by Robert W. Mackenna
Alan Troquoir is a hunted man. Once a respected son of a wealthy Scottish landowner, Alan is persecuted for his faith because he joined the Covenanters. These godly people will give their very lives to defend the right to worship God according to their conscience. However, the king of England has given his orders. These rebels must be hunted down and killed. At a nearby estate, David Lansburgh and his daughter Margaret are caught up in the controversy. On the one hand, they feel compelled to be loyal to the king, and they know that their beloved family estate will be stripped from them if they oppose him. On the other hand, both father and daughter strongly question the barbaric treatment of these men of faith. And as far as Margaret is concerned, matters of doctrine combine with matters of the heart to endear the Covenanters to her. [T.C. Farries]

THUNDER COUNTRY
written and illustrated by Armstrong Sperry
How would you like to camp in a jungle inhabited by poisonous snakes, crocodiles, and savages? Chad and his father are on a canoe trip in search of rare birds deep in the heart of Indian country—Venezuela. But they also have a more exciting mission, to find a man who has been captured by savage Indians. Along the way, they dine on monkey—fricasseed, roasted, stewed, or simmered whole in a soup—and experience one hair-raising moment after another: a plane crash, a journey through leech-infested swamps, an encounter with a ruthless Indian chief who means to kill them, and an attack of the dreaded tropical disease, malaria. [Macmillan]

TOM BROWN'S SCHOOLDAYS
written by Thomas Hughes, illustrated by Arthur Hughes
When Tom Brown arrives at Rugby, an English boarding school for boys, a boy named East adopts him as a chum and shows him the ropes. Tom and East soon become friends and co-conspirators. Despite the duties required of younger boys—they are forced to be the slaves of older students, for example—Tom and East rise above their oppressors through sheer pluck. Unfortunately, these boys also manage to get into one scrape after another, and it seems that Tom is fast becoming a

thorough scalawag. However, the headmaster of the school sees potential in Tom and devises a plan to cure him of his pranks. [Oxford]

THE TOURNAMENT OF THE LIONS
written by Jay Williams, illustrated by Ezra Jack Keats
During a tournament of knights in 1448, two young squires hear the Song of Roland for the first time. A knight tells the story of how Charlemagne rides out to conquer the Saracens with his nephew Roland and Roland's friend, Oliver, and how the traitor knight Ganelon betrays them. When Roland's men are greatly outnumbered by the Saracens, Oliver urges Roland to blow his horn in order to summon the help of the Frankish king. Roland refuses, believing that his honor is at stake and that he must discharge his duty without calling for aid. Both Roland and Oliver die in battle. The squires, fascinated by the tale, debate about who was right—Oliver or Roland. During the tournament, as the knightly virtues of both squires are tested, they gain a deeper understanding of chivalry. This book colorfully describes a medieval tournament and is a fine prose retelling of a great romance. [Henry Z. Walck]

> "Brother," said Oliver, "small wisdom is it to fight against such numbers. . . . Sound your horn, that Charlemagne may hear it and return."
> "Not I," said Count Roland. "If I did so, I'd be forever shamed."

TREASURE ISLAND
written by Robert Louis Stevenson, illustrated by N.C. Wyeth
Narrated by a young boy, Jim Hawkins, this story tells of pirates and buried treasure and includes many exciting plot twists. First, a sinister blind man, Pew, mysteriously dies. Then, while Jim hides in an apple barrel, he overhears Long John Silver's plans for mutiny. Jim's part in a desperate search for treasure puts his life in danger. Stevenson wrote this adventure story in response to his stepson's request to "write something really interesting." [Aladdin]

> "Budge, you skulk!" cried Pew. . . . "Scatter and look for them, dogs! Oh, shiver my soul," he cried, "if I had eyes!"

TWENTY THOUSAND LEAGUES UNDER THE SEA
written by Jules Verne
This book is a fine work of science fiction. Professor Aronnax leads an expedition to destroy a sea monster that has sunk ships around the world. When the creature is sighted, Aronnax and his crew discover that their harpoons are useless. The men end up in the water and later find themselves imprisoned by the mysterious Captain Nemo on his submarine *Nautilus*. Thus begins a series of exciting adventures and hairbreadth escapes for Captain Nemo's "guests." [Scholastic]

WHERE THE RED FERN GROWS
written by Wilson Rawls
Billy badly wants to own two coon hounds, an impossible dream for a boy whose parents are poor hillbillies in the Ozark Mountains. But Billy finds a way to buy two pups, and he trains them to be the best coon hunters in the country; in fact, they become such a good team that Billy enters them in the Championship Coon Hunt with a chance of winning the Gold Cup. This is a moving story of a boy and his dogs and the hair-raising adventures they share. [Laurel Leaf]

> I could see that Rainie was paralyzed with fright. His mouth and eyes were opened wide, and his face was white as chalk.

THE WHITE COMPANY
written by Sir Arthur Conan Doyle, illustrated by N.C. Wyeth
You may have read some Sherlock Holmes stories, but Sir Arthur Conan Doyle also wrote this lengthy and challenging historical novel set in fourteenth century England. Alleyne Edricson is an orphan brought up by monks who leaves his monastery to explore the world. He becomes squire to the worthy knight Sir Nigel Loring, leader of the White Company, and falls in love with Sir Nigel's daughter, the fair Lady Maude. Alleyne must prove himself a worthy cavalier and win his lady's love with knightly deeds. He risks his life to ensure victory for the White Company. [William Morrow]

THE WHITE MOUNTAINS
written by John Christopher
In this exciting science fiction story, Will, Henry, and Beanpole are running for their minds (not their lives) from the monstrous Tripods. These hideous creatures seek to control the world by implanting steel caps in the skulls of all fourteen-year-olds to make them obedient and docile. To avoid being "capped," the three boys escape to the White Mountains. At one point, Will realizes that a Tripod has implanted a tracking device in his arm and the only way to escape is for Beanpole to cut it out. In spite of this painful operation, however, Will is actually caught by a Tripod and whirled up into the air. What a terrible fate may await him! This is the first of the Tripods trilogy. The other titles are *The City of Gold and Lead* and *The Pool of Fire*. [Simon Pulse]

WILDERNESS VENTURE
written by Elizabeth Howard
Delia is sixteen when her widowed mother announces to her ten astounded children that she has swapped their farm for some land in Michigan Territory sight unseen. Delia, Ezra, Reuel, and Job leave immediately to clear the land and build a house, leaving Mrs. Clark and the other children to join them later. However, on the steamboat to Detroit, Ezra disappears. Apparently he has been murdered, robbed of their money, and thrown overboard. Delia and her two other brothers are devastated, and Reuel cannot forgive himself for talking about the money on the night Ezra disappears. But Delia is determined to carry out her mother's wishes. Together, she and her brothers courageously face disaster, and Delia finds romance in the Michigan wilderness. Another excellent book by Elizabeth Howard is *Winter on Her Own*. [William Morrow]

> We aren't going home!" Delia said and was surprised to hear her voice so loud and sure. "Ma has sold the farm. She'll have to leave it in the fall. . . . [W]e'll make some kind of home for her and the little ones. We have to."

THE WINGED WATCHMAN
written and illustrated by Hilda Van Stockum
This story takes place in German-occupied Holland during World War II. During the German occupation, the people of Holland lose their money and their food, and many starve to death. The Verhagen family—Joris, Dirk Jan, and their devout Catholic parents—risk their lives time and again working for the Dutch Underground. But in their midst is a spy who will not hesitate to turn the Verhagens over to the German authorities if he discovers that they work for the Resistance. Suspense mounts when Dirk Jan sends a signal across the countryside with the help of a windmill's wings, right under the nose of sleeping German guards. [Farrar, Straus & Giroux]

A YANKEE MUSKET
written by Hildreth T. Wriston
Stephen lives with his parents and older brother in frontier country, just after the War for Independence. These are exciting and dangerous times. Not only must Stephen and his family defend themselves from bobcats and Indians, but they must also worry about the instability of the war years. Stephen wishes that his father would give him his own musket, so he can help defend his family from all the threats around them, but it takes time to earn someone's trust. The British are approaching from Canada, and some say that the Yankee army will never hold their line. When Stephen sees soldiers retreating from Fort Ticonderoga, leaving it in British hands, he knows that he must fight—for his country and for freedom. [Abingdon Press]

THE YEARLING
written by Marjorie Kinnan Rawlings, illustrated by N.C. Wyeth
Jody Baxter lives in the backwoods of Florida. Disaster strikes one day when Jody's dad is bitten by a rattlesnake. In order to draw out the poison, Mr. Baxter shoots a doe and applies its liver to the snakebite. Jody is allowed to keep the doe's fawn because he wants "something to foller me and be mine." Jody and his parents live a hard but happy life raising corn, hunting in the woods, and trailing and shooting Old Slewfoot the bear. But when the fawn grows up and starts eating the Baxters' crops, Jody's dad is forced to take drastic measures. [Simon Pulse]

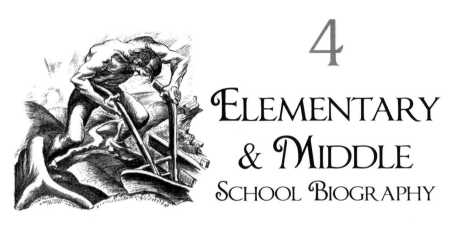

4
ELEMENTARY & MIDDLE
SCHOOL BIOGRAPHY

CONFEDERATE LEADERS
A CONFEDERATE TRILOGY FOR YOUNG READERS
written by Mary L. Williamson
This volume contains the biographies of three distinguished leaders of the Army of Northern Virginia: Robert E. Lee, Thomas "Stonewall" Jackson, and J.E.B. "Jeb" Stuart. General Lee provided brilliant leadership of the Confederate Army during the War Between the States. The soldiers loved this kindhearted Christian gentleman. General Stonewall Jackson was Lee's "right arm," a God-fearing military genius. During the Battle of Bull Run, someone saw Jackson "standing like a stone wall," and after that, his Stonewall Brigade was praised by friend and foe alike. Jeb Stuart was Lee's "eyes and ears." As chief of cavalry and commander of the famous Stuart Horse Artillery, Stuart was a courageous leader who inspired the devotion of his men. [Sprinkle Publications]

PILGRIMS
HOMES IN THE WILDERNESS
written by William Bradford and Others of the Mayflower Company, edited by Margaret Wise Brown, illustrated by Mary Wilson Stewart
This beautiful book includes the very words of the Pilgrims as they embark upon their voyage to the New World. Go with them as they draw up the Mayflower Compact and establish a new life for their small band

Illustration: *Daniel Boone*, illustrated by James Daugherty (New York: Viking Press, 1939), see page 166. Used by permission.

at Plymouth Plantation. Discover how the Pilgrims find an amazing
stash of corn and how they explore Cape Cod Bay looking for the best
place to settle. This small band of travelers overcomes many trials by
trusting in God to protect them. [Linnet Books]

THE LANDING OF THE PILGRIMS
written by James Daugherty
This is the story of the Pilgrims' settlement in the New World. First
the Separatists left England and then Holland to embark on a perilous journey across the Atlantic. They faced many trials such as lack of
food and shelter, biting cold, hostile Indians, and sickness. However,
William Bradford and his Plymouth colony gradually carved a home
out of the rugged New England wilderness and throughout their many
hardships placed their trust in God for survival. We recommend other
Landmark Books such as *The American Revolution* by Bruce Bliven,
Jr., *Our Independence and the Constitution* by May McNear, *The
Pioneers Go West* by George R. Stewart, *The Story of Thomas Alva
Edison* by Margaret Cousins, and *The Wright Brothers* by Quentin
Reynolds. [Random House]

THE PILGRIMS OF PLIMOTH
written and illustrated by Marcia Sewall
This wonderful description of Plimoth Plantation is told by the Pilgrims
themselves. They explain the specifics of their bold voyage and dangerous settlement of an untamed New
World. The trials of the harsh winter
and sickness come alive through the
perspective of these brave souls; they
realize their lives are safe in God's
hands. Daily life is full of hard work;
menfolk, womenfolk, and children
in turn describe the chores that fill
their days. They form compacts with
the local Indians, cultivate their fields, build homes, praise God, enjoy
a harvest festival, and gradually begin to "feel the sweetness of the
country." [Aladdin]

> Though the English were still strangers in it, this was for them the Promised Land.

ALCOTT, LOUISA MAY
INVINCIBLE LOUISA: THE STORY OF THE AUTHOR OF LITTLE WOMEN
written by Cornelia Meigs
Louisa May Alcott was the author of the Little Women series and other excellent books. Determined to help the depleted family finances, Alcott taught school, sewed, published her early writing, and very nearly sold her hair like Jo in *Little Women*. The Alcott family firmly believed that no matter how poor, one always has something to give away. During the War Between the States, Louisa nursed soldiers and traveled as the companion of an invalid girl to Europe where she met the Laurie of her famous novels. Finally, with the publication of *Little Women*, Louisa achieved fame and financial security for her beloved family. Cornelia Meigs gives us a vivid picture of Louisa, who is so like Jo—headstrong and temperamental, but loving and lovable. [Little, Brown]

AYLWARD, GLADYS
GLADYS AYLWARD
written by Catherine Swift
Gladys Aylward dreamed of becoming a missionary to China. She was determined to pursue her goal, so she saved her meager earnings to pay for the long and dangerous journey. When she finally arrived in China, Gladys was jeered at, but she and another missionary opened an inn where they befriended their guests and told Bible stories. Later, the Mandarin of the province gave Gladys a strange job—she became his Foot Inspector and traveled around China preventing foolish parents from binding the feet of

> China had many gods; people prayed to the sun, the moon, the god of the harvest, and the god of the rain. Now they were learning that a single God gave them all of these things and more.

their girl babies. This job allowed her to make many friends and bring the Gospel to the Chinese people. Her life in China was full of danger and amazing escapes, but the Small Woman, as she was called, proved time and again that she could do all things through Christ who gave her strength. [Bethany House Publishers]

AUGUSTINE OF HIPPO
AUGUSTINE: THE FARMER'S BOY OF TAGASTE
written by P. de Zeeuw, illustrated by Hein Kray
When he was a boy, Augustine led a wild life. He was constantly beaten for cheating, stealing, and getting into fights. Augustine lived for pleasure while his devout mother prayed for her pagan son. Sometimes her prayers lasted half the night. His mother was even forced to turn her pagan son out of the house. Eventually, however, Augustine was converted to Christianity. The unregenerate boy became a godly man, the Bishop of Hippo, and one of the great Church Fathers. [Inheritance Publications]

BELL, ALEXANDER GRAHAM
THE TALKING WIRE: THE STORY OF ALEXANDER GRAHAM BELL
written by O.J. Stevenson, illustrated by Lawrence Dresser
Alexander Graham Bell invented the telephone with the help of a gruesome piece of apparatus: a dead man's ear! In fact, he spent much of his time shouting into the corpse's ear and getting no reply. Bell had an extensive knowledge of anatomy, physics, and acoustics—everything he needed to conduct his research. After years of work with his assistant, Thomas Watson, he accidentally discovered how to make an undulating current. Alexander Graham Bell had invented "electric speech." [Julian Messner]

BOONE, DANIEL
DANIEL BOONE
written and illustrated by James Daugherty
This is the story of the famous frontiersman who blazed a trail west along the Wilderness Road from North Carolina. With his tomahawk and rifle, Daniel Boone wrestled with bears, eluded savages, and discovered an old Indian trail through the unexplored wilderness of Kentucky. Indians scalped his son, captured Boone himself several times, and staged a hair-raising attack on the settlement at Boonesborough. Daniel Boone's life was filled with danger and personal tragedy. [Viking]

BOWDITCH, NATHANIEL

CARRY ON, MR. BOWDITCH

written by Jean Lee Latham, illustrated by John O'Hara Cosgrave II

Nathaniel Bowditch, who lived in the 1800s, longed to follow in his father's footsteps and become a ship's captain, even though everyone said he was too small to be a sailor. When Nathaniel was still very young, he had to stop his schooling and become apprenticed to a ship merchant. He did not waste his time there but learned everything he could about astronomy and the sea. He was then able to carry out his ambition to go to sea. He amazed everyone with his ability to navigate even through thick fog, and he wrote a book on

> Nat's gaze never left his watch. He lifted one finger, as though with one finger he could control the wind and the waves that hurled a ship, a crew, and three hundred tons of cargo toward the waiting rocks.

navigation which any sailor could understand and which seamen still use today as a textbook at the U.S. Naval Academy. Jean Lee Latham has written other biographies of famous men, such as *Drake: The Man They Called a Pirate*, which is an exciting story of Queen Elizabeth I's favorite "Sea Dog." [Houghton Mifflin]

BUNYAN, JOHN

JOHN BUNYAN: AUTHOR OF THE PILGRIM'S PROGRESS

written by Sam Wellman

John Bunyan, a tinker's son, was a rebellious young ruffian with a foul mouth. When he enlisted in Cromwell's army to help fight the Royalists during England's Civil War, he saw a great deal of bloodshed and had many brushes with death. Eventually, God saved him, and Bunyan discovered that he had a great gift of preaching. He started preaching up and down the country lanes to whoever would stop and listen. However, since he was not a licensed minister, he was arrested and thrown into jail—twice. Bunyan was not discouraged but continued to preach God's Word to other prisoners. During his second imprisonment, he wrote his great Christian allegory, *The Pilgrim's Progress*. God used this humble tinker to teach countless thousands about God's mercy and grace. Other biographies in the "Heroes of the Faith" series describe the lives of Jim Elliot, John Knox, C.S. Lewis, Martin Luther, John Newton, and Corrie ten Boom. [Barbour]

COLUMBUS, CHRISTOPHER
COLUMBUS
written and illustrated by Ingri and Edgar Parin D'Aulaire
Other children laughed at Columbus when he said the earth is round, but he persevered because he knew it was true. When he was thirteen, Columbus sailed away from his home in Italy to make his fortune at sea, and he became a very good sailor. Unlike other people of his day, he was sure that you could cross the big ocean to the west and that there were lands on the other side. He believed that God had chosen him to find the fabulous riches of the East and take his Christian faith to heathens across the sea. Because of his faith and courage, Christopher Columbus discovered a vast new continent. This biography with its beautiful illustrations is for older elementary students. [Beautiful Feet Books]

THE COLUMBUS STORY
written by Alice Dalgliesh, illustrated by Leo Politi
Christopher Columbus poured his life and his dreams into finding a new route to the fabled lands of the East. He finally got funding from the king and queen of Spain and set sail with three ships into the unknown sea. The voyage was tense as the sailors longed for sight of land. At last, they found land and came to the lovely island of San Salvador. There they met people who fed them and exchanged gifts. When Columbus traveled back to Spain, he returned a hero, the Admiral of the Ocean Sea. This biography is for the youngest readers. [Charles Scribner's Sons]

DRAVECKY, DAVID
COMEBACK
written by Dave Dravecky with Tim Stafford
When Dave Dravecky, star pitcher for the San Francisco Giants, discovered he had cancer in his pitching arm, the doctors removed the tumor and half his deltoid muscle and told Dave that, short of a miracle, he would never pitch again. Well, the miracle happened. Dave returned to

the major leagues and won again and again. Then he broke his pitching arm—twice. After that, he had to face the fact that his baseball career was over. After each setback, Dave Dravecky kept coming back because he trusted God and knew that God controlled his life. In the inspiring sequel, *When You Can't Come Back*, Dravecky says, "What do you do when you can't come back? May God give you the grace to put your hand in His—even if you have only one hand to give—and there may you find peace." [Zondervan]

> My part, I believed, was to do everything possible, to try with all my might. Then, if I could not pitch, God would have other, better things for me to do.

FARADAY, MICHAEL
MICHAEL FARADAY AND THE DYNAMO
written by Mabel Miller
Michael Faraday was poor, uneducated, and suffered from a severe speech defect, but he overcame these impediments to become a great scientist. He was apprenticed to Sir Humphry Davy, first as a janitor but later as Davy's personal assistant. Faraday helped his employer invent the Davy Safety Lamp for coal miners, but his crowning achievement was the electric motor that he made from bits of string and strips of cloth from his wife's apron. His discovery of electromagnetic induction paved the way for the modern age of electricity. [Chilton Book Company]

FORTUNE, AMOS
AMOS FORTUNE, FREE MAN
written by Elizabeth Yates, illustrated by Nora Spicer Unwin
This book is based on the true story of an African prince who was captured by slave traders and sent to America to be sold. He did not become a free man until he was almost sixty. As a slave, Amos learned to read by studying the Bible. He became a Christian and a tanner with a thriving business and worked hard to save money in order to buy freedom for several slaves, including the woman whom he married. Amos Fortune was a godly man with a big heart and a dedication to freedom. [Puffin]

FULTON, ROBERT
ROBERT FULTON, BOY CRAFTSMAN
written by Marguerite Henry, illustrated by Lawrence Dresser
Robert Fulton always wanted to know how things worked. When

> All eyes were looking down at a strange boat tied to the dock. . . . "That snub-nosed little steam boat! It will sink before it reaches Albany."

he was a boy, he was full of ideas; he made one of the first pencils in America, cast bullets, repaired old rifles, and designed new guns while he was working for a gunsmith. One Fourth of July, he made some fireworks. Fulton invented many other things, but the invention that has made him famous is his steamboat, which ignorant men called "Fulton's Folly." You will admire this man's hard work and determination, and his story may inspire you to look around like he did and find ways to improve our world. If you like this story, you will enjoy reading about the childhood of other famous people in the Famous Americans series. [Bobbs-Merrill]

HANDEL, GEORGE FRIDERIC
GEORGE FRIDERIC HANDEL: COMPOSER OF MESSIAH
written by Charles Ludwig, illustrated by Arthur Schneider
Handel's father was determined that his son would become a lawyer, but God destined Handel for the world of music. This biography describes Handel's daily life and includes interesting anecdotes about his music. Handel suffered many disappointments and physical handicaps, but God protected him in amazing ways. At his lowest ebb, when he was paralyzed and owed so much money that he faced debtor's prison, Handel composed his greatest oratorio, the *Messiah*. With tears running down his cheeks, he cried out to a servant as he finished the "Hallelujah Chorus," "I did think I did see all heaven before me and the great God Himself." [Mott Media]

JACKSON, THOMAS
STONEWALL
written by Jean Fritz, illustrated by Stephen Gammell
Although Thomas "Stonewall" Jackson became one of the heroes of the War Between the States, he did not have a promising beginning.

An impoverished orphan, he graduated with a great deal of effort from West Point, and after seeing some action in the Mexican War, he became a mediocre teacher at a military school. At the first Battle of Manassas, however, Jackson saved the Confederate army and earned his nickname when he and his men held their position just like a stone wall. Stonewall Jackson was a devout Christian and believed that "every thought should be a prayer. The attitude of prayer should become a habit." He was a God-fearing, disciplined, determined man whose first rule of conduct was to acknowledge that God is in charge of all battles. This enjoyable biography is slightly flawed by a simplistic perspective on the reasons for the War Between the States. [Putnam Juvenile]

Another excellent biography of Jackson for older readers is Allan Tate's *Stonewall Jackson: The Good Soldier*. [J.S. Sanders]

KELLER, HELEN
THE STORY OF MY LIFE
written by Helen Keller
Because of a serious illness, Helen Keller lost her sight and hearing before she was two years old. For the next few years, she lived in a world of darkness and silence. Then Anne Sullivan, herself partially blind, became her lifelong tutor and taught her to perceive the world around her. In her autobiography, Helen describes that unforgettable moment when she first understood that the letters w-a-t-e-r, which Anne spelled out on her hand, meant the cold liquid gushing over her skin. Then "the mystery of language was revealed to me." From that moment on, Helen was an able student. She entered Radcliffe College and, with Anne Sullivan's help, mastered French, German, and Latin, as well as English literature and history. Helen Keller's courage and determination to overcome her severe handicaps is an inspiring story. [Bantam Classic]

KEPLER, JOHANNES
JOHANNES KEPLER: GIANT OF FAITH AND SCIENCE
written by John Hudson Tiner, illustrated by Rod Burke
As a result of childhood smallpox, Kepler had poor vision, but God still allowed him to see well enough to make his marvelous discoveries that revolutionized the science of astronomy. This brilliant German astronomer and mathematician discovered that the planets follow not circular but elliptical orbits around the sun; he also discovered two other laws

of planetary motion. Kepler taught at a Lutheran school in Graz but left rather than convert to Roman Catholicism. After becoming an assistant to Tycho Brahe, he continued Brahe's work. As a young man, Kepler intended to become a theologian. Instead he dedicated his life to astronomy for "the heavens declare the glory of God." [Mott Media]

LEE, ROBERT E.
ROBERT E. LEE
written by Guy Emery
Robert E. Lee, one of America's most loved heroes, was a true Christian gentleman. At the outbreak of the Civil War, he faced an agonizing decision: should he remain loyal to the Union or to his native state, Virginia? Lee decided to resign his commission in the United States army in order to become Commander of the Confederate forces. Throughout the long and bloody war, Lee acted with compassion, outstanding valor, and inspiring leadership. When defeat came, Lee accepted it with his customary dignity: "We have appealed to the God of battles and He has decided against us." General Robert E. Lee is remembered not for his defeats but for his virtues. [Julian Messner]

ROBERT E. LEE: CHRISTIAN GENERAL AND GENTLEMAN
written by Lee Roddy, illustrated by A.G. Smith
Another fine biography of the great Confederate general of the War Between the Sates. Lee was fortunate in his parents: his father was a Revolutionary War hero, and his mother was a godly woman who taught him the principles of the Christian religion. His military career began when he was admitted to West Point. When war broke out between the U.S. and Texas, Lee was sent to Texas where his superior officers were impressed by his bravery and military strategy. When the War Between the States broke out, Lee chose to stand with his native state of Virginia because he could not fight against his fellow Virginians. [Mott Media]

LEWIS, C.S.
C.S. LEWIS
written by Catherine Swift
C.S. Lewis, the great Christian writer, philosopher, and scholar, is the author of the popular Narnia books, the famous space trilogy, the cele-

brated *Screwtape Letters,* and many other inspiring non-fiction works. Lewis's childhood was not happy. The tragic death of his mother shattered his faith in God, and his father never gave him the guidance and affection he craved. He also suffered from nightmares and loneliness. In fact, some of his only happy hours as a child were spent writing stories with his brother. After serving in the army during World War I, Lewis endured years of domestic drudgery as servant and nursemaid to the mother of a dead war companion; at the same time, he became a tutor at Oxford University. Only after his father's death did Lewis become a believer and author of the books that would help strengthen the faith of thousands. [Bethany House]

LIDDELL, ERIC
ERIC LIDDELL
written by Catherine Swift
Eric Liddell was the unassuming Christian runner so devoted to his faith that he refused to run on the Lord's Day, even when that conviction meant the loss of a Gold Medal in the 1924 Paris Olympics. This is the story of Scotland's greatest athlete, hero of the film *Chariots of Fire,* who thrilled the world with his running and disappeared to China as a missionary. Liddell's life as a missionary in war-torn China is in itself a moving story. His faith, courage, and compassion never failed as he sacrificed everything for his missionary work. [Bethany House]

LUTHER, KATHERINE
QUEEN OF THE REFORMATION
written by Charles Ludwig
From her convent cell, Katharine von Bora secretly studied the writings of the "heretic" Martin Luther. Katharine risked severe punishment for reading Luther's attacks on the Roman Catholic Church. Eventually, Katie and eleven other nuns planned

In a half-scream, she continued: "We can no longer suffer the serpent to creep through the field of the Lord. The books of Martin Luther are to be examined and burned."

their escape from the convent, with the help of Dr. Luther. Hidden inside empty barrels, the girls held their breath until they came to safety. From then on, the lives of these former nuns were dramatically changed. The girls soon adapted to their new lives, most of them finding new homes and husbands. However, Katie, strong-willed and eager to serve Christ, took a little longer to find her niche. Dr. Luther attempted to find her a suitable husband, but in the end, he married her himself! Katharine and Luther's life together was full of joys and trials, and through it all Katie was a source of encouragement for her husband. [Bethany House]

MADISON, JAMES
THE GREAT LITTLE MADISON
written by Jean Fritz
Although James Madison was a puny child with a weak voice, he didn't let physical handicaps hold him back. He is known today as "the Father of the Constitution" because, before he was thirty, he worked out a clever system of checks and balances that controls our three branches of government. Madison was Jefferson's Secretary of State and America's fourth President. This biography lets you experience what life was like in colonial America and what a major contribution James Madison made to the shaping of our country. [Putnam & Grosset]

MAGELLAN, FERDINAND
FIVE SHIPS WEST: THE STORY OF MAGELLAN
written by Charles E. Israel
The story of Ferdinand Magellan and his famous voyage. Magellan developed exact plans about what he wanted. He would be the first man to sail around the world! His own country, Portugal, rejected his schemes and refused to give the explorer the necessary funding. However, Magellan was not daunted. He went to the king of Spain and found support. This was just the beginning of his adventures. The voyage of this courageous explorer brought him face-to-face with danger, starvation, and even death. [Macmillan]

MOODY, D.L.
D.L. MOODY
written by Faith Coxe Bailey
D.L. Moody was an uneducated farm boy with a rough-and-ready manner who came to Chicago to make his fortune. Somewhere down the line, he switched from selling shoes to selling Christianity, but his

efforts were still directed toward making himself rich. One day, his eyes were opened to his self-centeredness, and he dedicated the rest of his life to the glory of God. This is a short biography of a nineteenth-century evangelist. [Moody]

MUELLER, GEORGE

GEORGE MUELLER
written by Faith Coxe Bailey

George Mueller wanted to become a missionary, despite the wishes of the girl he loved and his father. So he gave up the girl and ignored his father's counsel because he believed that this goal was God's will for his life. Mueller traveled from Germany to London as a missionary to the Jews but was soon convinced that God wanted him to take the Gospel to all men. When Mueller became the pastor of a church in Southwest England, he told his tiny congrega-

> George kept his word; he never talked about money in public; he refused to ask anyone for a donation.

tion that he would be supported not by the old mandatory pew rents but by their voluntary contributions. To the amazement of the church members, the collection money never failed to pay for his needs. Mueller also opened five orphanages in Bristol, rescuing 2,000 children from hideous almshouses. [Moody]

NEWTON, JOHN

JOHN NEWTON: THE ANGRY SAILOR
written by Kay Marshall Strom

Kidnapped and forced to be a menial worker on a warship, John Newton tried to escape and was brutally whipped. In his misery, he bitterly rejected God and went on to live a thoroughly wicked life. He eventually became the cruel captain of a slave ship. During a violent storm at sea, he nearly drowned and cried out to God to help him. God saved

> Amazing grace! How sweet the sound
> That saved a wretch like me!
> I once was lost, but now am found;
> Was blind, but now I see.

him, body and soul. After his conversion, Newton became a famous preacher and hymn writer, the author of "Amazing Grace." Based on Newton's journals, this exciting biography describes Newton's life from his rebellious youth, through his experiences as a slave trader, his conversion, and later years as a dedicated Christian saved by God's grace. [Moody]

NIGHTINGALE, FLORENCE
FLORENCE NIGHTINGALE: GOD'S SERVANT AT THE BATTLEFIELD
written by David R. Collins, illustrated by Edward Ostendorf
Florence Nightingale met with a lot of opposition when she decided to become a nurse. Her wealthy family thought her ambition was shocking: English hospitals were filthy and the nurses often drunk. In addition, doctors were resentful and hostile. Florence persevered, however. She studied nursing in Paris and was appointed superintendent of a London hospital. When the War in the Crimea broke out, she nursed thousands of wounded solders in appalling conditions. The Turkish hospital where she worked was so overcrowded that dying and wounded soldiers were left outside, and the bed linen crawled with lice. But Florence dealt with the filth and horror and reorganized all the army hospitals in the Crimea, saving countless lives. Florence Nightingale brought about worldwide hospital reforms, and even Queen Victoria recognized the successes of "the Lady with the Lamp." [Mott Media]

PASCAL, BLAISE
A PIECE OF THE MOUNTAIN: THE STORY OF BLAISE PASCAL
written by Joyce McPherson
Pascal was a great seventeenth-century scientist, mathematician, and man of God. From childhood, he loved to study, and his father encouraged and supervised his learning. His scientific accomplishments have greatly affected our daily lives. The scientific principle called Pascal's Law now has hundreds of everyday applications from driving machinery to activating car brakes. Pascal also invented the theory of probability

> O Lord . . . help me to do the right thing. I want to seek the truth.

and the calculator, as well as the world's first mass public transportation system, the omnibus. He invented the omnibus because he wanted to help the poor who could not afford coaches. Above all, Pascal wanted his work to glorify God, and he is well known for his *Pensées*, the thoughts he wrote down for his *Defense of the Christian Religion*. Pascal spent his life trying to honor God with everything he did. [Greenleaf Press]

REVERE, PAUL
PAUL REVERE: THE MAN BEHIND THE LEGEND
written by Margaret Green
Paul Revere's midnight ride, immortalized in Longfellow's poem, was only one of many contributions this patriotic American made to the Revolutionary War. This biography describes the role Paul Revere played in the events which led up to the war, including the part he played in the Boston Tea Party and his famous ride to Lexington and Concord to alert patriots of the proposed British attack. Revere's accomplishments were many. He designed and printed the first Continental paper currency; he made gunpowder, bronze cannons, and bells; and he designed Massachusetts' state seal as well as his beautiful silverware. But what this book makes clear is that this simple craftsman was also one of America's most loyal and dedicated patriots. [Julian Messner]

ROOSEVELT, THEODORE
BULLY FOR YOU, TEDDY ROOSEVELT!
written by Jean Fritz, illustrated by Mike Wimmer
Teddy Roosevelt had a tremendous zest for life. When he developed an interest in natural history, he filled his parents' house with all kinds of animals, alive and dead—some chained to the stove and some in the icebox. He never walked if he could run; when he met an obstacle, he charged right through it. During his years at university, he wrote books, got married, and was elected to the

A Chicago newspaper-man wrote an article in praise of Teddy, addressing him directly. . . . "Dancing down the road—you came with with life and love and courage and fun stickin' out all over you. How we loved you at first sight! And how you loved us!"

New York State legislature. And he worked hard, sometimes eighteen hours a day. His volunteer cavalry regiment, his "Rough Riders," defeated the Spanish ("a bully fight"), and he was the youngest, as well as probably the most exuberant, American President. Roosevelt attacked the presidency with the same vigor he applied to everything else he ever did, and his political creed is legendary: "Speak softly and carry a big stick." [Putnam]

SHAKA
SHAKA: KING OF THE ZULUS
written by Diane Stanley and Peter Vennema, illustrated by Diane Stanley
This is the story of Shaka, who was born into the small tribe of the Zulus. Rejected by everyone except his mother, Shaka grows up determined to make an impact on the clans around him. He grows strong and courageous and forges ahead with innovative ideas about how warriors can fight better. Soon Shaka is leading the soldiers of his tribe, and before too long he becomes leader of the Zulus. His armies are known for their fierce and tactical fighting strategies, and the Zulu strength grows. Even when the English come, they cannot intimidate the great Shaka. [William Morrow]

SPURGEON, CHARLES
CHARLES SPURGEON
written by Kathy Triggs
Charles Spurgeon was blessed with godly parents, a love of reading, and a cook who taught him all about Calvinism! Amazingly, while Spurgeon was still a child, a missionary predicted that he would become a great preacher. He preached his first sermon at age sixteen and was still a teenager when he was given his first pastorate. He later pastored a London congregation where he remained for thirty-eight years. Spurgeon's popularity spread until he was preaching to thousands. Spurgeon founded a college where he taught theology students, and he also established day schools, homes for the elderly, and "Ragged Schools" for poor children. He published his sermons, a magazine, and his famous devotional book, *Morning and Evening*. In fact, Spurgeon's influence was so great that preachers throughout England claimed to have become "Spurgeonized." [Bethany House]

TYNDALE, WILLIAM

THE BIBLE SMUGGLER

written by Louise A. Vernon

William Tyndale was determined to translate the Bible into English, the language of the common people. However, Cardinal Wolsey and other influential English churchmen believed that Tyndale's ideas were heretical. In spite of the real possibility of being burned at the stake, Tyndale began his translation while Wolsey's spies stopped at nothing to prevent his sacred task. When they burned his house down, Tyndale and his page fled to Germany. The print-

> There's a special kind of louse that eats only type. This one's been eating up the New Testament as fast as I can set it up.

ing of Tyndale's New Testament was strictly forbidden, and all that remained was his handwritten manuscript. Tyndale had to smuggle the precious manuscript from one German city to another in search of a publisher. When it was finally printed, Tyndale smuggled the Bibles back to England so that all Englishmen could read God's Word for themselves. [Herald Press]

Two fictionalized biographies of Tyndale are Abert Lee's *Thrilling Escapes by Night* [Rod and Staff] and Scott O'Dell's *The Hawk That Dare Not Hunt by Day*. [Dell]

WASHINGTON, GEORGE

GEORGE WASHINGTON: MAN OF COURAGE AND PRAYER

written by Norma Cournow Camp, illustrated by Diane Manderfield

George Washington loved adventure. Before the French and Indian War, he went on a dangerous journey in order to carry a message to the French demanding that they leave the Ohio River Valley. During the War, he led a wilderness expedition to drive the French from the Ohio territory. Many times, his life was threatened, but God preserved this brave soldier. The height of his military career came when he was elected Commander-in-Chief of the Continental Army to fight the War for Independence. It was this position that firmly established Washington as "first in war, first in peace, and first in the hearts of his countrymen." [Mott Media]

WEBSTER, DANIEL

DANIEL WEBSTER: DEFENDER OF THE UNION
written by Robert Allen
Daniel Webster, the son of a New England farmer, loved to read and had a prodigious memory. As a boy, he could recite long passages from the Bible and entire chapters from Latin grammar books. He worked hard to receive a good education. His tutor insisted that he translate ten pages from Virgil and ten from Cicero—before breakfast! But when he was young, Webster hated to speak in public. He overcame his reserve, however, by studying the speeches of great orators like Edmund Burke. Webster delivered his first public address while a student at Dartmouth College, and he used his great gift of oratory throughout his distinguished career. When he was elected to the U.S. Senate, he gave passionate speeches in defense of the Constitution. [Mott Media]

> Our fathers came here to enjoy their religion free and unmolested; and, at the end of two centuries, there is nothing upon which we can pronounce more confidently . . . than of the inestimable importance of that religion to man, both in regard to this life and that which is to come.

WESLEY, SUSANNA

SUSANNA WESLEY: MOTHER OF JOHN AND CHARLES
written by Charles Ludwig, illustrated by Tim Bowers
The family life of Susanna Wesley was a turbulent one because her father was a dissenting minister who refused to conform to the Church of England. After she married, adversity continued to follow her. Of her nineteen children, only nine survived to adulthood. The Wesleys' house burned down—twice. In addition, the family's financial hardship became so severe that once Mr. Wesley was imprisoned for debt. But through all these troubles, Susanna's faith remained steadfast. She was a godly wife and mother and taught all of her children to serve God. Two of her sons, John and Charles, grew up to become preachers and hymn writers for America and the world. [Mott Media]

WILLIAM OF ORANGE
WILLIAM OF ORANGE: THE SILENT PRINCE
written by W.G. Van de Hulst
William of Nassau was Father of the Dutch Republic and a sixteenth-century Protestant hero. But he had a powerful enemy, King Philip of Spain, who did his evil best to stamp out the Protestant religion in the Netherlands. Prince William led a rebellion against Spain but did not manage to unite his beloved countrymen. Philip exiled William, confiscated his lands, and even sent his son away. This godly man was willing to sacrifice everything—even his life—for the sake of his people and his faith. [Inheritance Publications]

WRIGHT, ORVILLE & WILBUR
THE WRIGHT BROTHERS: THEY GAVE US WINGS
written by Charles Ludwig, illustrated by Barbara Morrow
This is the dramatic story of two dedicated young men who applied God's laws to their experiments in aeronautics. On the way to Kitty Hawk, North Carolina, Wilbur nearly drowned, but he survived to test the brothers' first passenger glider. However, neither that glider nor a subsequent larger model had the necessary lifting power, so Wilbur and Orville began experimenting

> The slender Bible-believing Bishop's kids had presented the world with wings.

with air pressure on model wings in a six-foot wind tunnel. The tables they derived from these tests allowed them to design a machine that could fly. They then set to work on a powered airplane and were eventually successful. [Mott Media]

ILLUSTRATIONS
The Hound of the Baskervilles, originally illustrated by Sidney Paget
(New York: Grosset & Dunlap, 1902), see page 195
for an unillustrated edition.

5

𝓗IGH SCHOOL
𝓕ICTION

ADAM BEDE
written by George Eliot
Adam Bede is a strong, honest, hard-working carpenter. He has earned the devotion of his mother, the affection of his brother Seth, and the respect of everyone in the village—but he has yet to win the love of his heart, Hetty Sorrell. Hetty is a beautiful girl, but her mind is occupied by self-centered concerns. Her attention can be caught by any bright ribbon or pretty bauble, and when dashing Captain Donnithorne starts to show her some attention, her mind is filled with foolish dreams. Dinah Morris, a young Methodist woman, tries to warn Hetty that foolishness will lead her into trouble, but Hetty refuses to listen. The resulting sequence of events brings Hetty to despair and causes Adam pain that only time can heal. [Penguin Classic]

THE ADVENTURES OF HUCKLEBERRY FINN
written by Mark Twain
Huckleberry Finn, a homeless boy and a rebel against respectable society, is being "sivilized" by Widow Douglas and Miss Watson. Huck cannot stand being stifled, so he escapes with Miss Watson's runaway slave, Jim. Together, they float down the Mississippi River on a raft toward freedom and experience some unforgettable adventures. Murder (both fake and real), mistaken identity, practical jokes, hair-breadth escapes, violence, and superstition are all crammed into this action-packed, humorous book. At the end of his escapades, Huck comments, "I reckon I got to light out for the territory . . . because Aunt Sally, she's going to sivilize me, and I can't stand it. I been there before." [Penguin]

ALL CREATURES GREAT AND SMALL
written by James Herriot
The first of five books describing the hilarious adventures of an English vet. Imagine the scene: A bleary-eyed doctor climbs out of bed at 2:00 a.m. and bumps over twelve miles of snow-covered country lanes to the difficult birthing of a calf. Then he grovels for two hours on a filthy stable floor, one arm up inside the cow while a know-it-all farmer keeps up a non-stop stream of criticism. All in a day's work for James Herriot. He and his partners run a brisk practice in the Yorkshire Dales. They have some amusing experiences, like the day they arrive at a farm to perform a post mortem on a dead sheep. They demand from the startled farmer's wife a sharp carving knife and ask the whereabouts of her husband. As she cowers in a corner clutching her children to her, he realizes it's the wrong farm! The other four titles in this series are *All Things Bright and Beautiful, All Things Wise and Wonderful, The Lord God Made Them All,* and *Every Living Thing.* [St. Martin's Press]

ANIMAL FARM
written by George Orwell

> No animal shall kill any other animal without cause.
> No animal shall drink alcohol to excess.
> All animals are equal, but some animals are more equal than others.

A clever political satire in which some foolish farm animals overthrow their brutal master, Mr. Jones, and establish a model community in which all animals are equal. To their chagrin, however, the animals eventually realize that some animals are more equal than others. They also discover that although they have removed their cruel overlord, Mr. Jones, he is replaced by another tyrant—a pig who walks on his hind legs and carries a whip. [Plume]

BEN-HUR: A TALE OF THE CHRIST
written by Lew Wallace
A great historical romance set at the time of Christ. Judah Ben-Hur is a nobleman of Jewish blood whose bitter enemy is Messala, a Roman. Because of a freak accident, Ben-Hur kills a Roman official, and Messala arrests the whole family, imprisons Ben-Hur's mother and sister,

and seizes his home. Imprisoned for years, his mother and sister contract the dreaded disease of leprosy. Unaware of their terrible fate, Ben-Hur races against his old antagonist Messala in the chariot races at Antioch. Messala will stop at nothing to throw Ben-Hur out of the race. Filled with desire for revenge upon Messala, Ben-Hur plots to overthrow the Roman rule and recruits an army to follow Christ, the Deliverer of the Jews. Throughout his life, Ben-Hur sees Jesus many times, such as when Jesus turns water into wine, feeds the five thousand, and when He performs the most wonderful miracle of all. [BiblioBazaar]

> Down on its right side toppled the bed of the Roman's chariot. . . . [T]he car went to pieces, and Messala, entangled in the reins, pitched forward headlong.

BILLY BUDD, SAILOR
written by Herman Melville
A short novel about a young, good-hearted sailor whose innocence and good looks inspire the hatred of a petty officer named Claggart. Claggart falsely accuses Billy of attempted mutiny, and Billy's outrage results in a tragic destiny for this young seaman. Readers of this novel should be aware of Melville's belief in arbitrary fate, a belief that conflicts with Christian belief. [Pocket]

THE BRIDGE OF SAN LUIS REY
written by Thornton Wilder
"On Friday noon, July the twentieth, 1714, the finest bridge in all Peru broke and precipitated five travelers into the gulf below." So begins this thought-provoking novel. Brother Juniper, a Franciscan missionary, witnesses the event and decides to find out why the tragedy occurred. When the bridge collapses, one of the victims is estranged from her daughter, another is a lonely orphan, and another is contemplating suicide. Brother Juniper hopes the accident will prove that men are not victims of meaningless events but part of God's sovereign plan, so he investigates the lives of the five victims. [HarperCollins]

BRIDGE OVER THE RIVER KWAI
written by Pierre Boulle
A great World War II story. A regiment of British POW's is forced to build a railway bridge for the Japanese. The British Colonel Nicholson, a brilliant and courageous leader, has to supervise a challenging feat of engineering for the hated Japanese army. A tense confrontation takes place between Nicholson and the Japanese commandant when Nicholson heroically refuses to allow his officers to engage in manual labor. He submits to torture rather than to compromise his principles. The tension becomes unbearable when Nicholson learns that an allied mission is about to blow up his beautifully constructed bridge. [Presidio Press]

THE CALL OF THE WILD
written by Jack London
When Buck is stolen from his master, he suffers many trials. He is sold to two French Canadians in Alaska as part of their dog sled team. There Buck learns that men and dogs often act little better than savages. After biding his time, he attacks and kills the mean lead dog. Buck soon becomes the leader of the team. He is sold again to brutal owners who almost club him to death. Then he falls into the hands of John Thornton, a kind man whose life Buck saves twice. But Buck's new owner comes to a tragic end, leaving his broken-hearted dog to respond to the call of the wild. [Aladdin]

THE CELESTIAL RAILROAD
written by Nathaniel Hawthorne

> "Is that," inquired I, "the very door in the hill-side which the shepherds assured Christian was a by-way to Hell?"
> "That was a joke on the part of the shepherds, said Mr. Smooth-it-away, with a smile.

Hawthorne's amusing satire is based on *The Pilgrim's Progress*, and it describes a pilgrimage from the infamous City of Destruction to the Celestial City. The gullible pilgrim in Hawthorne's tale happily notices the improvements made since Bunyan's day. The journey by foot, for example, has been updated to a comfortable train ride, and the burdensome luggage once carried on one's back is now safely deposited in the baggage car. His fellow passenger is sweet-talking Mr. Smooth-it-away, who points out other refinements such as the tunnel that has been dug right through Hill Difficulty and the convenient leveling of the Valley of Humiliation. As for his pleasant sojourn in Vanity Fair, this pilgrim is so diverted by the wise maxims of Rev. Mr. Clog-the-Spirit and Rev. Mr. Stumble-at-Truth that he almost decides to stay there! [Signet Classic]

THE CHOSEN
written by Chaim Potok
When Reuven Malter is hit in the eye with a softball by Danny Saunders, little does either boy know that this is the beginning of a strong friendship. Danny is a member of a Hasidic sect, a branch of Orthodox Judaism that demands strict observance of the Talmud. Danny's father is the revered leader of this sect, and Danny has been chosen to take over after his father. Reuven, on the other hand, is a more liberal Jew, the kind that Danny's sect abhors. Despite the two boys' different backgrounds, however, they become close friends. It is ironic that while Danny never wanted to be his sect's leader, Reuven hopes someday to become a Rabbi. Danny must now decide whether he should abandon his "secular" interests or whether he should follow in his father's footsteps. Also look for Chaim Potok's *My Name Is Asher Lev*. [Ballantine Books]

CHRISTY
written by Catherine Marshall
Christy is only nineteen years old when she leaves her home to teach school at a mission in the Smoky Mountains. She is young but full of determination and vision. Her imagination is charged with the idea of sacrificing her secure and wealthy home in order to minister to the needs of these backwoods Appalachian folk. Christy soon learns, however, that her romantic notions of self-sacrifice will be harshly tested. She lives in the most primitive of communities, where filthy homes lack any modern conveniences and the people dislike strangers. But in that secluded community, Christy discovers a people whose traditions are untouched by the modern world and whose hearts yearn for the knowledge she can share. [Avon Books]

THE CITADEL

written by A.J. Cronin

Andrew Manson is a young doctor fresh out of medical school, full of new ideas and enthusiasm. He starts to practice medicine in a Welsh mining village. There he serves as assistant to a bedridden doctor whose greedy wife pockets most of the fees and keeps Manson underpaid and overworked. His life, however, is full of interesting events, like the time he dynamites a sewer in the dead of night in order to prevent a typhoid epidemic. He faces ignorance, jealousy, and medical incompetence and makes courageous, life-or-death decisions. Later, he is charged with abusing the animals he uses to conduct research into miners' lung disease. Manson eventually abandons his integrity in a mad pursuit of wealth and success. When a patient dies on the operating table, however, he finally recognizes the corrupt man he has become. [Back Bay Books]

DAVID COPPERFIELD

written by Charles Dickens

Like all Dickens's stories, this lengthy novel will make you laugh and cry and keep you in suspense. Much of what happens to David Copperfield happened to Dickens himself. David is packed off at a tender age to work at a factory. In London, he meets all kinds of odd characters including Mr. Micawber, an easygoing spendthrift, and Uriah Heep, an oily lawyer's clerk whose fingers make clammy tracks along the page like a snail. The story also includes other unusual characters like Betsy Trotwood, David's eccentric aunt, who has a heart of gold beneath her formidable exterior; Barkis, who courts his girl via a single message, "Barkis is willing"; and Mr. Creakle, a headmaster whose chief interest in education is flogging his students. Of all his novels, Dickens himself liked this one the best. [Signet Classic]

DON QUIXOTE DE LA MANCHA

written by Miguel de Cervantes, translated by William Starkie

Cervantes's classic work about the "never-before-imagined" adventures of a would-be knight-errant is a dauntingly long but thoroughly entertaining novel. Don Quixote is a dreamer: He sees armies, castles, highborn ladies, and giants where Sancho, his faithful squire, and other realists see sheep, inns, farm girls, and windmills. The Don is never deterred by the considerable injuries he sustains, but, after each hilarious encounter, he picks himself up and ambles off on Rozinante, his nag—er, steed—to pursue yet another perilous quest and to right the world's wrongs. [Signet Classic]

EMMA
written by Jane Austen

Emma Woodhouse is a young lady who is intent solely upon matchmaking. After her best friend marries a neighboring widower, Emma focuses her considerable energies on a new friend, Harriet Smith, specifi-

> Were I to fall in love, indeed, it would be a different thing; but I never have been in love,—it is not my way or my nature,—and I do not think I ever shall.

cally to find her a husband. After many entanglements with various suitors for Harriet's hand, Emma finds that her plotting has served only to confuse matters and hurt other people's feelings. In the end, she is amazed to realize that the turn of events in her own life is beyond her control. [Penguin Classics]

ENTER JEEVES: 15 EARLY STORIES
written by P.G. Wodehouse

Of all the hilarious pieces of literature available to mankind, the writings of P.G. Wodehouse certainly rate up there with the best. Perhaps Wodehouse's most well-loved and comic characters are Bertie and Jeeves. Here is a collection of short stories about Bertie Wooster, an aristocratic loafer with no brain, and Jeeves, his erudite, resourceful valet. On several occasions, Bertie finds himself putting up unwelcome guests at his flat, or alternatively, moving out of it himself in order to help friends out of various scrapes. On one occasion, a friend's aunt arrives at the flat assuming it belongs to her nephew. The aunt takes an instant dislike to Bertie. "She looked at me in rather a rummy way. It was a nasty look. It made me feel as if I were something the dog had brought in and intended to bury later on when he had time." Bertie offers the gorgon a cup of tea. "'Tea?' She spoke as if she had never heard of the stuff." The situation assumes ghastly proportions when Bertie realizes the aunt has come to stay and decides that Bertie is a decadent sponger of the worst sort. [Dover]

EVERYTHING THAT RISES MUST CONVERGE

written by Flannery O'Connor

This is a collection of short stories set in the South. O'Connor describes a world full of freaks and hypocrites running away from God. The stories in this collection deal with self-righteous, self-deceived folks like Mrs. Chestney: "If you know who you are, you can go anywhere. I know who I am" (she doesn't, of course); Mrs. May: "She was a good Christian woman with a large respect for religion though she did not, of course, believe that any of it was true"; and Mrs. Turpin: "If it's one thing I am it's grateful. When I think who all I could have been besides myself and what all I got and a good disposition besides, I just feel like shouting, 'Thank you, Jesus!'" O'Connor's fiction will show you that without Christ, men and women are downright grotesque and the world is an ugly place. [Farrar, Straus & Giroux]

> The woman with the snuff-stained lips turned around in her chair . . . "You can get you one with green stamps. . . . Save you up enough, you can get you most anythang. I got me some joo'ry." Ought to have got you a wash rag and some soap, Mrs. Turpin thought.

FAHRENHEIT 451

written by Ray Bradbury

Guy Montag has a strange job—he's a fireman who burns books in a world where books and all intellectual pursuits are forbidden. He starts to become concerned about his job, especially when he meets a girl who makes him think. After an old lady is burned along with her books, Montag becomes increasingly alarmed about his culture's values until eventually he's on the run, chased by the firehouse's Mechanical Hound, a man-destroying robot. This is an exciting sci-fi novel that is hard to put down. [Del Rey]

FAR FROM THE MADDING CROWD

written by Thomas Hardy

This is the story of a simple shepherd named Gabriel Oak who falls in love with capricious but beautiful Bathsheba Everdene. Two other men love Everdene: wealthy Squire Boldwood and Sergeant Troy, a philanderer. Troy, however, is also involved with a servant girl whom he betrays most wretchedly. Enormous conflicts emerge as these characters interact with one another. Passion and melodrama abound, although this novel is much less pessimistic than most of Hardy's other works. For mature readers. [Modern Library]

A GOOD MAN IS HARD TO FIND
written by Flannery O'Connor
Some more bizarre short stories of the South. O'Connor has a humorous way of showing "good country people" in their true light. Those who rely on social respectability are actually lost. The grandmother in *A Good Man is Hard to Find* is obsessed with her collars, cuffs, and handkerchiefs because she wants to be sure that "in case of an accident, anyone seeing her dead on the highway would know at once that she was a lady." A crazed killer called the Misfit in the same story has more of a grasp on eternal issues. In his words, Jesus "thrown everything off balance. If He did what He said, then it's nothing for you to do but throw away everything and follow Him, and if He didn't, then it's nothing for you to do but enjoy the few minutes you got left the best way you can—by killing someone or burning down his house or doing some other meanness to him." The Misfit follows his own advice in this shocking story. [Harvest Books]

GOOD-BYE, MR. CHIPS
written by James Hilton, illustrated by H.M. Brock
A sentimental story about a well-loved teacher at an English boarding school who has taught generations of boys. The point of view is that of Mr. Chips, who reminisces about all the heartache and fun of his years of teaching. As Mr. Chips grows old, someone says it's sad that he's never had any children, to which the aging schoolmaster replies that he's had hundreds of children, and all of them boys! [Little, Brown Young Readers]

> You're past the age when people get these horrible diseases; you're one of the few lucky ones who're going to die a really natural death. That is, of course, if you die at all. You're such a remarkable old boy that one never knows.

THE GOOD SHEPHERD

written by C.S. Forester

An exciting sea adventure and World War II thriller. Commander George Krause of the U.S. Navy is captain of a destroyer, in charge of thirty-seven ships and three thousand men. He must guide his convoy across the freezing North Atlantic through a maze of deadly Nazi U-boats waiting their chance beneath the cold waters to blow the convoy apart. As George Krause faces one crisis after another, makes instant decisions, and issues commands, passages of Scripture pass through his head and give him guidance and support. This man of faith is a brilliant commander who, every minute of his three-day ordeal, looks steadily at the face of death. [Simon Publications]

THE GOVERNOR OF ENGLAND:
A NOVEL ON OLIVER CROMWELL

written by Marjorie Bowen

This is a fictionalized biography about a Puritan of strong convictions, a military genius, and a devout Christian who ruled England as Lord Protector during one of the most turbulent periods of her history. It describes the tyrannical reign of Charles I whose unwavering belief in the Divine Right of kings eventually resulted in his death in 1649. Unlike many other historical accounts, however, you really come to know the characters—the king's indecisiveness and his love for his catholic wife, his close friends' loyalty, and Cromwell's uncompromising faith. The description of Charles's execution is heartbreaking. [Inheritance Publications]

THE GREAT DIVORCE

written by C.S. Lewis

The imaginative concept behind this intriguing book is a bus ride several souls make when they have been temporarily released from a very dreary hell to visit a very beautiful heaven. The folks released from hell are a touchy, quarrelsome lot who cling tenaciously to their own pet peeves. When they get to heaven, they do nothing but complain: "I don't like it. It gives me the pip!" and "What's the sense of allowing all that riff-raff to float about here all day? Look at them. They're not enjoying it. They'd be far happier at home. . . . It's rather unpleasant on one's first day to have the whole place crowded out with trippers." Lewis is not attempting to make a theological statement about the afterlife, but rather to show us the chilling effects of holding stubbornly to our sinful nature. The appalling alternative to repentance and eternal life in God's heaven is a bus ride back to hell. [HarperOne]

> What they call Hell? Yes. It's a flop too. They lead you to expect red fire and devils and all sorts of interesting people sizzling on grids.

GREAT EXPECTATIONS
written by Charles Dickens
One of the most popular of Dickens's novels, *Great Expectations* opens in a churchyard near some lonely marshes where a young boy is visiting his parents' grave. Suddenly, a wretched-looking convict starts up from the graves, grabs the boy by the throat, and threatens to cut out his heart and liver unless he returns with a file and some "wittles." This is a fearful errand for Pip since he lives with his shrewish sister, who brings him up "by hand" with the frequent application of "Tickler," as well as his faithful friend, dear old Joe. Through an extraordinary set of circumstances, Pip finds that he is a young man of great expectations and soon becomes an insufferable snob. This book is crammed with mystery and suspense. [Bantam Classics]

GREAT GHOST STORIES
edited by John Grafton
Here are ten bone-chilling ghost stories written by the finest practitioners of the genre including Bram Stoker, J. Sheridan LeFanu, and Charles Dickens. Each tale involves some macabre goings-on. Just be sure not to read them when you're alone on a dark and stormy night. [Dover]

> Although the corner in which he sat was so dim that I could distinguish none of his features very clearly, I saw that his eyes were still turned full upon me. And yet he answered never a word.

GREENMANTLE
written by John Buchan

The second Richard Hannay World War I adventure. Hannay is sent on a dangerous mission for the British foreign office. Disguised as a Dutchman, Hannay travels right into the heart of enemy territory and has the audacity to pretend to the Germans that he is on their side. Soon, however, the Germans are pursuing him, so Hannay's friends arrange for the Dutchman's "death," and Hannay dons another disguise. With only three mysterious clues, Hannay and company must complete their mission against impossible odds. [Oxford University Press]

THE GUNS OF NAVARONE
written by Alistair MacLean

During World War II, the Germans build a heavily defended fortress off the coast of Turkey on an island called Navarone. Keith Mallory, a famous mountaineer, and four other men must dismantle this fortress and silence the guns that guard the harbor of Navarone. Their goal is to release 1,200 Allied soldiers from imprisonment on the besieged island. Mallory's rock-climbing skills are crucial since they must approach the island via a four-hundred-foot-high sheer precipice. As the team of handpicked men attempt to scale the rock wall, one of them is badly injured and becomes an intolerable burden to the others. Meanwhile, the men find a traitor in their midst. [HarperCollins]

You will also enjoy MacLean's *Fear Is the Key* [Fontanta Press] and *Ice Station Zebra*. [HarperCollins]

HEART OF DARKNESS
written by Joseph Conrad

The theme that Conrad explores in this novel is the evil that lurks in the heart of man. Charlie Marlow, an ivory trader, tells a group of fellow sailors the strange tale of his journey into the heart of Africa. As Marlow's steamer crawls sluggishly up the Congo River, he witnesses appalling sights—corrupt white traders, emaciated black laborers dying

> His was an impenetrable darkness. I looked at him as you might peer down at a man who is lying at the bottom of a precipice where the sun never shines.

of disease and starvation, and dried heads on stakes. But it isn't until Marlow meets the company manager, a mysterious and savage man named Kurtz, that he is brought face-to-face with the vilest human depravity. And only then does Marlow come to understand the darkness of his own soul. [Oxford University Press]

THE HOUND OF THE BASKERVILLES
written by Sir Arthur Conan Doyle

When Sir Charles Baskerville mysteriously dies on the grounds of Baskerville Hall, apparently killed by an enormous black hound, Holmes agrees to investigate the case. The mysterious hound continues to terrify the rest of the family, especially the current heir, Sir Henry Baskerville. On Holmes's behalf, Dr. Watson travels to Baskerville Hall in Devonshire to become entangled in a series of further mysteries, including a lonely figure that is seen keeping watch over the surrounding moors. Soon Holmes and Watson are hot on the trail of the prime suspect! [Modern Library]

HOWARD'S END
written by E.M. Forster

Helen Schlegel's sudden engagement to Paul Wilcox is the beginning of the Schlegel family's persistent connection with the Wilcoxes. Helen and her sister, Margaret, had met the Wilcoxes while traveling abroad, and ever after, their lives have been intertwined with the Wilcox family and their delightful home in the county, Howard's End. The Schlegels' heritage is German, and although Margaret, Helen, and their placid brother, Tibby, grew up in England, they don't seem to fit in with the staid British culture around them. Margaret and Helen are idealistic girls, enthusiastic for new causes.

What's an engagement made of, do you suppose? I think it's made of some hard stuff that may snap but can't break. It is different to the other ties of life.

One of these causes is Mr. Bast, an unsuccessful clerk who appreciates poetry. The girls attempt to lift him out of his drab life by cultivating his artistic interests and finding him a new job. Unfortunately, their well-intentioned efforts create tragedy for everyone involved—Basts,

Schlegels, and Wilcoxes alike—and the only place of lasting peace is Howard's End. [Modern Library]

HOW THEY KEPT THE FAITH
written by Grace Raymond
A mother gives up her beloved baby girl in order to save her; a man surrenders his career and his fiancée, and thousands sacrifice their homes, their families, and their lives for the cause of Christ. As the Catholic authorities increase their persecution of the Protestant Huguenots in France, the Huguenots uphold the doctrines of their faith. They refuse to bow to crucifixes and statues of saints, and for this they suffer untold sorrow and pain. Many are forced into slave labor, others waste away in dungeons, and still others are sent to convents and monasteries. Even beautiful Mademoiselle Eglantine, dashing Captain LaRoche, and the good doctor René Chevalier are caught up in the traumatic conflict. [Inheritance Publications]

> If your sister has succeeded in reaching you, which I can scarcely believe, hide her in the depths of the earth, and watch your opportunity to escape across the border. It is your only hope.

I CAPTURE THE CASTLE
written by Dodie Smith
"I write this sitting in the kitchen sink. That is, my feet are in it; the rest of me is on the draining-board, which I have padded with our dog's blanket and the tea-cosy." From this first sentence, Cassandra Mortmain draws you into her story. She lives with her very poor and very odd family in a six-hundred-year-old English castle. There's her pretty sister, Rose, her stepmother, who used to be an artist's model, her younger brother, a servant who's secretly in love with Cassandra, and her father, a well-known writer who, inexplicably, has stopped writing and who was wrongly sent to prison for supposedly attacking their mother with a kitchen knife. Into this unusual family stride two young American men, and life for Cassandra will never be the same again. [St. Martin's Griffin]

Note: Although this is a charming book, you should be aware of occasional flippant references to God and prayer.

JANE EYRE
written by Charlotte Brontë
Brontë's largely autobiographical novel is one of the world's great love stories. Jane, an impoverished orphan, spends her loveless childhood in the home of a hateful aunt. Her school days are punctuated with grief (the death of a close friend) and hardship (the cruel punishments meted out by a hypocritical superintendent). As an adult, Jane falls in love with her employer who is tormented by a terrible secret about his past. She is compelled to leave him but can never forget the mysterious Mr. Rochester. In addition to its romantic plot, this suspenseful novel includes madness, attempted murder, and all the trappings of the true gothic tale. [Penguin Classics]

> Wicked and cruel boy!" I said. "You are like a murderer—you are like a slave-driver—you are like the Roman emperors!"

KING SOLOMON'S MINES
written by H. Rider Haggard
In the late nineteenth century, three Englishmen make a harrowing trek across Africa to find the legendary treasure of King Solomon. After nearly dying of thirst in the desert and freezing to death in the mountains, the three friends face almost certain death during a monumental civil war during which thousands of Africans die. When they finally reach the treasure, they are buried alive deep in the diamond mines without hope of rescue. A first-rate adventure story. [Barnes & Noble Classics]

A LANTERN IN HER HAND
written by Bess Streeter Aldrich
Abbie, a pioneer girl, dreams of doing great things. She plans to "sing before vast audiences and paint lovely pictures in frames and write things in a book," but she does not foresee the life of hardship that lies ahead. Abbie and her husband, Will Deal, travel west across the endless prairie which never ceases to wave in ripples under the hot sun. They come to live in a tiny sod house in Nebraska. Together, Abbie and Will raise five children, and together they tame the wild prairie. Throughout those

struggling years, Abbie suffers much hardship, but she makes light of her trials and remains strong for her children. The eighty years of love she gives to her family is like "a lantern in her hand." [Puffin]

LEAVE IT TO PSMITH
written by P.G. Wodehouse

Miss Peavey was the sort of woman who tells a man who is propping his eyes open with his fingers and endeavoring to correct a headache with strong tea, that she was up at six watching the dew fade off the grass.

Psmith (pronounced "Smith"—"the *p* is silent, as in phthisis, psychic, and ptarmigan") is a debonair young Englishman who has recently quit the fish business because the trade sickens his soul. As a result, he quickly ends up cold stony broke. His solution is to hire himself out to do anything for anyone: "Psmith will do it, crime not objected to!" With his air of sophistication, sharp mind, and irrepressible gift of the gab, Psmith is ready for any job that comes along (unless it has to do with fish). The fantastic adventures that follow include a cast of unforgettable characters, such as doddering Lord Emsworth, formidable Lady Constance, ethereal Miss Peavy, and dim-witted Freddie Threepwood. *Leave It to Psmith* is a marvelously funny read. [Overlook Press]

LES MISÉRABLES
written by Victor Hugo, translated by Charles E. Wilbour, abridged by James K. Robinson

A moment afterwards, a tall and black form, which from the distance some belated passer-by might have taken for a phantom, appeared standing on the parapet, bent towards the Seine, then sprang up, and fell straight into the darkness.

Jean Valjean is a social outcast, an ex-convict imprisoned for nineteen years for attempting to steal bread for his sister and her starving children. A saintly bishop takes pity on Valjean and inspires him to live a life of integrity. Valjean spends the rest of his days helping others and saving lives, while he is constantly pursued by a ruthless police inspector who believes he is a dangerous criminal. Always on the run, Valjean rescues and raises up a motherless child, Cosette. Despite Valjean's dedication to sacrifice for the sake of others, he seems destined to meet constant rejection and persecution. [Ballantine Publishing]

Note: This abridged version cuts out the book's digressions and philosophical sections, so that what remains for you to enjoy is the story itself.

LITTLE BRITCHES
written by Ralph Moody
This is the first of eight novels based on the author's early years. When Ralph is eight years old, his family moves to Colorado to live at a run-down ranch. While Mr. Moody struggles to make a living at ranching, the family endures hardship as well as tornados and dust storms. During one dust storm, Ralph remembers his father tying everyone together with rope and ordering them to crawl on their stomachs away from the ranch while their barn and wagon hurtle through the air above them. Ralph's father is decent and honest and just about the smartest man around. He passes on to his son principles of honor and duty during long talks over the milk pails and occasionally with some sound thrashings. Ralph's school of hard knocks matures him into one sharp cowboy and, over time, a responsible rancher like his father. [Bison Books]

Note: The Lord's name is taken in vain several times in this book, mainly by a friend who is otherwise a good neighbor. Other than this flaw, however, this series of books is excellent, enriching reading.

LORD JIM
written by Joseph Conrad
A great adventure story full of suspense. A young naval officer commits an act of cowardice and is stripped of his rank. For years, he is haunted by guilt but eventually finds fulfillment as ruler of a remote Malay village. His problems, however, are far from over, and he faces the greatest challenge of his life in the form of an unscrupulous pirate named Gentleman Brown and his crew of cutthroats. [Bantam Classics]

> There was a buzz. One of the small boys, Henry, said that he wanted to go home. "Shut up," said Ralph absently. . . . "Seems to me we ought to have a chief to decide things."

LORD OF THE FLIES

written by William Golding

This novel was inspired by an earlier survival story, R.M. Ballantyne's *Coral Island,* but Golding's book is a disturbing variation on the traditional castaway theme. To this group of English schoolboys, the unpopulated island onto which their plane has crashed appears at first to be a paradise—non-stop fun with no grown-ups. But the boys quickly degenerate into ruthless savagery. Their adventures convey an important truth about what happens to people with no authority figures in control. In fact, the book is a thought-provoking exploration of human depravity. However, Golding does not include in his study of human nature any discussion of sin, repentance, or redemption. Thus, this is a novel for mature readers. [Penguin]

MAMA'S BANK ACCOUNT

written by Kathryn Forbes

This mother of a Norwegian immigrant family is resourceful. Every week, she takes Papa's wages and sorts the money into piles to pay for things the family needs. When she's finished her accounting, Mama announces that they don't need more money from the bank downtown, and everyone heaves a sigh of relief. Years later, Kathryn realizes that they never owned a bank account. Mama just doesn't want her children to worry. There is no problem that Mama can't fix. When Papa gets sick and needs an expensive operation, Mama cleverly outwits the greedy doctor's wife, and Papa has his operation. On another occasion, Christine is in labor and decides she's going to die. Mama calmly sits down by her bedside and eats her daughter's lunch. "You are just like me," Mama declares. "I could never eat either." Soon afterwards, Christine delivers a healthy baby. Her family will always remember Mama. [Harvest Books]

MAN OF THE FAMILY

written by Ralph Moody

This is the sequel to Ralph Moody's first book, *Little Britches.* Ralph's father has recently died, and at age eleven Ralph becomes head of the household. With his new responsibilities, Ralph doesn't think he should keep going to school, but no one wins an argument with his mother. Ralph and his sister set to work earning money for the family. They trudge around town delivering food their mother bakes; Ralph picks up coal along several miles of railway tracks and helps drive the drovers' cattle through town. Despite hard lessons learned, this family shares wonderful times together. Their mother is a rock. She holds them all together and trusts in the Lord to protect and provide for them. Two other titles in the series are *The Fields of Home* and *The Home Ranch*. [Bison Books]

THE MASTER'S QUILT
written by Michael Webb
Deucalion Cincinnatus Quintus, Pilate's Commander of the Roman Garrison, is the soldier who pierces Jesus' side at the crucifixion. It is Deucalion who visits the empty tomb and knows the truth about the Resurrection, but to acknowledge this truth means certain death for a Roman soldier. An added danger for Deucalion is his love for Esther, a beautiful Jewess and a believer. Deucalion, Esther, and other followers of Jesus face almost certain death at the hands of Saul of Tarsus, their brutal persecutor. The story comes to a head when Pilate, who loves Deucalion as his own son, must give the order to kill him. [Morningstar Publications]

MEG ROPER
written by Jean Plaidy
Sir Thomas More has three daughters: Alice, who wants to marry into high society (and does), Mercy, who tends to sick and starving London paupers, and Meg, More's favorite daughter, who marries Will Roper. Will is More's protégé, a law student who disagrees with More over the "heretical" writings of Martin Luther. While Luther's books are publicly burned, Roper adopts the German monk's convictions and is imprisoned. Meanwhile, More rises in the king's favor to achieve the powerful position of Henry's Lord

> We all have to die at some time, and I would not barter my honor for a few more years.

Chancellor. But when every Englishman must sign the Oath of Supremacy making Henry head of the English church, More cannot sign the document. [Roy Publishers]

Robert Bolt's play about Sir Thomas More, *A Man for All Seasons*, is superb. [Vintage]

MISS BISHOP
written by Bess Streeter Aldrich
Ella Bishop is a friendly, energetic, happy young woman. She works hard at college and becomes a dedicated teacher. But she must face one disappointment in life after another: her pretty cousin marries the man she loves, and after her cousin's death, circumstances dictate that she must raise the child of the man she had hoped to marry. Later on, Ella falls unhappily in love again. You will love Ella Bishop, and you will admire the way she deals with heartbreaking events in her life. [Bison Books]

MY ÁNTONIA
written by Willa Cather
Ántonia Shimerda's family moves from Bohemia to settle in a pioneer town in Nebraska. But Mr. Shimerda, homesick and miserable, cannot make a living and takes his own life. Despite her grief, Ántonia is strong and continues to work hard. She finds a faithful friend in Jim Burden, who lives on a neighboring farm. Jim and Ántonia grow up together on the Nebraska prairie, along with the rattlesnakes and wolves and brown earth-owls that fly home to their nests under the ground. Slowly Jim comes to love Ántonia, but they are parted for many years. During these long, hard years, they cherish memories of the happy childhood they shared on the prairie. [Mariner Books]

1984
written by George Orwell
This great modern anti-utopian novel is Orwell's nightmare vision of what could happen to the human race. The world Orwell envisages is one in which all man's actions, even his thoughts, are controlled by a totalitarian state. Two lovers attempt to evade the control of Big Brother with horrifying results. Orwell's book expresses the mood of hopelessness so prevalent in a world that rejects God. His predictions contrast

with the Christian faith in a sovereign God, but this is an important book that deepens our understanding of totalitarian government. For mature readers. [Plume]

THE OLD MAN AND THE SEA
written by Ernest Hemingway
A fast-paced, short adventure story about the struggle between an old Cuban fisherman and the fish he finally spears after eighty days of fishing without a catch. The giant fish is larger than any other fish ever caught in the waters off Havana. [Scribner]

> "Fish," he said softly aloud, "I'll stay with you until I am dead."

OLIVER TWIST
written by Charles Dickens
Oliver Twist, an orphan, creates a scandal in the poorhouse when, as spokesman for the other starving children, he asks for more food. Oliver is confined by the authorities and hastily sold as an apprentice to an undertaker. He has to sleep in the room that contains the coffins and the corpses. From then on, his fortunes decline even further until he is drawn into a gang of pick-pockets supervised by a master criminal, Fagin. Fagin coaches the homeless boys—the Artful Dodger and the rest—in the finer points of theft. In Fagin's den, Oliver "passes his time in the improving society of his reputable friends" until a miraculous event changes his life forever. [Signet Classic]

> "Please, sir, I want some more." . . . The master aimed a blow at Oliver's head with the ladle, pinioned him in his arms, and shrieked aloud for the beadle.

PEARL MAIDEN
written by H. Rider Haggard
This is the story of Miriam, a young Christian woman living in the Roman Empire during the first century A.D. and the two men who seek to

win her hand in marriage: Marcus, a kind-hearted Roman officer and Caleb, a bitter man whom she has known since her youth. The story is set in the context of the persecution of the early Church, and events culminate in the fall of Jerusalem in A.D. 70. Miriam is a devout Christian, but her faith is tested by fiery trials and deep conflicts of the heart. [Christian Liberty Press]

You may also enjoy another fine historical novel by H. Rider Haggard, *Lysbeth: A Tale of the Dutch*. [BiblioBazaar]

PRIDE AND PREJUDICE
written by Jane Austen
One of the most popular of Austen's books, this novel portrays two self-willed protagonists, proud Mr. Darcy and prejudiced Elizabeth Bennet, whose courtship is hampered by their persistent misunderstanding of each other's actions and personalities. In this novel, Austen examines the strengths and weaknesses of human beings against a background of refined eighteenth-century society. The book is filled with unforgettable characters: foolish Mrs. Bennet who is preoccupied with marrying off her five daughters, a formidable dowager aunt who dominates everyone except Elizabeth, and a ridiculously conceited clergyman who rehearses his speeches to young ladies before making them. The book contains a lively plot, much dry humor, and great insights into the genteel English society of Austen's day. [Bantam Classics]

THE PRISONER OF ZENDA
written by Anthony Hope
This romance is also a swashbuckling adventure story set in the nineteenth century. A carefree vacationer, Rudolf Rassendyll, arrives in Zenda, Ruritania, and meets his cousin Rudolf who will soon be crowned king and is his identical double. When the King is kidnapped by the villainous Black Michael, Rassendyll impersonates his cousin at the coronation and falls in love with Princess Flavia.

> He put spurs to his horse, and I, turning to look, saw him ride, full gallop, to the edge of the moat and leap in.

Meanwhile, the King is imprisoned in the Castle of Zenda, Black Michael pursues his evil schemes to become king, and the people demand that Rassendyll marry Princess Flavia. Although Rassendyll loves her, he knows it would be dishonorable to deceive the Princess and betray the king. In the end, the lovers must decide between love and honor. [Penguin Classic]

QUO VADIS
written by Henryk Sienkiewicz
Set in Rome during the era of the early church, this is a great love story. Vinicius, a Roman patrician, falls in love with Lygia, a beautiful foreign princess. Lygia is a devout Christian, and eventually Vinicius also becomes a believer and goes to live with other Christians in the catacombs, hiding from the debauched emperor Nero and the atrocities of the arena. There Vinicius listens to the sermons of Simon Peter and Paul of Tarsus. Rome burns, and the Christians are blamed and endure horrible persecution. Many are fed to starving lions; others are burned alive. One of the book's most dramatic moments occurs when Lygia is tied to Saul's back and a bull is sent into the arena. This is a magnificent portrayal of pagan Rome and the faith of the early Christians. The length of the book might deter some readers, but it is an inspiring historical novel. [Norilana Books]

> I am he who during the stoning of Stephen kept the garments of those who stoned him; I am he who wished to root out the truth in every part of the inhabited earth; and yet the Lord predestined me to declare it in every land.

REBECCA
written by Daphne du Maurier
When the wealthy widower Max de Winter remarries, his new bride soon realizes that something is very wrong about her situation as mistress of Manderley. The new Mrs. de Winter is timid and nervous, not a grand lady like Rebecca, the late mistress of Manderley. This is the opinion of Mrs. Danvers, Manderley's housekeeper and Rebecca's devoted servant. In fact, the sinister Mrs. Danvers rapidly becomes the

new bride's relentless enemy. An atmosphere of evil pervades the estate as a horrifying mystery about Rebecca unfolds. [Harper Paperbacks]

THE RED BADGE OF COURAGE
written by Stephen Crane
One of the best war stories ever written. Henry Fleming rushes to enlist on the Union side during the Civil War, expecting to fight like a hero. At the critical moment, however, he acts like a coward and flees from the enemy. Crane gives us an intense look into war from the inside as he powerfully probes the emotions and thoughts of a raw recruit. [Modern Library]

THE REMAINS OF THE DAY
written by Kazuo Ishiguro
Mr. Stevens is head butler of Darlington Hall, the grand home of one of England's most revered and influential men, Lord Darlington. Stevens records years of memories and all the events of his service, which are set in the post-World War II era. These events include critical meetings of powerful officials and foreign dignitaries. Stevens is keenly aware that any flaw in the housing or dinner arrangements could upset these leaders' negotiations for world peace. Throughout his entire life, Stevens is consumed with one passion: professionalism. His rigid control over his emotions affects his relationships with everyone, including Miss Kenton, Darlington Hall's housekeeper. Could Stevens' friendship with Miss Kenton ever develop into anything more than professional regard? [Vintage]

> **D**emetrius slowly bowed his head and handed Marcellus the Robe. . . . "Take that out into the courtyard," he muttered hoarsely, "and burn it!"

THE ROBE
written by Lloyd C. Douglas
Marcellus Lucan Gallio is one of the Roman soldiers in charge of the crucifixion of Christ. His legionaries put Jesus to death while he sits at the foot of the Cross casting lots for Christ's garment with the other drunken soldiers. After Marcellus wins the Robe, he is never the same again. Devastated by guilt and remorse, he contemplates suicide. He

leaves his noble family and the woman he loves and, with a devoted slave, travels to Greece. But wherever he goes, he hears about Jesus—His disciples, His love, His miracles. The miracle of Lydia healed by merely touching Jesus' garment is especially moving to Marcellus, and after witnessing the brutal stoning of Stephen, he becomes a believer. Eventually, Marcellus gives up everything he has to follow Jesus. [Mariner Books]

A ROOM WITH A VIEW
written by E.M. Forster

Traveling in Florence with her chaperone and cousin Charlotte, Lucy Honeychurch meets George Emerson, who promptly falls in love with her. When Lucy witnesses a violent street murder and is later embraced by the impulsive George, Charlotte

> Though life is very glorious, it is difficult. . . . Life, wrote a friend of mine, is a public performance on the violin, in which you must learn the instrument as you go along.

hastily removes her from Italy's "unhealthy" environment. Back in England, Lucy becomes engaged to a priggish snob, but she gradually begins to question her choice. Against a background of tennis and tea parties, Lucy wrestles with her emotions to know her own heart. [Bantam Classics]

THE SCARLET LETTER
written by Nathaniel Hawthorne

This novel explores the effect of sin on the lives of three New England Puritans. Hester Prynne has committed adultery and is condemned to wear a scarlet letter "A" and be publicly disgraced; Roger Chillingworth is Hester's revengeful and jealous hus-

> That old man's revenge has been blacker than my sin. He has violated, in cold blood, the sanctity of a human heart.

band determined to discover her lover; and Arthur Dimmesdale is the community's beloved pastor who is torn apart by a guilty secret. You may prefer to ignore the introduction, entitled "The Custom House," which does not affect the plot, and begin this novel at chapter 1, "The Prison Door." [Oxford University Press]

> **I**f people knew how much ill-feeling Unselfishness occasions, it would not be so often recommended from the pulpit.

THE SCREWTAPE LETTERS
written by C.S. Lewis

This book is a one-way correspondence from a retired devil to a junior devil just learning his trade. The master devil, Screwtape, advises his nephew Wormwood on the art of devilry and in so doing alerts the reader to many of the subtle tricks and temptations that Satan ceaselessly uses against Christians. Lewis's approach to this serious topic is insightful and hilarious. [HarperOne]

SENSE AND SENSIBILITY
written by Jane Austen

Elinor and Marianne Dashwood are two sisters with very different personalities. Elinor is a sensible young woman, while Marianne is sensitive and emotional. Since the death of their father, the two girls, their mother, and younger sister must survive on a meager income, and they are forced to move to a small cottage in the country. Both girls fall in love with eligible bachelors, but both of them experience heartbreak. Marianne is so wretched that her health breaks down, and she hovers near death, while sensible Elinor quietly endures her disappointment. You will also enjoy Jane Austen's other novels: *Mansfield Park, Northanger Abbey,* and *Persuasion.* [Penguin Classics]

A SEPARATE PEACE
written by John Knowles

A novel about growing up. More specifically, it is about the friendship between two sixteen-year-old boys at a New England boarding school during World War II. One of the boys, Gene, is an excellent student who studies hard and obeys the rules. The other, Phineas, is a superb athlete and a rebel. Gene fights a war within his own mind: Should he continue to live by the book, or should he adopt the rebellious lifestyle of his friend? What happens between the boys that summer brings the conflict to a tragic climax and changes their lives forever. [Scribner]

SHANE

written by Jack Schaefer

"Call me Shane," he says, as he walks into the lives of the Starretts, a homesteading family. Shane is a mysterious and dangerous stranger, although he soon proves to be invaluable to the family as their farmhand and their friend. But trouble is brewing for the Starretts. A mean rancher named Fletcher wants to buy up all the land thereabouts, including their land. And Fletcher has a way of forcing men's hands. He provokes them to a fight, then shoots them dead. When Fletcher faces a showdown with Joe Starrett, Shane steps between them, and he is carrying a gun. This is one tough western you won't want to miss. [Laurel Leaf]

SILAS MARNER

written by George Eliot

Silas Marner, a linen weaver who lives in England during the early years of the nineteenth century, is wrongly accused of theft. Heartbroken by a friend's treachery, Silas leaves his home in disgrace to become a wretched recluse with nothing to live for but the gold he accumulates as payment for his weaving. When an orphaned child mysteriously finds her way into Silas's cottage, his love of money is transferred to love for the golden-haired child. This story, part fairy tale and part realistic fiction, is a gripping story of guilt, betrayal, and love. [Penguin Classic]

> He himself was unaware that there was something more than the bush before him—that there was a human body with the head sunk low in the furze and half covered with the shaken snow.

THE SILVER CHALICE

written by Thomas Costain

This novel is set in the period following Christ's death and resurrection and is woven around the lives of men like Peter, Paul, Luke, and Joseph of Arimathea. It tells the story of a young man named Basil who is sold into slavery and commissioned to design a vessel worthy of holding the cup from which Jesus drank at the Last Supper. Basil must design the vessel by engraving upon it the likenesses of Christ's disciples. As he seeks out these men, he encounters many dangers. This great Christian novel is full of action and suspense. [Buccaneer Books]

SINK THE BISMARCK!
written by C.S. Forester
At a point in time during World War II, England stands all alone surrounded by her enemies. The Nazi conquest of Europe seems certain. Now Germany plans a massive attack against British shipping in order to end the war. The *Bismarck* is the largest, deadliest battleship ever built, and it is this foe that engages the Royal Navy in the Atlantic. Suddenly, Britain's largest battle cruiser, the *Hood*, is hit by a shell that crashes through her decks and bulkheads to explode among 300 tons of high explosives. Two thousand British sailors die in an instant. Now the *Bismarck* plows relentlessly on towards the other British ships. Churchill's order is legendary: "Sink the *Bismarck!*" [Bantam]

SIR GAWAIN AND THE GREEN KNIGHT
translated by J.R.R. Tolkien
This is Tolkien's accurate and lively translation of a medieval English poem written by an unknown Christian poet. The story recounts a bizarre incident that takes place at King Arthur's court when a knight dressed all in green with rolling red eyes challenges Sir Gawain to a duel. When Arthur's brave knight beheads his opponent, the Green Knight nonchalantly retrieves his head, tucks it under his arm, and gallops off. And that is only the beginning of this fantastic tale. [Del Rey]
    You may also enjoy *The Sword in the Stone* by T.H. White. *See Middle School Fiction.*

THE SOLDIER OF VIRGINIA
written by Marjorie Bowen
This is a fictionalized but accurate portrayal of George Washington during the Revolutionary War. The book describes Washington's courtship of his beautiful Martha, his defeats, and his legendary courage as he faces enormous odds before winning America's war for independence. Another fascinating section of the book deals with his close friendship with Benedict Arnold. Arnold is a fine soldier but suffers many disappointments and is eventually convinced that his country has treated him unjustly. He turns traitor, an action that leaves Washington devastated. This historical novel is a page turner. [Inheritance Publications]

A TALE OF TWO CITIES
written by Charles Dickens

Set in London and Paris during the bloody days of the French Revolution, this is an exciting historical novel. Dr. Manette, long-time prisoner in the Bastille, is restored to his daughter Lucie. A complication arises when Lucie's husband, a French aristocrat named Charles Darnay, is tried for treason against the French government. Darnay is acquitted and flees from France, but he returns to free a servant and is condemned to death. Lucie also inspires the love of another man, a dissipated lawyer named Sydney Carton, who finds meaning for his life in his love for Lucie while seeking to avert Darnay's tragic death. [Bantam Classics]

> The plaintive tone of her compassion merged into the less musical voice of the Judge, as he said something fiercely: "Answer the questions put to you, and make no remark upon them."

TALES OF MYSTERY AND IMAGINATION
written by Edgar Allan Poe

This collection of macabre short stories includes Poe's classic tales of horror and suspense. Stories such as "The Tell-Tale Heart," "The Black Cat," "The Fall of the House of Usher," and "The Pit and the Pendulum" reflect Poe's genius as the unsurpassed creator of horror fiction. [NTC Publishing]

THE THIRTY-NINE STEPS
written by John Buchan

An exciting spy thriller. The excitement of the first of Richard Hannay's adventures begins when Hannay finds a stranger lurking in his apartment. The stranger tells Hannay about an international plot, and, days later, he is found stabbed to death in Hannay's lodgings. Hannay is wrongly targeted as the murderer and escapes from London with the whole British police force, plus some dangerous thugs, at his heels. Hannay must avert the start of a war between England and Germany, and he has three weeks and a day to complete this vital mission. Meanwhile, he must escape the clutches of an evil group known as The Black Stone. [Penguin Classics]

THREE BLIND MICE AND OTHER STORIES
written by Agatha Christie
The short story entitled "Three Blind Mice" contains the plot of the longest running play in British theater, *The Mousetrap,* which has been playing in London continuously since 1952. In this story, a young couple starts a guest house, but one of their first guests is a murderer. Having killed once, this ruthless killer is ready to pounce on his next victim, then the next. The other mysteries in this collection are just as spell-binding. Agatha Christie has written dozens of murder mysteries and is the most popular mystery writer of all time. [Berkley Books]

THE THREE HOSTAGES
written by John Buchan
The fourth of the Hannay thrillers. World War I is over, and Hannay lives peacefully in England with his wife and son. He hears about an international plot and the kidnapping of three young people. His attempts to solve the crime and save the victims involve Hannay in some spine-chilling adventures that include a sinister hypnotist. Hannay must place himself in his enemy's hands and pretend to be in his power, knowing that the lives of three innocent people depend upon his retaining full control of his mental faculties. Like all Buchan's spy novels, this is "a rattling good yarn." Also in this series: *Mr. Standfast* and *The Island of Lost Sheep.* [NTC Publishing]

> Suddenly the rope scorched my fingers and a shock came on my middle which dragged me to the very edge of the abyss.

TILL WE HAVE FACES: A MYTH RETOLD
written by C.S. Lewis
A retelling of the myth of Cupid and Psyche told from the perspective of Psyche's ugly but loving sister Orual. Psyche is so beautiful and good that she is offered as a sacrifice to the Brute in order to appease the gods. She becomes the Bride of the Brute (no one knows if he is monster, god, or villain), and Orual tells her sister what she must do to save herself

from her terrible fate. But the suffering for Orual and Psyche has only just begun. [Harvest Books]

  Note: Lewis's wonderful space trilogy—Out of the Silent Planet, Perelandra, *and* That Hideous Strength—*is reviewed in Middle School Fiction.*

TO KILL A MOCKINGBIRD
written by Harper Lee
This is the moving childhood memory of a spunky little girl named Scout. It is also a novel about bigotry and hate in an old Southern town. When Scout's father, Atticus Finch, decides to defend an innocent black man against a false criminal charge, he does so at enormous cost to his family. As a result of their experiences, Scout and her brother Jem learn a great deal about prejudice and malice on the one hand and wisdom and compassion on the other. [Harper Perennial]

UNNATURAL DEATH
written by Dorothy Sayers
Lord Peter Wimsey, an elegant and aristocratic sleuth, hears about the death of a rich, bedridden old lady and, although the verdict of natural death is rendered and there appears to be no motive or opportunity, Lord Peter is certain that murder most foul has been committed. He sets out on a very dangerous path to discover the murderer, but not before his prey commits several other murders. Dorothy Sayers's other intriguing mysteries include *Strong Poison, The Documents in the Case,* and *Have His Carcase.* [HarperCollins]

  Note: We warn readers that the characters' dialogue is occasionally blasphemous. The profanities in this intriguing novel are unfortunately typical of the speech of its worldly cast.

UP A ROAD SLOWLY
written by Irene Hunt
This is a story that will make girls laugh and cry. Julie's mom dies when she is young, and she is brought up by a stern, unmarried aunt. Growing up is a painful business for Julie. She suffers the pain of her father's remarriage, a schoolmate's tragic death, and the agony of first love. And when her sister Laura gets married, Julie realizes that she is no

longer the center of Laura's attention. But Julie learns a lot of important lessons; above all, she learns that, in order to be happy, you must first concentrate on the happiness of those around you. [Berkley]

VERY GOOD, JEEVES!
written by P.G. Wodehouse
This is another of the many amusing novels about idiotic Bertie Wooster and his incomparable manservant, Jeeves. When Bertie is not passing an idle hour at the Drones Club, he is being summoned by one of his demanding aunts to rescue a member of the "fam" from a scrape. After Bertie unfailingly devises an elaborate, imbecilic scheme that fails, Jeeves shimmers in at the eleventh hour with a brilliant, unbeatable plan. On one occasion, Bertie is called upon to aid an old school chum, Bingo Little. The driving force of their plan is to rescue a marooned judge, "a tubby little chap who looked as if he had been poured into his clothes and forgotten to say 'when!'" Bertie manages to totally bungle the assignment, and Jeeves must insinuate himself into the situation and once again save Bertie's skin. [Overlook Press]

A WHITE BIRD FLYING
written by Bess Streeter Aldrich
The sequel to *A Lantern in Her Hand*. Abbie Deal's granddaughter, Laura, longs to carry out her grandmother's dream of becoming famous, so she determines to pursue a writing career. "If love comes by," she vows to herself, "I shall spurn it." Love does come by in the form of Allen Rinemiller, grandson of her grandmother's neighbors. Laura and Allen's friendship grows, but Laura's mind is fixed upon her goal. Meanwhile, life constantly gets in the way of her dream—sorority life at the University of Nebraska, visits to her cousin Katharine, trips with rich Uncle Harry Wentworth who lures her with money and fame, and warm and wonderful family reunions. And what about Allen? Well, Laura soon understands the wisdom of her old neighbor, Oscar Lutz, who once chuckles to himself, "He was warned agin' the woman; she was warned agin' the man. And if that don't make a wedding, why there's nothing else that can." [University of Nebraska Press]

WUTHERING HEIGHTS

written by Emily Brontë

Set against the rugged Yorkshire moors, this romance explores the stormy relationship of strong-willed Catherine Earnshaw and Heathcliff, a ragged urchin adopted by Catherine's father. Their tempestuous love is destined to end in grief, but happiness is eventually achieved by the next generation, the children of Catherine and Heathcliff. A complex but moving novel for mature readers. [Bantam Classics]

You teach me now how cruel you've been—cruel and false. Why did you despise me? Why did you betray your own heart, Cathy?

ILLUSTRATIONS
Patrick Henry, Firebrand of the Revolution, illustrated by Victor Mays
(Boston: Little, Brown & Co., 1961), see page 224.

6
HIGH SCHOOL
BIOGRAPHY

CHRISTIAN MARTYRS
FOXE'S BOOK OF MARTYRS
written by John Foxe, edited by W. Grinton Berry
Foxe's Book of Martyrs did more to spread Protestantism throughout England than any other book apart from the Bible. Here you will read of the martyrdom of great men of faith such as Hus, Tyndale, and Wycliffe. You will read of Tyndale's death at the stake and of Luther's words when he was accused of heresy and threatened with excommunication and death: "My conscience is so bound and captived in these Scriptures and the Word of God that I will not nor may not revoke any manner of things." Foxe also includes the account of Cranmer who had signed a refutation of his support of the Protestant Church and then, at the stake, put the hand that had signed the recantation into the flames to be burnt first. These men and many others endured a martyr's death rather than deny their belief in God's Word. Their stories are an inspiration to all believers. [Baker]

FOUNDING FATHERS
A WORTHY COMPANY
written by M.E. Bradford
This volume contains detailed biographical sketches of the framers of the United States Constitution. As a result of meticulous research, Dr. Bradford contends that at least fifty of those fifty-five men were Christians who understood well that those who govern are accountable to God for their actions. After reading this book, the reader must surely

conclude that this country was founded upon the Christian religion. [Plymouth Rock Foundation]

ADAMS, JOHN

JOHN ADAMS
written by Alfred Steinberg
This biography describes the long and colorful career of America's second President. Steinberg brings to life Adams's vigorous efforts to repeal the hated Stamp Act, to adopt the Declaration of Independence, to negotiate peace with Britain, and to give birth to the U.S. Navy. Adams's political life was crammed with energetic activity. A brilliant writer, orator, and diplomat, this godly man did more than almost any other man to secure American independence. [G.P. Putnam's Sons]

ADAMS, SAMUEL

SAMUEL ADAMS: SON OF LIBERTY
written by Clifford Lindsey Alderman
Samuel Adams, a hero of the American Revolution and cousin of John Adams, organized the group of patriots who called themselves the Sons of Liberty in order to incite resistance against the injustice dealt the colonists by the British. With his emotional rhetoric, Adams became a leading spokesman for independence, and his activities, especially his masterminding of the Boston Tea Party, forced England into war. This biography tells the story of Samuel Adams's single-minded fight for liberty. [Holt, Rinehart & Winston]

ALFRED THE GREAT

ALFRED THE GREAT: THE KING AND HIS ENGLAND
written by Eleanor Shipley Duckett
Alfred is deservedly the only English king to be called "the Great."

> To learn was indeed in itself a joy, but to teach his people was the duty of a king.

Alfred's England was constantly ravaged by Vikings, and at one time the Vikings conquered all Wessex (the part of England ruled over by Alfred), except Alfred and his personal warriors. But Alfred converted the Viking leader to Christianity, and to subdue further attacks, he built a navy to free England from the grip of the Northmen. Alfred was dedicated to learning; he founded free schools, translated into English the "books most needful for all men to know," and was the first man to write powerful English prose. Alfred also reformed England's legal system by drawing up a series of laws based upon the Ten Commandments. This biography deals with a great ruler who in all his endeavors sought to be faithful to God. [University of Chicago Press]

BUKER, RAY
AGAINST THE CLOCK
written by Eric S. Fife
Ray Buker was a staunch Calvinist and athlete who ran for the Lord. After he won a gold medal at the 1924 Paris Olympics and became the mile champion for the American Athletic Union, Ray traveled with his twin brother as a missionary to Burma and China, preaching Christ to Buddhists resistant to the Gospel message. Fighting frequent bouts of malaria, insomnia, and depression, Ray worked on church development, Bible translation, and the organization of a leper colony until the Japanese invasion of Burma during World War II forced him to return to America. Back in the United States, Buker became a popular preacher and teacher and a missions executive. [Zondervan]

BUNYAN, JOHN
JOHN BUNYAN
written by Ola Elizabeth Winslow
John Bunyan, a humble tinker, became the author of *The Pilgrim's Progress,* the book that, after the Bible, is the most well-read book ever written. This biography tells the story of Bunyan's conversion, his career as a soldier in Cromwell's army during England's civil war, his preaching to the common folk of Bedford, his separation from his family, and his two periods of imprisonment. Winslow describes the turmoil surrounding Bunyan during a turbulent period

> His language was not ours. 'Tis my belief God spake: No tinker had such powers.
> —Robert Browning

of England's history and emphasizes his desire to make God's Word understood by all men. [Macmillan]

CALVIN, IDELETTE
IDELETTE: THE LIFE OF MRS. JOHN CALVIN
written by Edna Gerstner
Although the marriage of John and Idelette Calvin did not begin with a traditional courtship and romance, their wedding brought them both years of joy and fulfillment. Idelette was actually a widow with two children of her own when Calvin's friend Martin Bucer came to Idelette with the suggestion that she consider marrying the great reformer. At first, Idelette was surprised by the suggestion, but after much prayer, she realized that she had every biblical reason to marry this godly man. Their lives were not easy because of opposition to John Calvin's reform work and many personal sorrows. But they were strengthened by one another and by their faith in a sovereign God. [Soli Deo Gloria Publications]

For a biography of the great reformer, read *This Was John Calvin* by Thea B. Van Halsema. [IDEA Ministries]

CAREY, WILLIAM
WILLIAM CAREY: FATHER OF MISSIONS
written by Sam Wellman
William Carey was a poor English cobbler who taught himself Hebrew and Greek by studying the Old and New Testaments. He was ordained as a Baptist minister and was sent to Bengal as a missionary to the Hindus. After a dangerous sea voyage, he arrived in a pagan land without friends or any means of supporting his growing family. Coerced into accompanying her husband, Carey's wife became very bitter and suffered hideous fears in this strange land with its cobras, tigers, and yellow-eyed crocodiles. Carey had to face heart-wrenching trials in India, including death and insanity among

> "Tigers killed twenty people last year in this district alone."
> "I see." Fear crawled on William.
> "Needless to say, you will have to keep your boys close to the house."

members of his own family. But he endured. Carey, who called himself "a wretched, poor, and helpless worm," labored for forty years in India translating the Bible into countless languages. He strived to end the barbaric practices of infant sacrifice and widow burning, and he laid the foundations for generations of future missionaries. [Barbour]

CARVER, GEORGE WASHINGTON
Dr. George Washington Carver, Scientist
written by Shirley Graham and George D. Lipscomb
George Washington Carver's life did not begin happily. He was the sickly child of slaves. As a baby, he was stolen and returned in exchange for a horse. He was accepted at a good college on a full scholarship but was turned away because he was black. The college president told George he would be wasting everyone's time by attempting to pursue an academic career. Carver replied, "Time belongs to God. I am going to college because there is work for me to do, and I must be ready." And to college—another college—he went. After he had graduated from Iowa State College, he continued to excel. He became a professor at Tuskegee Institute and received countless awards for agricultural research. Ignoring prejudice, poverty, and physical handicaps, George Washington Carver became one of America's most revered scientists. [Julian Messner]

COLUMBUS, CHRISTOPHER
The Last Crusader: The Untold Story of Christopher Columbus
written by George Grant
In their zeal to manipulate the past, modern historians have seen fit to rewrite history, and in doing so have attacked, even condemned, the accomplishments of a great Christian explorer. This biography sets the record straight. It brings to life Columbus the man, and it explains Columbus's motivation: to open trade routes to the Indies, certainly, but more importantly, to free the Holy Land from the Turks and evangelize the nations for Christ. Grant recounts how Columbus's idea took shape and was finally realized, and he explores the controversy that continues to surround this zealous crusader. [Crossway]

Other good biographies of Columbus include Samuel Eliot Morison's *Admiral of the Ocean Sea: A Life of Christopher Columbus*

[Little, Brown] and John Eidsmoe's *Columbus and Cortez, Conquerors for Christ.* [New Leaf Press]

CROMWELL, OLIVER

THE PROTECTOR: A VINDICATION
written by J.H. Merle D'Aubigné

> *C*romwell, our chief of men, . . . has rear'd God's trophies, and his work pursued.
> —John Milton

Although Oliver Cromwell is often maligned, D'Aubigné describes the achievements and true character of the Lord Protector of England. Cromwell was a Member of Parliament and a man who was dedicated to promoting biblical Christianity as well as England's prosperity. Cromwell was all too aware of the tyranny of King Charles I and the persecution Christians endured: Their ears were severed, nostrils slit, and cheeks branded. He knew that unless England regained her faith, she would die. Cromwell and other Puritan leaders denounced the king's tyranny and upheld constitutional liberty and, as a result, sparked a revolution. This meticulously researched biography shows us Cromwell's faults as well as his outstanding virtues, especially his devotion to God. [Adamant Media]

ELIOT, JOHN

JOHN ELIOT: "APOSTLE TO THE INDIANS"
written by Ola Elizabeth Winslow
John Eliot was a missionary to the Massachusetts Indians. He sailed with John Winthrop's family from England in the seventeenth century and lived for the rest of his life in America. Eliot had a burning desire to bring Christianity to the Indians, and he mastered the Algonquian language—a remarkable feat since the Algonquian language had no written alphabet and there were no grammar books or dictionaries to help him. He worked entirely by ear and translated the Bible into Algonquian so that he could preach to the Indians in their native tongue. He founded fourteen "Praying Indian" villages where Indians discontinued their pow-wows, punished those who profaned the Sabbath, and catechized their children. This is a lively story of a saintly man who obeyed God's command to win the nations to Christ. [Houghton Mifflin]

ELLIOT, JIM
THROUGH GATES OF SPLENDOR
written by Elisabeth Elliot
Jim Elliot, along with five fellow missionaries, went to Ecuador to bring the Gospel message to a primitive Auca tribe who had always attacked strangers. Their initial contacts with the tribesmen were successful: they lowered gifts from an airplane and shouted messages in the Auca language into the wilderness. The tribesmen's reactions were apparently friendly, and the missionaries actually befriended three natives long enough to take one up for a ride in their plane. On an appointed day, the five missionaries set out to make contact with the whole tribe, and their wives awaited the outcome, listening by radio for news of their husbands. What happened to these five brave men is horrifying, but what is so inspiring for Christians is the reaction of their wives who thanked God for all things. Elisabeth Elliot makes it clear that their sorrows were not in vain, that "Operation Auca" continued, and that eventually some of this savage tribe came to know the Lord. This is a moving biography filled with photographs which give testimony to five men who sacrificed their lives so that others might know Jesus. [Tyndale House]

> When thou passest through the waters, I will be with thee, and through the rivers, they shall not overflow thee.

GALILEI, GALILEO
GALILEO: FIRST OBSERVER OF MARVELOUS THINGS
written by Elma Ehrlich Levinger
Galileo, Italian inventor and mathematician, discovered the law that all falling bodies, regardless of their weight, fall through the air at the same speed. He also invented the compass and was the first scientist to use the telescope in the field of astronomy. His discoveries revealed that the earth revolves around the sun. Galileo was slandered for his

> The moon revolves around the earth; the four moons of Jupiter revolve around the planet; the earth, Jupiter, and other planets revolve around the sun.

claims because the seventeenth-century church viewed them as false and dangerous. Again and again, weakened with disease and sobbing like a child, Galileo was forced to appear before the dreaded Inquisition. Then came the day when he was told to recant his "heretical" theory. [Julian Messner]

HENRY, PATRICK

GIVE ME LIBERTY
written by David J. Vaughan
No one would have expected when Patrick Henry was a lad apprenticing to be a shopkeeper that he would become one of the most important leaders of the American Revolution. However, even in his early days, God's providential hand was upon him, instilling in him a deep love of his country and the values that made her great. This biography is an excellent look at the mind and heart of this champion of liberty. It is amazing how an obscure, failed shopkeeper could turn his keen mind to the study of law, and thereby gain such respect that he soon was elected to the Virginia House of Representatives and then to the Continental Congress. Facing some of the most highly respected, aristocratic statesmen of his day, Henry swept all of them off their feet with his uncompromising stand for freedom. His brilliant oratory was no match for any of the seasoned legislators, and his cry for release from British tyranny soon echoed throughout America. [Cumberland House]

> Adversity toughens manhood and the characteristic of the good or the great man is not that he has been exempt from the evils of life but that he has surmounted them.

Note: All the Leadership in Action biographies published by Cumberland House are highly recommended.

PATRICK HENRY: FIREBRAND OF THE REVOLUTION
written by Nardi Reeder Campion, illustrated by Victor Mays
Even as a boy, Patrick Henry dared to be different. Everyone thought he was doomed to failure because he failed at schoolwork, store keeping, and farming, but a meeting with Thomas Jefferson and the knowledge

that he had a golden tongue inspired Henry to become a lawyer. He rose to prominence as an orator with a speech in the House of Burgesses against the Stamp Act. The author relates Henry's immortal speech: "Why stand we here idle? What is it that gentlemen wish? What would they have? Is life so dear, or peace so sweet, as to be purchased at the price of chains and slavery? Forbid it, Almighty God. I know not what course others may take, but as for me, give me liberty, or give me death." Henry's stirring rhetoric determined the course of history. [Little, Brown]

HUS, JOHN
ON FIRE FOR GOD: THE STORY OF JOHN HUS
written by Victor Budgen
John Hus, a humble peasant's son, lived in rural Bohemia (modern-day Czech Republic) during the thirteenth and fourteenth centuries. He became a Christian at the University of Prague where he was heavily influenced by the writings of the English Reformer John Wycliffe, "the Morning Star of the Reformation." He began preaching and writing and spoke out vehemently against the false teachings and corruption of the Roman Catholic Church—the trafficking in relics, for instance, and the selling of indulgences. Only God can remit sin, said Hus. The officials of the Roman Catholic Church vainly sought to silence this zealous Reformer. After lengthy papal proceedings against him, Hus was excommunicated, imprisoned as a heretic, tried, and burned at the stake. He died singing praises to God. Of John Hus, Luther said, "If only my name were worthy to be associated with such a man!" [Evangelical Press]

KNOX, JOHN
JOHN KNOX, APOSTLE OF THE SCOTTISH REFORMATION
by George Barnett Smith, adapted by Dorothy Martin
When Knox was a young man, Scotland was turning away from Catholicism because of the corrupt doctrines and practices of the Roman Catholic church. Because of his powerful preaching, which God used to convert thousands to the Protestant faith, Knox had to flee to Europe where he became a close friend of John Calvin. His courage and zeal never deserted him. Can you imagine the nerve of a man who wrote

> The godly in the land rejoiced that Mary had heard the gospel from Knox and hoped she would give heed to it. Their hopes were dashed when the queen continued to observe the mass and mocked Knox's words.

against women leaders at a time when both England and Scotland were ruled by queens? (Knox would doubtless have endeared himself to modern feminists with his title *The First Blast of the Trumpet Against the Monstrous Regiment of Women!*) He was so diligent in his attacks on the Catholic Church that Catholics offered a substantial reward to his killer. But it was largely due to the efforts of this tenacious Scottish reformer that Protestantism became the state religion of his country. [Moody Press]

LEE, ROBERT E.

CALL OF DUTY: THE STERLING NOBILITY OF ROBERT E. LEE
written by J. Steven Wilkins

Robert E. Lee possessed in abundance all the qualities of a Southern gentleman; he was a military genius but a humble man. Although Lee hated the idea of secession, he placed his loyalty to his native state of Virginia above his loyalty to the Union. Rather than taking up arms against Virginia, Lee refused the prestigious command of the United States troops and resigned his commission in the army. During the War Between the States, Lee continually demonstrated his love for his men. For example, after Gettysburg, he was so anxious to protect the reputations of his generals that he shouldered the entire blame for his devastating defeat. Even at the tragic end of the war, Lee surrendered with his customary dignity.

> Often to his opponents it seemed that [Lee] was privy not only to their counsels of war but to their thoughts as well!

To a friend, he wrote, "We failed, but in the good providence of God, apparent failure often proves a blessing." And to his wife he wrote, "I trust that a merciful God, our only hope and refuge, will not desert us in this hour of need." [Cumberland House]

Another excellent biography of Robert E. Lee is Rev. J. William Jones's *Life and Letters of Robert Edward Lee*. [Kessinger Publishing]

LEWIS, C.S.

NOT A TAME LION: THE SPIRITUAL LEGACY OF C.S. LEWIS
written by Terry W. Glaspey
Although C.S. Lewis is one of the most well-known Christian writers, it was not until his thirties that he became a believer. He remained a skeptic for years until God used the influence of friends such as Tolkien to convert him. Lewis's life was punctuated with suffering; after the death of his mother, his misguided father sent him away to a wretched boarding school where the boys were beaten by a brutal headmaster. Lewis did not marry until his sixties, but after three brief years of happiness, his wife died in agony of incurable cancer. Lewis was also a rare breed—a thoroughly unselfish man; he cared for years for the invalid mother of a friend, placing her chores before his important work. Glaspey helps you get inside Lewis and his books. You will come to know this man who was so brilliant and yet so humble and funny and giving of all he had. Lewis lived life to the fullest. His writing gives you fresh understanding about daily living and, above all, about the God he tirelessly served. [Cumberland House]

THROUGH THE SHADOWLANDS
written by Brian Sibley
The life story of the distinguished Christian author and scholar. Sibley traces Lewis's boyhood in spartan English boarding schools and his university days at Oxford, which Lewis found "absolutely ripping." At Magdalene College, Cambridge, where he had received a fellowship, Lewis's atheistic ideas were challenged by the writings of Tolkien, MacDonald, and G.K. Chesterton. Finally, God brought him to his knees, and he was converted to Christianity. His illustrious writing career begins with his space adventures, and his BBC talks catapulted him overnight

The marriage took place in the stark, sanitized setting of the Wingfield Hospital. . . . The bride lay propped up on pillows and the bridegroom sat on the side of the bed.

to fame. Meanwhile, in America his fans grew, and among them was Joy Davidman, a converted Jew. Lewis and Joy met and were married, and in the description of their whirlwind courtship and marriage and her illness and death, you will feel their joy and grief and be deeply moved as Lewis wrestled with his last battle. [Revell]

Also read Lewis's autobiography, *Surprised by Joy: The Shape of My Early Life.* [Harcourt Brace]

LINDBERGH, CHARLES

THE LAST HERO: CHARLES A. LINDBERGH
written by Walter S. Ross

Lindbergh always knew where his talents lay and what he wanted to do. His father did not want him to become a pilot because he knew the risks, and Charles was his only son. However, in the face of his son's determination, the father gave in and helped Charles borrow money to buy his first airplane. Lindbergh trained in the Army Air Corps to become a veteran pilot, and, after completing 2,000 hours in the air and barnstorming over half of America, he was ready for his great challenge: the first nonstop New York-Paris flight.

> It is a mark of the man that he traded fame for privacy, to safeguard his family and explore his concerns. It is a comment on society that he had to.

In his airplane, the *Spirit of St. Louis,* Lindbergh successfully completed this historic flight. When he landed, he became an instant celebrity, but fame resulted in the tragic kidnapping and murder of his infant son. However, Lindbergh survived this tragic loss and went on with his life. He made many great contributions to aviation and other areas of benefit to mankind. What you will most admire about Lindbergh are his courage, integrity, commitment to his goals, and his faith in God. [Harper & Row]

LIVINGSTONE, DAVID

THE LIFE OF DAVID LIVINGSTONE
written by Mrs. J.H. Worcester, Jr.

David Livingstone believed that salvation of the lost must be the chief goal of every Christian. At an early age, he determined to evangelize

South Africa. But only his strong faith and dedication sustained this brave man throughout his hard, dangerous, and heartbreaking missionary career. Once he almost died when a lion sprang on him and permanently maimed his arm. Livingstone had to endure constant debilitating sickness, as well as hatred and suspicion, and—worst of all—constant separation from his wife and children. His wife's death nearly broke him, but he wrote, "I try to bend to the blow as from our heavenly Father." Livingstone would have been much safer if he had been content to evangelize a small region, but he courageously set out to explore the whole mysterious continent and to convert the people of Africa to Christianity. [Moody Press]

LUTHER, KATHERINE
KITTY MY RIB
written by E. Jane Mall
This fictionalized biography captures the courageous personality of Martin Luther's wife. Katharine grew up in a convent where she realized that the church was becoming corrupt and that a monk in Wittenberg was working to purge the church of corruption. She prayed for freedom, and Martin Luther helped Katharine and several other nuns escape. Everyone told Luther, a confirmed bachelor, that he should marry, and Luther married Katharine "so as to set an example" for others. As Luther's wife, Katharine had to make many sacrifices. In order to avoid charges of greed, she was compelled to refuse gifts of food, but she herself offered food and shelter to all

> God never sends us more than we can bear, dear wife.

who came to her door. Katharine worked hard at being a good wife while Luther translated the Bible. When Luther died, worn out with hard work and physical infirmities, Katharine faced loneliness, poverty, and danger. Katharine Luther was truly a godly helpmeet for the great Reformer. [Concordia]

LUTHER, MARTIN

HERE I STAND: A LIFE OF MARTIN LUTHER
written by Roland H. Bainton
Luther exhausted a great deal of time and energy attempting to merit God's grace. He failed miserably and then grasped the central truth of justification by faith alone. After this revelation, Luther lashed out at the corrupt practices of the Roman Catholic Church, especially the selling of indulgences that falsely claimed to pardon people from the penalty for sin. Luther's attacks on the Church culminated in his Ninety-five Theses that began the Protestant Reformation. Although he was branded a heretic and excommunicated by the Pope, Luther would not recant. Bainton takes us step by step through Luther's arguments with the Catholic Church; he discusses at length Luther's debates with other theologians and humanists, his theological works, and his translation of the Bible into German. This authoritative biography of a great leader of the faith is a work for scholars as well as mature students. [Plume]

MARSHALL, CATHERINE

CATHERINE MARSHALL HAD A HUSBAND
written by William J. Petersen
This is a brief but inspiring account of the marriages of five famous Christian couples. The wives of five Christian leaders—Elizabeth Bunyan, Mary Livingston, Mary Bryan, Susie Spurgeon, and Catherine Marshall—shared a common trial: frequent separation from their husbands. Elizabeth Bunyan, for example, had to take care of her children while her husband endured two long imprisonments for preaching God's Word. But the marriages of these godly men and women thrived in spite of affliction because their lives were marked by commitment and love. [Tyndale House]

TO LIVE AGAIN
written by Catherine Marshall
The death of Catherine Marshall's minister husband left her grief-stricken and poor, but she learned to rely upon God. And her faith sustained her so that she was able to continue her husband's ministry. She published a book of Peter Marshall's sermons, which sold thousands of copies, and she wrote her husband's biography, which became a best-

seller. The hero of this biography of her husband, *A Man Called Peter*, is not Peter Marshall, chaplain of the U.S. Senate, but our sovereign God. This book has given spiritual comfort to thousands all over the world.

Mrs. Marshall also tells the fascinating story of how the biography was made into a Twentieth-Century Fox record-breaking movie. Catherine Marshall overcame grief and loneliness, and by putting her trust in God, she found a new life to live. [Chosen]

> *L*ife is people—wonderful people, dear people, God's people. Could it have been that I—who had so valued solitude that I had fled up the back stairs to find it—had had to be stripped, reduced to aloneness, to discover how much I needed people, wanted them?

POTTER, BEATRIX
THE TALE OF BEATRIX POTTER
written by Margaret Lane

Beatrix Potter was a solitary child; in fact, she was alone a great deal and spent her time drawing plants, birds, and woodland creatures such as foxes and (of course) rabbits. Her delicate watercolors of Peter Rabbit and friends are as famous as her stories. She kept up a large correspondence with various children and illustrated her letters with little paintings. One of these letters begins, "I don't know what to write to you, so I shall tell you a story about four little rabbits whose names are Flopsy, Mopsy, Cottontail, and Peter." These letters launched Beatrix Potter into the career she was to pursue for the rest of her life. [Frederick Warne]

ROOSEVELT, THEODORE
CARRY A BIG STICK
written by George Grant

During a presidential campaign, Theodore Roosevelt was wounded by a crazy assassin firing at point blank range into his chest. Undaunted, Roosevelt staggered to his feet and

> *T*here is nothing in a leader at once so sane and so sympathetic as a good sense of humor.

gave his scheduled campaign speech. This amazing incident characterizes Roosevelt's life. Courageous and indomitable, Roosevelt is one of America's heroes. In private life, he was a devout man, a devoted husband, and a fun-loving father. In public life, he was a reformer, basing his reforms on God's principles. Roosevelt had an enormous zest for life. He was a fine writer, a highly successful legislator, and an intrepid explorer. Roosevelt's Rough Riders—whom Roosevelt trained in six weeks to fight in the Spanish-American War—have earned a rightful place of honor in history. [Cumberland House]

STUDD, C.T.

C.T. STUDD: CRICKETER AND PIONEER
written by Norman P. Grubb
Charles Studd was a born cricketer; he captained his teams at Eton and Cambridge and played for England. However, his brilliant athletic career was arrested by a brother's near-fatal illness and his realization that worldly success is an illusion. Under the influence of D.L. Moody's preaching, C.T. Studd came to realize that the only reality is an eternity with Jesus. It was easy after that to become a missionary to China. C.T. Studd gave his entire inheritance (the equivalent of $60,000) to the Lord's work. Some of this fortune was used to start the Moody Bible Institute, some to help George Mueller's orphans, and some to fund Hudson Taylor's China Inland Mission. C.T. Studd had to return to England because of ill health, but later he labored in India and in the heart of Africa. [Lutterworth Press]

TADA, JONI EARECKSON

JONI
written by Joni Eareckson Tada
Joni was seventeen when she broke her neck and was paralyzed from the neck down. When she learned that she would never walk again, Joni wanted to die. She rebelled against God and wondered why He allowed her to suffer so. She was consumed with self-pity and depression. Gradually, however, Joni made the long journey back to emotional and spiritual recovery. She enrolled in college, learned to paint with her mouth, and became a well-known speaker. Her message is one of God's mercy and sovereignty: all things work together for good for those who trust in Him. [Zondervan]

TAYLOR, HUDSON

HUDSON TAYLOR'S SPIRITUAL SECRET
written by Dr. and Mrs. Howard Taylor
Hudson Taylor was called to be a missionary to China while civil war and bloodshed were raging and no other Protestant missionary was in China's interior. Nothing deterred the young pioneer evangelist—not danger, lack of funds, heat, cold, the death of close family members, or ill health. Hudson Taylor was dedicated to his task. He used his medical skills to reach men with the Gospel message and ministered to the physical and spiritual health of the Chinese

> It was the exchanged life that had come to him— the life that is indeed "No longer I."

people. Although Hudson Taylor lost three of his children, and the surviving children were separated from him to be educated in England, he withheld no sacrifice to do the Lord's work. As a result of this man's dedication, between three and four thousand Chinese Christians minister today in the field where Hudson Taylor labored. [Moody Press]

TEN BOOM, CORRIE

CORRIE TEN BOOM: HER LIFE, HER FAITH
written by Carole C. Carlson
During her childhood, Corrie ten Boom's house in Amsterdam was a home to all who needed shelter. When she grew up, Corrie, her watchmaker father, and her sister continued to provide a home for missionaries' children. Then came World War II, the repressive German occupation of neutral Holland, and the deportation of all Jews. Corrie's home once again became a shelter, this time for Dutch Jews and Hollanders wanted by the German police. There they stayed until the ten Booms could find them homes in the country. A small group of them remained and were hidden in a secret room whenever the Gestapo invaded

> Today I heard that most probably you were the one who betrayed me. . . . I have prayed for you that the Lord will accept you if you will turn to Him.

the house. Inevitably, the day came when Corrie, her sister, and father were arrested and imprisoned. What happened to the ten Booms is a testament to human courage and faith. [Fleming H. Revell]

You will also enjoy *The Hiding Place* by Corrie ten Boom, with John and Elizabeth Sherrill. [Chosen]

TYNDALE, WILLIAM
GOD'S OUTLAW
written by Brian H. Edwards
William Tyndale lived during the reign of Henry VIII when men were tortured and burned at the stake for translating the Bible into English. But it was Tyndale's dream to "cause the boy who driveth the plow to know the Scriptures." He found it impossible to translate the Greek New Testament legally; he could not safely do his work anywhere in England, and certainly no one was willing to publish his translation. Tyndale fled to Germany where he was able to get the Bible published and smuggled back to England. Although many copies of the Scriptures were intercepted and burned, many survived. Because of Tyndale's dedication, every Englishman from then on would be able to read the Bible. [Evangelical Press]

VANAUKEN, SHELDON
A SEVERE MERCY
written by Sheldon Vanauken
This is an intensely moving love story that is also about courage and Christian faith. Van (Sheldon) and his wife Davy were unbelievers during the early years of their marriage. As students at Oxford University, they read about Christianity and were deeply influenced by the works of C.S. Lewis, soon to become one of their closest friends. After they were both converted, Davy became suddenly and fatally ill. C.S. Lewis was the friend Van needed in his terrible grief, and through his letters that were filled with wisdom and love, Lewis helped Van say, "Thy will be done." This book will strengthen the faith of any Christian. It contains eighteen of Lewis's previously unpublished letters. [HarperOne]

VAN DER BIJL, ANDREW
GOD'S SMUGGLER
written by Brother Andrew with John and Elizabeth Sherrill
After Brother Andrew, uneducated and lame, told God he would serve
on the mission field wherever God sent him, God miraculously healed
his leg. He trained at an unconventional seminary and began to travel
behind the Iron Curtain in communist countries. Andrew discovered
that Bibles were unavailable in these countries in spite of claims of
religious freedom, so he became "God's smuggler," smuggling Bibles
and Christian literature into communist lands. On the Yugoslav border,
his car and luggage loaded with Bibles, he prayed that God would make
"seeing eyes blind." God answered his prayer over and over again.
Other cars were torn apart while guides inspected their interiors and
interrogated the drivers, but Brother Andrew always passed through
with his precious cargo. This is an inspiring story of how a Dutch
missionary risked his life to spread God's Word. [Chosen]

VICTORIA, QUEEN
QUEEN VICTORIA
written by Noel Streatfeild, illustrated by Robert Frankenberg
This is a fascinating biography of a great queen who ruled England for
sixty-four years. When she was a child, Victoria had no idea she would
become queen, but she was trained for that great office by people who
loved her dearly. Victoria loved life; she loved being queen, although
she was constantly in and out of favor with her subjects. Her marriage
to her dearest Albert is a storybook romance; when he died, Victoria
mourned for years. When she died, England felt it had lost an old and
trusted friend and named the time in which she lived the Victorian Age.
[Random House]

WALLACE, WILLIAM
WILLIAM WALLACE: THE KING'S ENEMY
written by D.J. Gray
William Wallace was a valiant Scottish patriot. The thirteenth-century king of England, Edward I, was determined to get rid of the
Scottish king so that he could rule Scotland. Wallace raised an army
and achieved a stunning victory at Stirling Bridge. After that, all of

Scotland looked to Wallace as a savior who would free them from the cruel grip of English tyranny. Wallace's story has been brought vividly to life by the movie *Braveheart*, but you need to read this book to fully understand the glorious achievement of this brave Scottish warrior. [Barnes & Noble]

WASHINGTON, BOOKER T.
UP FROM SLAVERY
written by Booker T. Washington
Booker T. Washington was a slave until he was nine years old when the Civil War ended and slaves were freed. He was both student and teacher at an industrial school for black people in West Virginia, and from there he founded the Tuskegee Institute, a vocational school for black people. He started the school in a dilapidated hut. There was no large building at his disposal, just "hundreds of hungry, earnest souls who wanted to secure knowledge." His institute was unique: The students made the bricks, erected the buildings, and built wagons, buggies, and furniture. In addition to offering a practical education in specific trades such as farming and mechanics, the school also ministered to the spiritual well-being of its students through regular worship services and prayer meetings. Booker T. Washington will always be remembered as an inspiring leader and educator. [Modern Library]

> Merit, no matter under what skin found, is in the long run recognized and rewarded.

WASHINGTON, GEORGE
EPISODES IN THE LIFE OF GEORGE WASHINGTON
written by A.J. Cloud and Vierling Kersey
The authors of this biography present Washington in a series of events from his life: as a young surveyor, as an inexperienced soldier carrying out his first military commission, as America's leader in the Revolutionary War, and as our first President under the United States Constitution. The cumulative effect of these episodes captures a complete picture of a great American. Washington acquired his military prowess on the

frontier during the French and Indian War and was voted Commander-in-Chief of the Army during the Revolutionary War. The authors bring us face-to-face with the dangers and hardships Washington and his men endured and his clever military strategies. As President, Washington conducted the affairs of his country with exemplary dedication, and at his funeral oration, General Henry Lee spoke the words which accurately describe the man: "first in war, first in peace, and first in the hearts of his countrymen." [Scribner's]

WHITEFIELD, GEORGE

George Whitefield
written by Arnold A. Dallimore

George Whitefield was known for his bold, dramatic preaching and passionate oratory. He preached outdoors to thousands. In fact, the numbers of his congregations are staggering; Benjamin Franklin computed that Whitefield's organ-like voice could reach more than thirty thousand. He was a lifelong friend of Charles Wesley, also a powerful preacher, whom he persuaded to begin an open-air ministry. Whitefield, a Calvinist, founded the Methodist movement, although he disagreed with John Wesley over the doctrine of predestination that Wesley opposed. God used this popular preacher to bring countless thousands to Christ in both England and

> Eager he press'd to his
> high calling's prize,
> By violent faith resolved
> to scale the skies,
> And apprehend his Lord
> in paradise.
> —Charles Wesley,
> elegy on Whitefield

America. Whitefield had a deep compassion for his fellow man and the zeal to bring men to a saving knowledge of the Lord. [Crossway]

WILBERFORCE, WILLIAM

Amazing Grace
written by Eric Metaxas

This is the inspiring story of a courageous man who spent much of his life in pursuit of a noble but almost impossible goal: the abolition of the British slave trade and the abolition of slavery throughout the British colonies. Wilberforce faced fierce opposition—most of Parliament denounced and ridiculed his bill over and over again, but he had enormous compassion and the vision that others lacked. He saw great injustice being done and was determined to end it. His heroic struggle and ultimate victory clearly demonstrate that one man can accomplish much for God's kingdom. One man can change the course of history and create a better world for the suffering and the oppressed. If you have not already seen it, you will also be inspired by the movie that poignantly celebrates the amazing story of the man who freed the slaves. [HarperCollins]

WOMACH, MERRILL
TESTED BY FIRE: A TRUE STORY OF COURAGE AND FAITH
written by Merrill and Virginia Womach with Mel and Lyla White
Merrill Womach, a renowned singer, was involved in a terrible plane crash. He survived, but half his body was badly burned, and his face severely disfigured. Over the next fourteen years, Womach endured over fifty operations to graft skin onto his face, neck, and hands. Throughout the often dangerous surgeries, Merrill sang gospel songs. Gradually he recovered, resumed his singing career, and shared his faith. He and his wife told people all around America how God had allowed the accident to happen. Surely God's purpose for this couple was to bring the message of salvation to others as they shared their trial by fire. [Fleming H. Revell]

WURMBRAND, RICHARD
TORTURED FOR CHRIST
written by Richard Wurmbrand
Wurmbrand distributed thousands of Bibles and converted countless numbers of Russians to Christ under the pretext of buying watches. He labored in underground missionary work among the Romanians and Russian soldiers in Romania. Although he was captured by the secret police and endured hideous torture, God allowed him to survive in order to tell the story of the Underground Church in communist territory. Wurmbrand

> We shall win the Communists. First, because God is on our side.

was later able to leave Romania to preach Christ in the West but was threatened with more torture if he spoke out against the communists. This brave and faithful man risked his very life in order to preach the Gospel. [Living Sacrifice Books]

TITLE INDEX

G

H

I

M

N

O

P

ILLUSTRATIONS
Peter Pan, illustrated by F.D. Bedford
(New York: Charles Scribner's Sons, 1911), see page 100.

AUTHOR
INDEX

P

Page, Thomas Nelson 119
Payne, Emmy 42
Peters, Ellis 149
Petersen, William J. 230
Picard, Barbara Leonie 142
Piper, Watty 43
Plaidy, Jean 201
Poe, Edgar Allan 211
Porter, Gene Stratton 140
Potok, Chaim 187
Potter, Beatrix 54
Prins, Piet 64, 107, 108
Prokofiev, Sergei 50
Provensen, Alice and Martin 37
Pyle, Howard 148, 149, 155

R

Ransome, Arthur 156
Rawlings, Marjorie Kinnan 162
Rawls, Wilson 160
Raymond, Grace 196
Reeves, James 117, 137
Rey, H.A. 33
Richardson, Arleta 84
Richter, Conrad 147
Roddy, Lee 172
Ross, Walter S. 228
Rossetti, Christina 35, 80
Rouse, W.H.D. 140
Roy, Ron 55
Ruskin, John 87

S

Sabatini, Rafael 130
Salten, Felix 66
Sanders, Scott Russell 34, 57
Sayers, Dorothy 213
Sayers, Frances Clarke 71
Scarry, Richard 36, 57
Schaefer, Jack 209
Schindler, Regine 37

Seignobosc, Françoise 52
Selden, George 75
Sendak, Maurice 25, 31, 49
Seredy, Kate 80
Serraillier, Ian 127, 131, 136
Sewall, Marcia 164
Sewell, Anna 69
Sharp, Margery 105
Shecter, Ben 81
Sherrill, John and Elizabeth 235
Sibley, Brian 227
Sidney, Margaret 78
Sienkiewicz, Henryk 205
Silverstein, Shel 37
Slobodkina, Esphyr 30
Smith, Dodie 98, 196
Smith, George Barnett 225
Speare, Elizabeth George 110, 128
Sperry, Armstrong 127, 128, 158
Spyri, Johanna 82
St. John, Patricia 118
Stafford, Tim 168
Stanley, Diane 178
Steig, William 61
Steinberg, Alfred 218
Stevenson, O.J. 166
Stevenson, Robert Louis 31, 134, 145, 159
Stockton, Frank 81
Stolz, Mary 34
Streatfeild, Noel 76, 117, 235
Strom, Kay Marshall 175
Summers, Susan 35
Sutcliff, Rosemary 135, 147, 157
Swift, Catherine 165, 172, 173

T

Tada, Joni Eareckson 232
Taylor, Dr. and Mrs. Howard 233
Terhune, Albert Payson 87
Thomas, Dylan 74
Thurber, James 45, 149

ℐLLUSTRATOR
ℐNDEX

Illustration: *Cinderella*, illustrated by Arthur Rackham (London: William Heinemann, 1919), see page 75.

SUBJECT INDEX

Ilustration: *The Wizard of Oz*, illustrated by W.W. Denslow (Chicago; New York: Geo M. Hill Co., 1900), see page 122.

C

camping
Jem's Island [EL] 85
Pip Camps Out [PS] 50
Canterbury Tales
Canterbury Tales [MS] 129
Chanticleer and the Fox [EL] 30
captivity. *See also* escape
Calico Captive [MS] 128
Indian Captive [MS] 143
Light in the Forest, The [MS] 147
cats. *See* animals: cats
Christian fiction
Amahl and the Night Visitors [EL] 63
Anak, the Eskimo Boy [EL] 64
Augustine Came to Kent [MS] 126
Ben-Hur [HS] 184
Bronze Bow, The [MS] 128
Christy [HS] 187
Dutch Color [MS] 135
For the Temple [MS] 139
Fourth Wise Man, The [EL] 34
God's Creation—My World [EL] 37
Great Divorce, The [HS] 192
Hinds' Feet on High Places [MS] 141
How They Kept the Faith [HS] 196
Huguenot Garden [EL] 83
King's Daughter, The [EL] 87
Lion, the Witch, and the Wardrobe, The [EL] 89
Master's Quilt, The [HS] 201
Pearl Maiden [HS] 203
Pilgrim's Progress, The [MS] 151
Quo Vadis [HS] 205
Robe, The [HS] 206
Scottish Seas [MS] 154
Screwtape Letters, The [HS] 208
Silver Chalice, The [HS] 209
Story of the Other Wise Man, The [EL] 113
Tinker's Daughter, The [EL] 117
Treasures of the Snow [EL] 118
Wise Words [EL] 122
Christmas. *See* holidays
class conflict. *See also* slavery

Great Expectations [HS] 193
Howard's End [HS] 195
Pride and Prejudice [HS] 204
To Kill a Mockingbird [HS] 213
colors. *See* first books
construction. *See* machinery
counting. *See* first books
cowboys. *See* ranch life *and* western

D

dance
Dancing Shoes [EL] 76
dogs. *See* animals: dogs
dolls and toys
Best-Loved Doll, The [EL] 68
Carolina's Courage [EL] 73
Corduroy [PS] 32
Doll's House, The [EL] 77
Dolls' Christmas, The [PS] 33
Laura Charlotte [PS] 42
Most Wonderful Doll in the World, The [EL] 94
Story of Holly and Ivy, The [EL] 112
dragons. *See* fantasy

E

escape. *See also* captivity
Count of Monte Cristo, The [MS] 133
Escape, The [MS] 136
Escape from Warsaw [MS] 136
Escape to King Alfred [MS] 137
Exodus [PS] 34
I Am David [MS] 142
Kidnapped [MS] 145
England. *See* historical fiction
Eskimos
Anak, the Eskimo Boy [EL] 64

F

fables, folklore, and legends
Aesop's Fables [EL] 62
Beowulf the Warrior [MS] 127
Giving Tree, The [PS] 37
Henny Penny [PS] 40
Hiawatha [EL] 83

Illustration, opposite: *The Wizard of Oz*, illustrated by W.W. Denslow (Chicago; New York: Geo M. Hill Co., 1900), see page 122.

THE
END